No Trophy, No Sword

NO TROPHY
NO SWORD

AN AMERICAN VOLUNTEER

IN THE ISRAELI AIR FORCE

DURING THE 1948 WAR

OF INDEPENDENCE

HAROLD LIVINGSTON

edition q, inc.
Chicago, Berlin, Tokyo, and Moscow

Published by edition q, inc.

Library of Congress Cataloging-In-Publication Data

Livingston, Harold.
    No trophy, no sword : an American volunteer in the Israeli Air Force during the 1948 War of Independence / Harold Livingston.
       p.   cm.
    ISBN 1-883695-03-1
    1. Livingston, Harold.   2. Israel-Arab War, 1948–1949–Personal narratives, American.   3. Israel-Arab War, 1948–1949–Participation, American.   4. Flight radio operators–Palestine–Biography.
5. Haganah (Organization)–Biography.   6. Israel. Hel ha-avir–History.
I. Title.
DS126.97.L57   1994
956.94'04'092–dc20
[B]   93-49571
                                                  CIP

Manufactured in the United States of America

To Those Who Were There

"They were all we had . . . "

–Yitzhak Rabin, in a 1983 interview, referring to the foreign volunteers of the Israeli Air Force of 1948.

BOOKS BY HAROLD LIVINGSTON

Pilotes Sans Visa
The Coasts of the Earth
The Detroiters
The Climacticon
Ride a Tiger
Touch the Sky
To Die in Babylon
No Trophy, No Sword

CONTENTS

His means of death, his obscure burial,
No trophy, sword, nor hatchment o'er his bones,
No noble rite nor formal ostentation.

William Shakespeare
Hamlet, Act IV

In Tel Aviv that year we sat on the hotel terraces along the Esplanade, the Park Hotel, or the Kaete Dan, or the Gat Rimmon. We took in the warm afternoon sun and sipped tea and talked of wives in New York and in London and Cape Town, of girls in Paris and in Rome. The weather over the Alps and fog around the Corsican coast and the breasts of a girl two tables away. Jerusalem last week, and Ajaccio tomorrow, and the valiant stand of the Palmach, and how last night the Lebanese were hurled back to the border.

". . . that blonde in Prague? Well, when you see her, tell her I went back to the States."

The Israeli officers stalked about with grim expressions, and little Skoda .32 pistols strapped over parade ground-neat uniforms. The Americans and Brits made a point of not wearing weapons. There was a joke, in Hebrew, about the Yankee and English pilots standing for hours in front of mirrors mussing their hair and rumpling their uniforms.

". . . Jesus Christ! They call this tea? My wife could make it better than this, even!"

Gordon Levett was not Jewish. He got into a minor hassle with a Tel Aviv bus conductor, who called him a Dirty Goy. Everyone said it was a very healthy sign.

". . . you know that fat-assed Gelfand? Not only are they paying him a grand a month, the slimy bastard's been smuggling gold in, too."

They said it was the best-press-agented-war-in-the-last-fifty-years. But the front was never more than ten miles away and at night you could hear the rattle of the guns.

". . . you Americans think you are so safe. The German Jews were much, much better assimilated. Believe me."

Ray Kurtz had been a Brooklyn cop. In the Big War he flew B-17s. One night he took an Israeli bomber over Cairo, a B-17 with the Star of David on its wings. He hit Farouk's palace from 15,000 feet and then went down to 10,000, headed for the military airfield at Fayid, radioed that he was a TWA airplane in trouble, and asked them to turn on their runway lights. They obliged. Ray Kurtz went down to 3,500 feet and plastered the main runway with five-hundred-pound HE bombs.

". . . no, I'm not. I'm not a Zionist. What am I doing here? You want the truth, I just don't know."

The population of Tel Aviv was 166,000. That year, more

than 300,000 lived in the city. At night the streets were crowded and every café jammed. Each night, in the swankest hotel lounges and the filthiest hashish joints, there was a serious brawl. The Haganah fought with the Irgun and the Irgun fought with the Stern Gang, and they all fought with the Americans. The Americans said it was like a frontier town of the Old West. The Englishmen said it was a wizard show. The South Africans were appalled.

". . . but they don't have any political history. Don't you see, they're bound to make mistakes!"

In Jerusalem they were on quarter rations and no water and the Israelis dug into a mountain to build a new road from Tel Aviv to get the convoys through. The Arabs shelled the New City, and the Israelis shelled the Old City, and each tried not to hit the holy places. They said it was as though it rained every day because the gutters ran with blood.

". . . you know something? This goddamned war has put aviation progress back fifty years!"

No one knew his right name, they called him the "Mad Russian." Every night, just before sundown, he climbed into an old Piper Cub and flew off toward Gaza. In his lap were two dozen hand grenades, and in the rear seat a burlap bag filled with empty bottles. He dived down to treetop level and hurled the grenades at the Egyptian troops. After exhausting the grenades, he would reach behind him for the burlap bag and bombard the enemy soldiers with the empty bottles.
One day he did not return.

". . . the best way I know to get your throat slit is call one of those big sabras a 'native.'"

"Michael of the Negev" was twenty-five years old. A Hungarian, he had survived Treblinka, and gone on to study engineering at the University of London. When the Negev was cut off and the only means of communication was by air they sent Michael to build an airstrip in the desert. They had made the desert bloom, so it was only logical that an airstrip could be built.

An airstrip requires concrete and machinery and the knowledge of how to build it. An airstrip must support thirty tons of aircraft. Michael had no concrete, no workers, no experience. But in two weeks there was an airstrip in the desert.

The supplies were flown in, and when the army broke out they chased the Egyptians all the way back to Suez, and Farouk accused the Jews of using atomic bombs and germ warfare.

Michael was killed in a crash, in the Negev.

". . . yes, everybody is fine. The kibbutz hasn't been attacked since about a week after you left. Oh, Rivka? Well, she had the baby, you know. A boy. Twelve pounds, so help me God. The next morning she was at her guard post."

Ben-Gurion's Foreign Legion. They took anyone. Misfits from America, English communists, South African Zionists, Soviet Army deserters, Polish noblemen, ne'er-do-well soldiers of fortune. If you want excitement and adventure, come on over. If you want to make money, come on over. If you want to write a book. If you're running from the police. If you want to get away from your wife. If you want to prove that Jews can fight. If you want to help build a new land.

No Trophy, No Sword

ONE

THE HANK GREENBERG SYNDROME

The landmark was off to the left, two miles ahead, three thousand feet below: two egg-shaped patches of sand on the beach. The navigator spotted it first. He was on the flight deck, standing directly behind the pilot, looking out the airplane's left side window. In the dark the patches of sand glowed with a dull iridescence.

"There it is," the navigator said quietly, his voice almost lost in the roar of the airplane's engines.

The pilot ordered the co-pilot to reduce power. "Twenty-three inches, twenty-one hundred r.p.m.!"

The co-pilot unlocked the engine manifold pressure and propeller speed controls and eased them back. Immediately, protesting its momentarily unsynchronized engines and propellers, the airplane vibrated from nose to tail. But quickly, deftly, the co-pilot adjusted the settings. The big airplane steadied and sped smoothly on through the night.

"Over the coast!" the navigator called out. He was a tall,

solidly built prematurely gray man of twenty-eight who only three months before had been dispensing prescriptions in the Chicago pharmacy he and his brother jointly owned. A laconic and oftentimes dismayingly cynical man, he was nevertheless a superb aerial navigator who had served two combat tours with the 8th Air Force in World War II. He said he volunteered for the second tour because he was Jewish.

At his station behind the co-pilot, the radio operator listened intently to a Morse signal in his earphones: V-R, V-R, V-R. It was a reply to the message he had tapped out a few seconds before, 9-9-3, 9-9-3, 9-9-3, which was that day's code advising the airfield of fuel required upon landing: nine hundred gallons. The return signal, V-R, meant "Message understood, you are clear to land."

"Clear to land!" the radio operator called to the pilot. Earphones still clamped to his head, he rose and stepped up on the pedestal behind the co-pilot. He gazed down at the beach below. Already now they were beyond the sand patches and over the blackness of land.

"We'll overfly the field at this altitude, then go back in and let down over the water," the pilot said. Two months ago he had worked in the scrap metal business in Los Angeles, a junior partner to his wife's brother. He was thirty, deceptively lean, with thick black hair and dark brown eyes and a heavy-boned, angular face. His life-long ambition had been to attend medical school but, as a Jew, they placed him on a quota. The war intervened, so he learned to fly B-29s instead. The airplane he flew now was not a bomber, but a twin-engined C-46 Curtiss Commando transport. It was just as demanding.

"Estimate two and one half minutes to the field," the navigator said.

"Let me know the minute you hear the 'engines-heard' signal," the pilot said to the radio operator.

"Engines-heard," radioed from the ground controller, would indicate that the airplane had been sighted directly over the airfield, which was unlighted.

They flew on now, the four young men, straining for a first glimpse of life on the ground below. The roof of a building reflected in the hazy moonlight filtering down through the overcast. A flicker of light from an opening door. Automobile headlamps.

Nothing.

A few more moments. On the flight deck, not a single word exchanged, the only sound the steady drone of the engines and the shrill rush of wind. And then, abruptly, the radio operator clamped his hand over his earphones. He listened. "'Engines heard!'" he shouted.

The pilot grinned at the navigator. "Nice work, Big Jules. You split it down the middle." He was already swinging the airplane into a tight bank, turning west, back toward the water. "We'll fly out three minutes," he said, hacking his watch. "Mark!"

"I wonder if the Arabs have any night fighters?" the radio operator said.

"You'll be the first to know," said the co-pilot. He was twenty-five, short, chunky, with red curly hair so coarse it resembled Brillo, and a face straight out of a Russian novel. Like the others, he was a World War II USAAF veteran. Unlike the others, he had logged considerable C-46 time, although not since 1945, three years ago. During those three years, and until the past five weeks, he had been a sales clerk in his father's Washington, D.C. jewelry store. Now he said to the radio operator, "I wish my old man could see me now!"

Mine, too, the radio operator thought. His father, a physician in a small northeastern Massachusetts shoe-manufacturing city, had made no attempt to conceal his distress at his son's volunteering to fight in a foreign war.

Foreign war?

The radio operator had reminded his father that he, the father, continually accused his son of turning away from

3

their Jewishness. "All right," the radio operator had told his father, "so now I'll be helping my fellow Jews."

In the father's eyes, this logic made the radio operator a "wise guy." He was a wise guy whenever he did anything his father was unable to understand or accept. Unfortunately, that was almost everything.

The radio operator was thinking all this gazing out the airplane's right front window, down at the city of Tel Aviv, which he could not see but knew was directly beneath them. Tel Aviv, the Jewish city hewn out of the desert and now the shining symbol of Jewish independence. He had been thinking about it almost all the way from the refueling stop at Corsica, all during the twelve-hour night flight over the Mediterranean. Of course his mind was also filled with other thoughts, the most prominent of which was trying to convince himself this was just another flight, a routine mission.

Routine mission?

You could not see the field, or the runway. And no runway lights until you radioed the appropriate signal, and then only at the last possible instant so that you knew this was the right airstrip and not the one held by the enemy only a few miles away. And the flight originated in Czechoslovakia, at an airfield that at one time, irony of ironies, was a *Luftwaffe* base.

"Two minutes," the navigator called.

"Let's slow her up," the pilot said, and gestured the co-pilot to adjust the power settings.

Just another flight? The radio operator knew better. In the cabin of this very airplane, this truck-like C-46, stacked along every available inch of cabin wall were boxes marked *Fragile–Glass!*, containing machine guns and ammunition. The remainder of the cabin, from bulkhead to tail, was occupied by the fuselage of–more irony–a Messerschmitt ME-109 fighter.

"Three minutes!" the navigator called. He gave the pilot a new heading. The radio operator tapped out the Morse signal notifying the field they were turning final. The airplane, descending now, once again approached the two white patches of sand on the beach.

Messerschmitts . . . ?

To Israel . . . ?

Jews flying Nazi fighter planes? The Star of David instead of a swastika? The radio operator wondered how a Star of David looked on an airplane's wings and rudder. It would look pretty good, he decided. It would look just fine.

"Coming up on the coast!" the navigator shouted.

Now, again, the coast was beneath, then gone. The constant whistle of wind was louder now than the roar of the engines. The airplane hurtled into the darkness.

"Twelve hundred feet!" the co-pilot called.

"Call for runway lights!" the pilot ordered the radio operator.

The radio operator tapped out another series of Morse numbers. Immediately below, a single row of lights appeared. The lights at first resembled a straight red line but quickly, as the airplane came lower and closer, you could see the spaces between each light.

"Full flap!"

"Six hundred!"

"Speed?"

"One-ten."

"Instruments?"

"Check."

"Landing lights!"

The co-pilot flipped the switch. The airplane's two landing lights flashed on, each light extending from the leading edge of a wing like a solid white beam, each trained on the ground below, on the near end of the runway, the huge white numbers: 2 7. The numbers grew larger, and whiter.

"Over the fence!" the co-pilot called. "Ninety!"

"Maintain power!"

The wheels felt for runway, touched, skimmed over the surface.

"Chop 'em!"

The first runway lights raced past in a blur of red as the airplane flew onto the strip. Then gently, ever so slowly, she settled, touched down on the Macadam with an almost quiet screech of rubber, and held. She rolled down the runway, slower, slower.

Another few hundred feet, and then the pilot switched off the landing lights. An instant later the runway lights went off. Immediately, out of the darkness, a jeep with an illuminated "Follow Me" sign on its rear appeared. The jeep led the airplane onto a taxiway, then onto the apron. The radio operator was already in the cabin and even before they stopped he had opened the rear cargo door. A breeze splashed over his face, cool, and fragrant with the scent of orange blossoms. Outside, from the jeep, a man in a rumpled khaki uniform called up to the radio operator.

"Shalom."

"Shalom," the radio operator replied.

"You are Americans?"

"Yes, American."

"It was a long journey," the man said.

"Yes," said the radio operator. "A very long journey."

2.

I was that radio operator. It was the night of May 24, 1948. My first flight into Israel. And it had indeed been a long journey. Simply as a point of departure I suppose you could say it began two and one half years earlier. On a drab early December morning in 1945 at Fort Devens, an equally drab New England U.S. Army base. The day I was discharged from the United States Army Air Force, at the very same place–Devens–where thirty-nine months before, at age eighteen, I had enlisted.

When I enlisted, my intention–no, my burning ambition,

my wildest fantasy—was to become a pilot, an Aviation Cadet. Even as a small boy, airplanes, flying, fascinated me. I built model Spads, Fokker D-7s, Stinson Reliants. I read *Flying Aces, Air Trails, Bill Barnes, Doc Savage.* It was *me* peering through the Sopwith Camel's gun sight at the red triplane dead-beaded in the cross hairs. Me, flying the Northrop Gamma through a killer storm to bring the lifesaving serum to the dying infant. Not to mention the Battle of Britain: the three Stukas I shot down over Romney Marsh before bailing out of my burning Spitfire.

Fantasies aside, I knew I was color-blind and knew it would wash me out of Cadets. But I also knew that the test administered for color blindness was an Ishihara color chart. I obtained one of these charts from an optometrist colleague of my father's. I memorized it thoroughly, and two weeks after completing basic training reported to Scott Field, Illinois, for my initial cadet physical. The flight surgeon had mislaid his Ishihara and used instead a batch of wool yarns of various colors he said were just as effective.

They were. My military pilot days were over.

I was assigned to radio operator's school. Some six months later, on July 9, 1943, I arrived in Prestwick, Scotland, as an Army Airways Communications System point-to-point radio operator. I served with AACS throughout the war. From England to the Normandy beaches, to a long, marvelous stint in Paris, and finally Germany. I finished out the war as a Master Sergeant: at twenty-one years old, I can immodestly say, no small accomplishment. I had been a communications chief, supervising the operation of all phases of airways communications facilities for transport aircraft. It was complex and demanding work. I loved it and I was good at it.

But now it was over. I was a civilian.

I floundered around a few months. Living at home, subsisting on the "52-20" Club (veterans benefits: $20 weekly for 52 weeks), plus whatever handouts cadged from my parents. Not an unpleasant life. Cigarettes twenty cents a pack, gasoline thirteen cents a gallon, an epicurean hamburger fifteen cents. Movies fifty cents, beer a dime, cocktails thirty-five cents. Take a girl to dinner, and I mean a first-class meal–lobster or steak or veal–drinks and tip included, you could not spend ten dollars; and then, if you got lucky, a comfortable motel room–in those days they called them "motor courts"–went for a dollar and a half, and you always signed a false name.

Pleasant as all that might be, you knew you should be thinking of making something meaningful of your life. Many of us, though, simply did not know what to do with our lives. Some returned to college. Not I. I wanted no college, not then, not even on the GI Bill. And I certainly was not interested in my prewar job as a *Boston Globe* copyboy.

Copyboy . . . ?

In the army I was a high-ranking executive, in charge of as many as one hundred men, in a difficult and responsible job. Go back to a copyboy . . . ? Never.

What I wanted, truly, was the war again.

The Old Days.

London, Paris, Rome, Vienna. Exotic, exciting places where each new day seemed to bring a new adventure, and being an American made you someone special.

Uncle Sam wanted me back. I could have my old army job, and my grade as Master Sergeant. And I would have gone back in an instant, but not as an enlisted man. I wanted officer's bars. But the army was being reduced, particularly the Air Force officer pool, and they said I was far more valuable as a communications chief than a second looey they wouldn't know what to do with. Of course, if I did go back in as a GI, they said they could practically guarantee that within a year I would have a commission.

Come on, I wasn't born yesterday, I knew all about army "guarantees." Thanks but no thanks.

Besides, I had a back-up plan.

TWA, Trans World Airline.

The airline had offered me a position as communications supervisor for their newly acquired North African–Middle Eastern routes. The same job I did for the air force during the war and, better yet, at three times the pay. The Old Days were not lost after all. I was saved.

The reason I say my journey to Israel began with my discharge from the army is, clearly, that had I received a commission and remained in the service, I would not have joined TWA. And it was in TWA I met the people who, two years later, brought me into the Israeli Air Force.

Although in that spring of 1946 I surely could not have anticipated Israel. There was no Israel, only Palestine. Palestine, as alien a word and image to me as Mars. More so.

It meant, then, embarrassingly Jewish old men with tobacco-stained beards and shiny-shabby black frock coats knocking at your door with little tin boxes called *pushkes* into which you were expected to place a small donation for the Jewish people of the Holy Land. For a more substantial sum a tree might be planted in your name.

As a youngster growing up in a small Massachusetts city–Haverhill, on the New Hampshire border, thirty miles north of Boston–while I knew I was a Jew, and all my friends were Jews, my only real relationship to Jews and Jewishness was the vague perception that this made us, me, somehow different. When Max Baer, a large white Star of David boldly emblazoned on his dark silk trunks, won the heavyweight boxing championship, or Marshal Goldberg made All-American, or the Detroit Tigers' Jewish first baseman, Hank Greenberg, hit fifty-eight home runs, I felt a strange tug of pride.

The Hank Greenberg Syndrome.

Certainly not confined to sports. Albert Einstein was a Jew. Movie mogul Louis B. Mayer was Jewish, and Supreme Court justices Louis Brandeis and Felix Frankfurter. George Gershwin, Bernard Baruch, and Sigmund Freud. So were the

Rothschilds, the Morgenthaus, the Marx Brothers, Eddie Cantor, Irving Berlin, Lauren Bacall, Jack Benny, George Burns, and Benny Goodman. Ernest Hemingway was not, which disappointed me.

I think we were conditioned to expect, and accept, Jewish suffering. From Moses fleeing Egypt, to Masada, to medieval inquisitions, all the way to the classic stories of grandparents leaving the old country to escape persecution. And, of course, Hitler's Germany. And I remember a definite sense of shame at wartime media references to "helpless Jews."

Helpless Jews.

Why helpless? Later, in high school and then the army, I prided myself on being an Anglicized Jew—as contrasted, I suppose, to Helpless Jew—although at the time I was unable to identify it in such sophisticated terms. To me, then, it meant not acting like a Jew. Whatever acting like a Jew meant.

My TWA salary was $450 monthly.

More money than I had ever earned in my life, more than I knew what to do with. And far more than I possibly needed, thereby permitting $213.45 to be painlessly and automatically deposited into my special checking account at the Bank of The Manhattan Company.

So not only had I retrieved the Old Days, they were paying me a fortune for the privilege.

After a brief orientation/training period in New York I was sent to Egypt and placed in charge of the seven-position airways radio station at Payne Field (now Cairo International). We lived near the field, in Heliopolis, at the Heliopolis Palace Hotel. Off duty we were either at the hotel bar, which was like a last outpost of the British Empire, or the USAAF Officer's Club at the field. Or in Cairo. In those days—before Nassar, Suez, Sadat, and Saddam—Cairo was an intriguingly exciting city.

Cairo meant Groppi's, the terazzo-floored café with the best ice cream east of Rome, where each afternoon at 4:00 a tuxedo-attired ensemble played soft violin tea-dance music. And the Kit-Kat Club and La Pigalle and the Club California, whose chorus lines seemed entirely comprised of high-breasted, long-legged French or Rumanian girls who never refused late supper invitations—in 1946, $20.00 American went a deliciously long way—and who all seemed to live in luxurious Nile River house boats with at least one servant. And Shepheard's Hotel, where you drank gin-and-tonics on the world's longest hotel veranda, and where downstairs in the arcade the old White Russian emigre who claimed to have been a genuine count or baron fashioned custom-designed eight-strand sterling silver puzzle rings that sold for $5.00.

Cairo, unhappily, was only a temporary assignment. My permanent station was Dhahran, Saudi Arabia. Dhahran, a euphemism for Hell. On the Persian Gulf, oven-hot, alien, hostile. Consisting, in 1946, of several dozen oil rigs, an airstrip, a few Quonset barracks, and the Arabian-American Oil Company (ARAMCO) club. That, plus a small Bedouin tent settlement you could have transported fourteen centuries back in time and never known the difference.

In truth, however, not really all that bad. Our Quonsets were air-conditioned and the food first rate: former Italian POWs operated the mess hall. And there were occasional "route-survey flights"—also a euphemism, for rest-and-recreation junkets—across the 1,200-mile desert to Africa, to Asmara in Italian Eritrea, where you could sit in a canopied sidewalk cafe and drink cold French or Belgian beer while leisurely awaiting the 7:00 p.m. opening hour of the famous House Of Mirrors, which they said was built especially for Benito Mussolini, and was certainly the most opulent brothel this side of Pompeii.

I was the Dhahran Station Chief, supervising all TWA communications in that region, and all operations at the airfield. Dhahran was not an important installation, but because I wanted it to be important—and because I wanted to be important–I worked hard to make it so.

I was not a good executive. I had no patience for what I considered inefficiency or ineptitude. I demanded perfection from those five American radio operators in my charge, and from the two operations specialists and the one mechanic. I drove them mercilessly. In no time I was faced with a full-scale insurrection. I was twenty-one years old and had never learned tolerance. I was unable to understand why others failed to attain my standards of performance. I was arrogant, and impatient, and insufferable.

And I was fired.

Back to the States I came, back to Haverhill, back to my parents' house. Three squares a day and comfortable digs. My father was delighted: I was safe, home where I belonged. He offered me $25 weekly to chauffeur him on his daily medical rounds. I took the money, but not the job. My father did not mind; he had me home, which was all he wanted.

He should have known better.

A month later I was in New York, living in a $3 per day room at the Shelton Hotel on Lexington and 49th. I nailed a job with a small advertising agency as an account executive. Fifty dollars weekly against commissions earned. Account executive meant knocking on the doors of various business concerns to solicit their advertising accounts. I seldom, if ever, earned the weekly draw and shortly found myself once again unemployed.

In the meantime I had moved from the Shelton to Greenwich Village, sharing an apartment with a struggling young writer named Everett Greenbaum, a former Navy fighter pilot. Although decades later Everett would win Emmies and Oscars for his television and film work, he was supporting himself then as a flying instructor at a private, civilian school in Teterboro, New Jersey. Through Everett, and the GI Bill, I finally won my wings. Not the coveted Air Force silver, of course, and at best a poor substitute. A kind of consolation prize. But at least, and at long last, I had my pilot's license.

Which with a nickel, as they not inaccurately said in those days, bought you a cup of coffee. The trouble was, I lacked even the nickel. I could not find another job. In truth, I never tried very hard. I loathed sales work; I was a clumsy salesman, anyway. I also disliked the Village and most of its inhabitants. "Bohemian," or "Beat," whatever the label, they and it were not for me. Too cerebral, too abstract. This unfortunately included the Village women, most of whom not only considered my advertising career as "distastefully materialistic," but seemed to demand intellectual stimulation as the preferred form of sexual foreplay. I never made out too well.

Back to Haverhill I came, supplementing–not too success-fully–my non-income at the weekly Thursday night dollar-limit poker games, hanging out at a nearby roadhouse called The Diamond Mirror, ineptly trying to write a novel, and only a little less ineptly trying to sleep with each one of The Diamond Mirror's four waitresses. Certainly, not worry-ing much about the future. It would take care of itself; it always did.

In between all this, however, I managed to obtain another advertising agency job. Two friends who had opened a shop specializing in retail store accounts gave me a part-time position. Part-time meant that whenever I felt like it I could go out and hustle new accounts on a commission basis. Not much of a job, but it provided a certain respectability that temporarily satisfied my parents. My mother less than my father: he did not care what I did as long as I was home, where I belonged. She on the other hand was very con-cerned for my future.

So acute was her concern, she allowed me to manipulate from her a "loan" of $1,500, making me a full partner in my two friends' advertising agency, Hoffman & Schiff, Inc.

Now it was Hoffman, Schiff & Livingston, Inc.

The infusion of new capital enabled us to move our offices from Lawrence, Massachusetts, into Boston. Into a seedy downtown section, in a cramped suite of tiny cubicles that resembled a bookie parlor more than an ad agency. The same rooms, perhaps prophetically, had once been occupied by the infamous Boston stock swindler, Charles Ponzi.

We had a few retail store accounts that barely paid the telephone bill. We sought new, bigger, consumer accounts. Acquiring these new accounts was my task. Each morning I rode the Boston & Maine commuter train from Haverhill to Boston. Before lunch I would prepare a list of prospective clients. After lunch I began telephoning them. (A partner now, you could hardly expect me to go knocking on doors!) I filled the days doing this, or trying to write advertising copy, or sometimes interviewing attractive and reputedly ambitious young models referred by a photographer friend. Of course we had no clients whose advertising required photography and the girls almost invariably caught on.

My partners claimed that my most creative contribution was dropping a set of engravings into a wet gutter. It turned out that the engravings were flawed, so my clumsiness saved us money. I might also note that this agency later grew into an organization known as Ingalls Associates, one of the largest and most prestigious of New England agencies, and was eventually sold to BBDO for a sum said to exceed $60 million. To illustrate my business acumen, when I resigned my "Vice Presidency" that same year, 1948, I sold my one-third share back to my partners for $500 cash, a desk, a chair, and a typewriter. I still have the chair.

3.

In December 1947, the United Nations Organization had voted to partition Palestine into separate Arab and Jewish states, effective May 15, 1948. I found this only mildly inter-esting. On a par with stories of "Jewish terrorists" blowing up British officers' billets, and of something called "Haganah," and phrases like "Jewish Homeland," or "Jewish Nation."

Interesting, but of little personal significance beyond being part of the Hank Greenberg Syndrome. I continued filling the days with those telephone solicitations, pursuing the ambitious young models, and awaiting the Big Break: a Class A consumer account. The fact that you had to go out and earn the Big Break, that you had to work for it, only vaguely occurred to me. I expected it to be dropped into my lap.

And then I received the letter.

It arrived just after breakfast one March day as I was leaving for the railway station—in 1948 mail was delivered twice daily: early morning, and mid-afternoon, and you could set your watch by it. A letter from a former colleague, a TWA Flight Radio Officer, Milton Russell. He had written hastily from London just prior to boarding his flight to Rome.

Would I be interested, he wrote, in joining an outfit being formed to fly munitions and refugees to Palestine? If so, I should telephone a number in New York City and ask for "Swifty."

I read the letter a second time, and then again, studying the blue tissue-thin airmail envelope and stationery. The British stamp and postmark. And then I read it again.

Was I interested?

A tantalizing image flashed into my mind. I have bailed out of my burning airplane and landed safely in the desert, and am detaching my parachute harness and gathering up the chute, and at the same time training my .45 on the band of howling Arabs rushing toward me.

On second thought—or third, or fourth—maybe I wasn't so interested. It was probably a joke anyway. Russell sometimes enjoyed such pranks. But I called the New York number. A very business-like woman answered.

"Service Airways, good morning."

Service Airways? What the hell is Service Airways?

I said, "Could I speak to . . . Swifty, please?" Now I knew it was a joke. "This is Harold Livingston."

He came on the line almost immediately. A crisp, resonant, executive voice. "This is Swifty."

"This is Harold Livingston," I said again, which was as far as I got because he brusquely interrupted to ask where in the name of God I was calling from.

"Boston," I said. "I'm in my office—"

"—is your passport in order?"

"Yes," I said. "It's good until—"

"—where the hell have you been?" he said. "We've been waiting for you more than a week! Now listen, we need you here right away. Now, today!"

I spoke into the phone, hearing my own voice, my own words, but it was like listening to someone else. If they needed me that badly, I said, I would get there.

And I did.

That very afternoon, reporting to Service Airways, Inc. A four-room suite of offices on the fifth floor of 250 West 57th Street. Reporting to Swifty.

Irvin Roland Schindler, "Swifty." Thirty-three years old, tall, dark haired, with a long bony face and wide-set, deep piercing eyes. He seemed to always be in a hurry, hence the nickname, but also seemed to always know where he was going. He was President of Service Airways, Inc.

Service Airways.

A company formed after the war by ex-USAAF ATC pilot Swifty Schindler, incorporated in the State of New York for the purpose of conducting aerial transport of passengers and cargo. But business was poor and after a few months' operation Swifty was forced to close down. He sold the firm's lone airplane, a four-passenger Beechcraft, and went to work flying co-pilot for a non-scheduled international carrier whose proprietor boasted that his company would never allow a Jew to fly Captain.

In the meantime, on paper at least, Service Airways still existed. Swifty had never bothered to dissolve the corporation, an oversight that proved most advantageous for a thirty-year-old former TWA Flight Engineer named Al Schwimmer.

Al Schwimmer, born and raised in Bridgeport, Connecticut, had some months before convinced Jewish Agency representatives of the feasibility of flying munitions into Palestine. With JA money he purchased ten C-46 Curtiss Commando transport airplanes, and three C-69 Lockheed Constellations. War-surplus aircraft, the C-46s cost $5,000 each, the Connies $15,000.

Now, possessing the airplanes, Schwimmer needed a "clean" corporate entity to shelter them.

Service Airways.

Whose new fleet of thirteen aircraft made it then, in March of 1948, the largest non-scheduled airline in the world. In theory, if not in practice: the airplanes were scattered at airports from Ontario, California to Teterboro, New Jersey. Scattered because no central base had yet been established; and, more important, there were no qualified air crews to fly them.

But in less than ten weeks, on May 15, the British were to evacuate Palestine. The combined Arab armies now massing on the partitioned borders would attack. Already, the British had imposed a naval blockade in concert with the U.S. embargo of military shipments to the Middle East. Not even inconsequential material was entering Palestine by sea. Unless Service Airways' ten C-46s and three Constellations began ferrying supplies there would be no Jewish state.

An overstatement as well as oversimplification, perhaps, but that was how Swifty presented it to me that afternoon in New York. And it could be dangerous. He could almost guarantee an unacceptably high percentage of combat casualties.

"Combat?" I said. The word contained a stomach-fluttering quality. "You're flying transports. What combat?"

Swifty's dark eyes narrowed with impatience. "The Arabs have fighters patrolling the whole Mediterranean. Do you think they'll just politely wave us on through?"

He knew his customer. The grimmer he described it, the

more glamorous and exciting it translated in my mind. And with precisely the correct proportion of ego-massaging: the project's success depended on the participation of seasoned professionals such as myself.

Swifty did not realize he was wasting his breath. He never had to sell me. I was sold long before this, the instant I read the first line of Milton Russell's letter. *"How would you like to fly munitions and refugees to Palestine?"*

It was unimportant that the "salary" consisted of a $25 weekly expense allowance, plus hotel accommodations and a $7 per diem food allowance. It did not matter that U.S. citizens were forbidden by law to serve in the armed forces of a foreign state. Nor did it concern me that this just might not be the Nice Little War I sought. All that mattered, I told myself, was that I was helping an oppressed people establish their own country.

This was what I told myself, and it was basically true, but I also wanted the action. The excitement. The Old Days. That it was a Jewish operation, to be sure, was much of the motivation. But I liked to believe that what really motivated me was that I, an American, would be helping those people fight for, and establish, a nation in the finest American tradition.

Those People.

They were *my* people, but I had chosen not to acknowledge it. I was an American, New Englander, a Yankee, my Jewishness purely coincidental, an accident of birth. I had last visited a synagogue eleven years before, at my own bar mitzvah. I believed that much so-called Jewish persecution was self-inflicted, and anti-Semitism a catch phrase for rabbinical breast-beating. I enjoyed the delusion that Jewishness and religion were one and the same, thereby providing me, as a resolute Unbeliever, further justification for denial. Looking back, it sounds so naive—even ignorant—and of course it was all of that, but it was a conflict of identity that had been raging within me for many years.

Whatever my motives, I was in. I was a qualified, experi-

18

enced aircrewman. I could have been an idealistic Zionist, or cynical soldier-of-fortune, or footloose neurotic adventurer (this latter category probably best describing me). It made no difference. I was desperately needed.

Some fifty additional qualified and licensed men were also desperately needed. Desperate, the operative word. We were so desperate for people that my first Service Airways assignment was not to fly, but instead to research "borrowed" New York Air National Guard personnel rosters for aircrewmen with Jewish names. I would telephone the selectee, vaguely query him concerning his possible interest in a flying job. What kind of flying job? Oh, with a new overseas airline. If he expressed interest I invited him to visit the Service Airways offices.

Whether this technique actually recruited anyone, I do not recall, but somehow we were finding more and more candidates. Friends of friends, or they had heard of the outfit, or been referred by other Zionist groups.

There was Norman Moonitz, a William Bendix look-alike, a former B-17 pilot now a Brooklyn fireman. Larry Raab, he of the baby face, from whom bartenders unfailingly demanded ID, an A-20 pilot in the Pacific, now flying a non-sked Puerto Rico run. Big Ray Kurtz, also a B-17 pilot, now a New York City cop. Milton Russell, my TWA friend who had recruited me. And, talk about small worlds, two men I knew in Cairo when both were still in the U.S. Army and I was with TWA. Sheldon Eichel, a pilot, and Steve Schwartz, a navigator. Steve, eggshell-bald at twenty-six, I knew particularly well: daily, at the Payne Field Officer's Club, we played gin rummy for lunch. I don't remember him ever once buying.

And others. Pilots, navigators, radio operators. But not enough, never enough, not to adequately crew thirteen transport aircraft. I tried to interest my former Greenwich Village roommate, the ex-Navy fighter pilot, Everett Greenbaum; he said he had had his war, and one war was more than enough. We began to take anyone with even minimal experience, even pilots. We could teach them what they did not know.

We awaited the east coast arrival of the three Constellations and remaining eight C-46s. One C-46 was already here, at Teterboro, New Jersey, the same airport where I had learned to fly. Another C-46–flown by veteran ATC pilot Leo Gardner, with Steve Schwartz as navigator–had left a week earlier for Italy, and now was grounded in Geneva, Switzerland, for mechanical repairs.

Once all aircraft were ready we planned to take off en masse for Italy, to Castiglione Del Lago, a small private airfield outside Perugia, north of Rome. Military supplies purchased by Haganah representatives throughout Europe were being stockpiled at this field. Service Airways airplanes would deliver the material to Palestine, landing at night at a secret airstrip.

By May 15, therefore, the new Jewish state would have acquired the means to defend itself against the initial Arab attack. And by then, pending successful completion of negotiations with the Mexican government, Haganah would have modern fighter planes: three squadrons of P-47s.

The Jews would give a good account of themselves.

But it all depended on us, Service Airways–ATC, as we had begun to call ourselves. ATC, Air Transport Command. With the Royal Navy blockading the Mediterranean, not a rifle, not a single cartridge, not even a screwdriver could arrive in Palestine unless we flew it in.

In the meantime, waiting, we lived at the Henry Hudson Hotel on West 57th Street–familiar to me from TWA days–a hotel that catered to transient airline crews. Perfect cover for us, for that is precisely what we were: transient airline crews.

During the day Chief of Operations Bill Gerson worked with the pilots at Teterboro, checking them out in that one available C-46. I organized a radio operator's orientation-refresher course. The navigators relearned their celestial and studied North Atlantic airways charts. In between, we scavenged Army & Navy stores from Brooklyn to the Bronx for flying boots, jackets, parachutes, Mae Wests, rafts, radio equipment, flashlights, emergency rations, first-aid kits. Someone even brought in two gross of Julius Schmidt & Sons "Ramses Brand" condoms. Swifty refused to reimburse the purchaser.

At night we hung out at the Henry Hudson's bar, "The Ferris Wheel." We got to know each other, formed friend-ships and cliques. We ate and drank together, chased women, argued fiercely–and unsuccessfully–with Swifty about money: $25 a week simply was not enough, not in New York. We exchanged rumors tirelessly: our phones were tapped, the FBI was tailing us, the Jewish Agency had pur-chased a war-surplus aircraft carrier, the U.S. government had clamped an embargo on all heavy aircraft leaving the country, the good-looking blonde who lived in the hotel was really a British agent.

In mid-March the first Connie arrived, flown by Sam Lewis, a former TWA captain, one of TWA's few Jewish cap-tains. Lewis, who had sacrificed his hard-earned airline seniority to fly for this Jewish cause, brought the Connie into a remote airfield in the New Jersey tomato country. The field, a wartime USAAF training base, was now privately owned and operated. Hangar space had been leased to Service Airways.

Called Millville Municipal Airport after the sleepy little nearby town, the field was ideal for our purposes, far enough from the metropolitan area not to attract attention, yet only a two-hour drive away. And its 5,000-foot concrete runway could accommodate our large airplanes.

A few days after the Connie's arrival three C-46s landed at Millville, bringing with them from California some dozen mechanics, non-Jews, top professionals hired by Al Schwim-mer. Simultaneously, all aircrewmen–all fifteen of us!–were transferred from New York to Millville. All at once the tiny airport bustled with activity.

Gerson assigned Raab, Eichel, and me to fly the Teterboro C-46 to Millville. Raab's total C-46 flying time was all of two hours. Eichel had never logged a C-46 takeoff or landing. Gerson personally drove us from the Henry Hudson Hotel to Teterboro Airport.

The entire forty-minute drive was consumed with a continual flow of C-46 advice from Gerson: " . . . she tends to yaw to the left on takeoff." "Keep a constant eye on the props. You just can't rely on those damned four-bladed Curtiss electric propellers!" "And, please, remember what I said about the fuel cross-feed!" "And for God's sake, if you should lose the left engine, you'll have only about three seconds to transfer control boost to the good engine!"

Thirty-five, Bill Gerson was the Old Man, the father figure, the voice of reason, the guy you told your troubles to. Balding, slight, with an almost stoic gentleness concealing great strength and style. He had served as a USAAF major in World War II. An ardent Zionist, he left a wife, two young daughters, and his prosperous Los Angeles flying school to join us. More accurately, we had joined him. He was one of the first to be recruited by Al Schwimmer.

That day at Teterboro he was like a father lecturing a son on the first solo with the family car; a mother bird preparing her chicks for their first flight. He boarded the airplane with us, ran through each single checklist item. He even started the engines for us, cocking an ear to each engine as it surged into life, listening for the slightest suspicious sound.

I accompanied him back through the cabin to the door. He climbed down the ladder to the ground, turned, and faced me. He started speaking, then stopped. For a long troubled moment, he peered at me and then, with a lame grin, gestured me to pull up the ladder. I closed the door and hurried back to the flight deck.

Through the left side window I glanced down at Gerson outside. He trotted doggedly alongside the taxiing airplane, directing Raab onto the access strip. He followed us all the way to the run-up area and, there, listened anxiously to each roaring engine as we executed the run-up checklist.

It was at that instant, standing behind Raab on the flight deck, gazing down at Bill Gerson outside, I thought, "This gigantic airplane—and three Jews are flying it!"

This had popped into my head with a totally unfamiliar sense of pride and achievement. Pride at being a Jew. No Hank Greenberg Syndrome this time. This time it was *me*, the first time I had ever known such pride. I, the "Anglicized Jew," always so careful to emphasize my Americanness. I, whose very name, Livingston, had always provided me the privilege of Passing. Now, suddenly, Passing was unnecessary. I did not want to Pass. I wanted to Belong. I did Belong.

Three Jews are flying it.

TWO

LAPSA

" . . . I think you're more comfortable writing about Jewish characters."

Forty-two years later, in 1990, in California, this was said to me by an editor in New York. He had just finished reading the first draft of a new novel and had phoned me, troubled by what he felt was a certain brittleness, a lack of compassion in my main character. This main character, an aviation pioneer-tycoon–a composite of Lindbergh, Boeing, Douglas, et al–obviously could not be Jewish.

I remember how the conversation brought to mind that 1948 day in Teterboro and the pride I felt of three Jews flying the airplane, and of being a part of what eventually would be the Israeli Air Force. And I remember, too, thinking about what had afterwards brought me to California, which had nothing to do with Jews, Jewishness, or Israel.

It was money.

In 1953, after a brief period in Europe flying for what can quixotically be called a "charter airline," and then nearly a year with the Korean Air Lift, and finally a belated education at Brandeis University, I had settled down in Massachusetts to make my living as a writer. In the six years from 1953 to 1959, I wrote dozens of short stories and three novels. I sold five of the stories and all three novels. It was all quite gratifying, but not very profitable. It was not the way to get rich. If you want to get rich, they said, write for the movies. For a writer, they said, Hollywood was a money tree.

So in 1959 I came and shared in the tree's fruit. I wrote some seventy-five television shows, a half dozen feature films, including one with the dubious distinction of being at the time the most expensive film ever made: $53 million, *Star Trek–The Motion Picture*, which ultimately became one of the highest-grossing pictures in history, and from which I personally earned close to a half million dollars.

The Money Tree.

There were times of course when the pickings were not so bountiful, but with persistence (meaning you kept churning out the stories and outlines) you always, somehow, hit with one project or another that helped make up for the fallow months. On the whole–albeit sometimes precariously–you lived pretty well. After almost a quarter century of this, however, I one day in effect peered into a mirror and saw a man whose productive time was running out and who was squandering whatever time remained as a journeyman movie and television writer.

In 1983, then, after twenty four years in Hollywood, I realized I had to return to where I started: writing novels. I had to write something I wanted to write, something that if successful would be wholly and totally credited to my own singular ability, not a director's or actor's, or just plain luck. Conversely, if I failed, I could not blame the director or actor or just plain luck. What I wrote would be mine. No one could rewrite me, fire me, or–even better–not hire me.

In Hollywood parlance, when a working screenwriter undertakes an endeavor such as writing a book, it is known as his "Fuck-you Project." It ostensibly frees him forever from the demeaning bondage of competing with a thousand other working colleagues for the handful of assignments.

While novels have been known to make some authors millions of dollars, gambling the year or more to write them is akin to buying a lottery ticket or pulling the handle on a progressive Las Vegas slot machine. Except that the lottery and slot odds are better.

A fact already well known to me.

The real question, though, was could I do it? Could I do it after nearly twenty-five years away from writing narrative, twenty-five years of writing screenplays, which are really "shorthand" and designed for a totally different medium. So I did not know if I could do it. I knew only that when I stopped writing novels I had just begun to learn how to write them. I would have to learn all over again.

I had had this idea about a "Jewish Godfather," a story inspired by the life and times of an infamous and excitingly enigmatic gangland figure, Meyer Lansky, who had only recently died. Of old age. The character in my book would embody much of the Lansky business brilliance, but would also be a man with vulnerability, a human being. I knew if I could humanize a gangster I would have a successful novel. It took me four long months to write the outline, but I knew it was a good story. I knew it worked.

And so did I.

Two and one half years, but the pages piled up. In January, 1987, *Ride a Tiger* was published, a 611-page saga of seven decades of a man's life. When I saw it between covers for the first time I felt a glow of achievement I had not felt for years. I did not care if the book sold one copy or 100,000. What mattered was that I had done it.

I thought of my father, dead some seventeen years. I saw him in my mind, my beautiful new book in his hand, proudly entering the barber shop or the hospital or a patient's home. "This is my son's," I could hear him saying. "His *fourth* novel! Quite a boy, isn't he?"

My father's proclivity for flaunting my accomplishments to everyone and anyone invariably embarrassed and angered me. I never really understood why. I think it was because I did not understand him. Just as he, I am sure, never really understood why I went to Israel.

But for that matter, then, neither did I.

My father was a man whose entire life and career was devoted to caring for the underprivileged. He enjoyed helping people. I think it was his only pleasure. A first generation American, the eldest of nine children of penniless Russian immigrants, he had worked his way through college with jobs ranging from hospital janitor to milkman.

He first earned a Bachelor of Arts degree from what was then called "Normal School," qualifying him to teach in elementary schools (where he found it expedient to change his name from Meyer Levinson to Myron Livingston).

Then, in World War I, on a U.S. Army program, my father attended Boston University Medical School. He completed his internship in 1923, married my mother, and a year later—the year I was born—settled in Haverhill. Not only did the small shoe factory town with its sizable Jewish population seem an ideal location for the young doctor, but he had been offered the post of City Physician: the welfare doctor. Lacking funds to purchase an existing practice, this at least provided a stipend sufficient to support his family while he established himself. He would remain City Physician—both officially and not—for forty-seven more years.

My father's ambitions were limited. He never aspired to anything more than the cautious, conservative general practitioner he was. Within those parameters, however, he proved eminently successful. Years after it was abandoned as a routine medical service, he continued to make house calls–and no matter what time of day or night. When other doctors were referring their delinquent lists to collection agencies, he still accepted five pounds of tomatoes for a fee, or a fence painted, a lawn seeded. An accountant once estimated my father's unpaid fees at more than $150,000–in 1945 dollars. He feared offending people. He was a small man among other small men, and in this he felt most comfortable and secure.

He also happened to be physically small: short, although quite well-proportioned so that one really did not notice. *I* noticed. To my great dismay, you see, I had inherited his height. One of my earliest memories is the wife of the pharmacist-owner of a drugstore asking my father if I wasn't small for my age. He replied, almost proudly it seemed to me, "Yes, he's going to be short like me." I hated him for that.

I resented my height. He did not. It never disturbed or inhibited him. He accepted it. I did not, and could not. He never attempted–nor, I am sure, ever felt any need–to compensate. I did, endlessly; it shaded and influenced my every act. From deliberately picking fights with anyone calling me "Shorty"–obviously they were always bigger–to developing a consummate preference for tall women to, I am certain, volunteering for the Israeli Air Force.

I was driven to do things better than the other, ordinary guy. More spectacular, more colorful, more eventful. It would be many painful years and experiences before I finally realized that I would not wake one morning to find myself six feet tall, or even five and one half. And even more years to realize that the only person giving a damn about it was me. Only me, no one else.

I think my father tried to convey all that to me, but failing to comprehend its significance (it never bothered *him*, why should it me?), he was unable to properly articulate it. And I suppose it might not have gotten through to me anyway. I would have given it no credence because I knew he did not understand me, and what he did not understand confused and intimidated him. Anything beyond his own field of vision was beyond his understanding. For my part, intuitively realizing all this, I never demanded more from him, never expected it, consequently was seldom disappointed not receiving it.

One of those infrequent disappointments was the day I informed him of my imminent departure for Palestine. After that first meeting with Swifty in New York I had returned briefly to Haverhill for clothes and other personal belongings and, of course, to say goodbye. This time, I wanted approval. This time, it was important. Important, I know now, because my own motives were so unclear. By convincing someone else—my parents in this case—I was doing it for a Jewish cause, I might somehow convince myself.

In 1937, for $6,000, my parents had purchased an early Colonial home. During the war, with many of the city's doctors serving in the military, my father's practice had boomed. The money made it possible for my mother to completely restore the house. It was her proudest possession, filled now with rare antiques and fine furniture. It was one of the few pleasures I enjoyed in Haverhill, that house—along with, I must confess, the Haverhill Country Club's incomparable golf course—and one of the few reasons I kept returning.

So I sat with my parents in that handsomely appointed and so very comfortable living room and attempted to explain my latest "fling." They always referred to my various endeavors as "flings"—the army, TWA, Saudi Arabia, advertising, New York. But never a fling as fanciful as this new one.

Flying supplies to Palestine.

"You're crazy!"

This, immediately, from my father. My mother quietly agreed, but I knew she was only placating him. She did not want to believe I was serious. It was her way. She always tried to avoid unpleasantness, hoping that left undisturbed it might somehow be transformed into something nicer. But once she realized it as a fact, that it was happening, she could accept the reality.

He could not.

And it led to an ugly, recriminatory scene. As with most confrontations with him, I handled it badly. I threw his own words back at him: " . . . you're always telling me how I'm ashamed of being a Jew. Now I want to help the Jews, and you call me crazy."

"You can help in a dozen other different ways," he said. "A hundred ways. You don't have to kill yourself!"

"But I'll be a Jewish hero!" I shouted back. "My son, the Jewish hero!"

"All right, never mind the wise guy stuff."

"I'm doing what he always wanted me to do," I said to my mother. "But because he doesn't like the way I'm doing it, I'm a wise guy."

"You have no respect for your parents," my father said. "You don't care how you hurt them."

"Respect is *earned*," I said.

He was outraged. "I haven't earned it?"

"You be the best judge of that," I said.

"What have I done not to earn respect?" He directed this to my mother. "I've worked my fingers to the bone!" He faced me again. "For *you*! To give you all this!" He waved his hand around the room, at the genuine Chippendale kidney-shaped desk, the deep-piled Persian rug, the authentic Queen Anne velour sofa. "You, your brother and sister. And what do I get for it?"

It grew worse; and finally, as always, he resorted to his ultimate weapon. Emotion. Tears, pleas. I was not thinking of him, of what would happen to him if anything happened to me.

So true, so true.

(Five years later, when I fell in love with a French girl, a non-Jew, he said that if I married her it would kill him. It turned out that I eventually married a hometown Jewish girl;

31

we eloped, and when we told him, he wept with joy, proclaiming it the best thing that had ever happened to *him*.)

Although he lived twenty-three more years, and there would be many more confrontations, I think Palestine was the one issue on which we might have broken through. We might have communicated. If I had managed it differently, if I had tried to understand him. But I did not want to understand him. I could not—or did not want to—make the effort. I did not perceive that he wanted me to understand him. When, decades afterward, I finally saw it, it was too late.

And in the end, that day in Haverhill, he simply collapsed, weeping. My mother looked helplessly at me and said, "Do what you have to do."

I kissed her goodbye and started out. I walked past my father. He sat, peering up at me, tears streaming down his cheeks. I stopped. We regarded each other silently. For some reason I suddenly remembered, as a child, the sandpapery feel of his beard stubble when at the end of the day sometimes he placed his cheek next to mine in a goodnight kiss. Now, looking at him, his eyes moist and red, his face contorted, I wanted to touch him. To ask him to please try to understand. But I did nothing and said nothing. I turned and left.

Feeling, then, no guilt. Only relief, freedom. I knew that when I returned safely from this "fling," my father—as he did almost ritually—would boast to his friends and patients of my adventures. "Can you imagine where the rascal was?" he would say, "rascal" uttered with affection and pride. "In Israel. In their air force, by God! Israel! That rascal!"

2.

And indeed I was in their air force. Which was corporately camouflaged in March of 1948 not only as Service Airways, Inc., but also, of all unlikely entities, *Lineas Aereas de Panama, S.A.*

Lineas Aereas de Panama, LAPSA, the airline of the Republic of Panama.

Panama . . . ?

Yes, Panama. Very much so and, in the winter and spring of 1948, for the most opportunistic of reasons: to help maintain the stability of the political party then in power in that country. Presidential elections were scheduled for late April but only a miracle, or a series of them, could save the incumbent government. A government racked with scandal from four years of unending brazen graft and corruption.

Among the more glaring boondoggles was a multimillion-dollar investment in the construction of a new airport on the Pacific side of the Isthmus, at Tocumen, an inconvenient distance from Panama City.

Tocumen Airport, now open for business, was virtually unused. Commercial airlines preferred the superior facilities and geography of the United States Air Force base at Albrook Field. Tocumen's very existence therefore totally justified the opposition party's charges of waste and cronyism. Tocumen was a serious political liability.

Into this situation stepped Service Airways Executive Vice President, Martin Bellefond. Big, blond, ruggedly handsome, Marty Bellefond was a disarmingly personable thirty-one-year-old Jewish ex-USAAF pilot with the nerve of a Mississippi riverboat gambler and the persuasiveness of a Klondike land speculator. He convinced the Panamanian government that he could turn Tocumen into a bustling and profitable enterprise; indeed, the hub of world-wide operations for a Panamanian flag airline.

They awarded him the franchise. Lineas Aereas de Panama, Sociedad Anonima.

LAPSA.

And Marty Bellefond, now as LAPSA's President and CEO, delivered.

An imposing fleet of large transport aircraft, the first of which, a Constellation, had already arrived at Tocumen. The remaining two Constellations and nine C-46s would soon follow. These were of course the very same Connies and C-46s registered to Service Airways. Service Airways and LAPSA were one and the same, although this pertinent fact was discreetly withheld from the Panamanians. Along with the fact that Service Airways was the Haganah air arm, and in a few weeks would be employed shuttling arms from a secret Italian airfield to a secret Palestinian airfield.

At the time, however, the arrangement proved enormously beneficial to the Panamanian government. It could demonstrate the viability of Tocumen Airport, perhaps in time to swing the elections. So it was a kind of quid pro quo, although far more beneficial to the new Jewish state whose vital supplies could now be funneled through an accredited international airline, thereby circumventing the U.S. State Department's embargo of arms to Palestine. Obviously, the embargo did not apply to foreign flag carriers.

LAPSA was a foreign flag carrier.

The Connie now at Tocumen bore on its outboard vertical rudder fins a Panamanian flag and Panamanian registration number, RX-121. Atop the fuselage, running the entire length from flight deck window to cabin door, were flowing blue scripted letters: *Lineas Aereas de Panama, S.A.* Behind the door, large blocked blue letters read L A P S A.

Sam Lewis had flown the Connie to Tocumen. RX-121, the proud flagship of the new international airline, was greeted by an enthusiastic welcoming committee of important Panamanian government functionaries.

In the meantime, at Millville, we worked on the second Constellation and awaited the arrival from California of the remaining Connie and five C-46s. We planned a mass flight to Panama in the next three weeks, before April 15. On that date yet another U.S. embargo would be imposed: aircraft weighing over 35,000 pounds, even those of foreign registry, could not be exported without proper State Department license.

We lived in a small Millville hotel, two and sometimes three to a room. We spent the days at the airport, flying, studying, crating the spare parts that would accompany us to Panama, helping the mechanics (more often, getting in their way). At night we hung around the coffee shop adjoining the Millville bus station, or played poker or gin rummy in our rooms.

We scoured the New York newspapers for news of Palestine: the British were evacuating in a slow, orderly fashion, "orderly" a euphemism for turning over to the Arabs surplus arms and installations, while confiscating all Haganah munitions they could find. Haganah elements and irregular Arab forces fought for control of the Tel Aviv–Jerusalem highway. For a few days Jerusalem was actually cut off. Jewish towns and kibbutzim under continual attack, heavy casualties. In Haifa, the British intervened to prevent a complete Arab rout. But it was all still so far away and hard to relate to, and the real war would not start until the British Mandate officially ended on May 15.

In seven weeks.

Each day at the field a parked black sedan overlooked the ramp area. In this car were two, sometimes three, grim men of indeterminate age. They wore overcoats and fedoras and sat patiently throughout the day observing our mechanics working on engines, our aircrews landing or taking off on training flights, our personnel coming and going. At night, another black sedan relieved the first one, other grim men in overcoats and fedoras.

But at night, too, yet another car appeared. This other car was parked in full view of the black sedan, but across the entire ramp distance. In this car were our own people, usually two of us, each pair assigned to the duty according to a rotating schedule composed by Bill Gerson. Our cars, depending on availability, were either Swifty's handsome new canary yellow 1948 Packard convertible, Schwimmer's disreputable old La Salle; or, now and then, a rented Chevy. We were watching the men in the black sedan, who were watching us.

They were T-men, U.S. Treasury Department agents. They

had served official notice that our airplanes were prohibited from leaving the continental United States. We, they officially informed us, were suspected of carrying contraband.

Contraband in our case probably meant anything from machine guns to ping-pong balls. We were watching them to make certain that they, in their zeal to enforce the law, were not tempted to take it upon themselves to assure the sudden and mysterious appearance of contraband on one of our airplanes.

We never spoke to them, nor they to us, or otherwise acknowledged each other. Except when their night shift, relieved by the day shift, drove past us leaving the airport. We always threw them crisp, exaggerated salutes. They pretended not to notice.

We played this game for several weeks. At least it broke the monotony. That, and infrequent commutes to New York. Trips for "morale purposes," thoughtfully arranged by Bill Gerson, either in whatever available car, or in an Ercoupe owned by Schwimmer.

It was in this Ercoupe that for the first and only time I saw Bill Gerson—the gentlest and mildest of all men—lose his temper. And I was the cause of it.

An Ercoupe is a tiny, low-winged, enclosed cockpit, two-place, single-engined airplane. It is dual-controlled, and uncomplicated. I was flying it, with Gerson, from Millville to Teterboro. The day was dark and overcast. Without a contact horizon I was unable to keep the little airplane on course.

Calmly, patiently, and at first with a tinge of amusement, Gerson corrected my errors: "Harold, this machine is supposed to be stall-proof, but somehow I think you're about to prove otherwise." Or, "Hey, son, the airplane has a compass, you know . . . " For a while he offered all this with affectionate indulgence. But I was all over the sky. Gradually, Gerson's face tightened with annoyance. His voice turned increasingly brittle.

The last thing on earth I wanted was Bill Gerson's displeasure. Him of all people. He had specifically requested me as his permanent radio operator. A signal honor because if our critical pilot shortage continued and no experienced co-pilot was available, I would sit in the right seat. I loved the idea and I loved Gerson for his confidence in me, especially his promise to begin checking me out. And here I was, unable to keep an Ercoupe, a toy, on course.

It was one of those days. The harder I tried, the tenser I became. I was blowing the whole show. Relax, I kept telling myself. Wiggle your toes, chew some gum, smoke a cigarette. Nothing helped. I awaited the ultimate humiliation: he would wrest the controls from me.

"Goddamit!" He finally exploded. He banged his fist on the instrument panel crash pad and prodded the yoke with his fingertip, pushing it slightly forward. "This," he said, his voice rising as the airplane's nose dipped, "this makes it go fast!" He wrapped the same finger around the yoke edge to delicately pull it back so the nose rose a few degrees. "And this makes it go slow!"

I peered at him, startled. He seemed equally startled and then, totally dismayed, looked away. I gripped the yoke even tighter—and completely overcontrolled, sending the airplane into a wide, sloppy turn.

"Jesus!" Gerson said, closing his eyes in abject pain.

I tried to level out, only to overcontrol on the opposite side. Another mushy turn. Gerson shook his head sadly, resignedly. He drew in his breath to speak and I knew it would be, "All right, Harold, I'll take it." But at that very instant, like Joshua at the walls of Jericho, the overcast all at once cleared. The horizon was brilliantly outlined. A marvelously definitive black line separated earth and sky. Immediately, I had the Ercoupe's nose lined up. Immediately, I was flying straight and level.

"Mr. Livingston," Gerson said slowly, wearily, "I will make a pilot out of you—even if it kills me!" And he turned away, muttering, " . . . and it probably will!"

I landed with no trouble, a "grease" job. We parked the Ercoupe at the Teterboro transient aircraft area and walked to Operations to close the flight plan. Just as we stepped inside, Gerson stopped. He studied me a brief, reflective moment. Then he grinned. He ruffled my hair and said, "On the way back, you'll do better."

I idolized him. He was like an older, wiser brother. He exemplified "idealist." His plan was to someday settle in Israel, contribute to its growth. He had already contributed to mine.

Some weeks before the Ercoupe incident he had saved me from a repetition of my TWA experience, that humiliating, ego-shattering dismissal.

Shortly after joining Service Airways I had found myself faced with another near insurrection. Again, as in TWA–and even before that, once in the army–my own impatience and intolerance created resentment and dissension among the radio operators I supervised. But this was not TWA. No one was expendable, not even me.

One night at the height of it Gerson took me to dinner. He said I was a professional with much to offer. My services were sorely needed. But I was making a mess of my job. I was dealing with human beings who deserved to be treated as such, not as inferiors simply because of their inexperience.

"Come on, Bill, I'm not running a charm school," I said. "I'm trying to turn a bunch of rabble into flight radio operators. Some of these heroes can't even spell their own names, let alone learn radio procedure. What I need is some people with half a brain."

"What you need," Gerson said quietly, "is a swift kick in the ass."

But Bill Gerson kicked ass with logic. He explained the realities and practicalities. We were engaged in an operation of unimaginable significance. We were helping build a nation for people who for 2,000 years had been denied a homeland. Success hung on a single, constantly unraveling wire no stronger than its weakest strand. Personalities must be swept aside, personal ambitions sacrificed, and sometimes even principles.

What he suggested–no, what he pleaded for–was a change of attitude. It might make all the difference; to me, more than anyone else. By change of attitude, he meant more patience, more tolerance. ("You don't teach people by clubbing them over the head.") I think he intuitively sensed some inner need of mine to assume responsibility, a need he was attempting to channel into a more constructive direction.

I was too young, too immature, to concede totally, but smart enough to recognize the logic–and the warning. So I changed my attitude. For the first time in my life I made a conscious, overt effort to make myself liked. It was hard, and frustrating, and entirely contrary to my nature. It caused me much discomfort. I felt I was being dishonest and hypocritical. But it worked. My "trainees" responded. I began getting along better with them, and with everyone else. It was a learning experience.

It also kept me busy those last two weeks of March and first week of April, and that was important for us all, keeping busy. Nothing seemed to be really moving. Although the airplanes and crews were ready to leave, Service Airways attorneys had made little progress obtaining proper clearance papers. One day the clearances would be issued, the next day revoked. It went on that way for weeks. We began doubting we would ever (literally) get off the ground.

Our "morale purpose" shuttles between Millville and New York continued, but that created yet another problem: security. We knew that not only were we under U.S. Treasury Department surveillance, but also the intelligence services of at least two other nations, Great Britain and Egypt. Actually, it was stimulating to sit in the Henry Hudson's "Ferris Wheel" a few tables away from a couple of poker-faced young men you recognized from the day before in the lobby of Radio City Music Hall. The very same pair who a few days later were standing outside Carnegie Hall when Gerson, Raab, and I attended a concert. (Gerson had to practically drag us there, he claimed a little culture would not kill us.) The poker-faced young men always wore narrow-brimmed fedoras and business suits with conservative ties; it was like a uniform.

As for uniforms, someone determined that we should eventually wear them. Milton Russell was assigned the task of purchasing appropriate garb. Not U.S. Army surplus, but custom-made by one of several, hopefully patriotic, Jewish tailors submitting the lowest bid. Russell decided on gabardine khaki Eisenhower jackets, cotton shirts, and poplin slacks. And USAAF silver pilots wings, whose air force medallion was to be replaced with an enameled world globe, over which would be superimposed the letters L A P S A.

Russell's clothing deal proved prohibitively expensive, so we never received those snappy uniforms. In the end we would wear a uniform of sorts: our own old army suntan shirts and slacks, and fur-collared all-weather nylon flying jackets Russell did manage to obtain. He also salvaged a few sets of sample wings, and on these–instead of L A P S A–he superimposed a *Magen David*, the six-sided Jewish star, the Star of David.

So much for Security.

Security also brings to mind a young woman named Ada White whom I like to recall as vaguely resembling Lana Turner. Tall, blonde, and certainly with Lana's figure, Ada lived at the Henry Hudson Hotel. She said she was from Cleveland, Ohio, a commercial artist, looking for a job in the big city. I had met her at the hotel bar one night, only to be quickly joined by Raab trying to move in, and then by Moonitz who moved us both out.

We told Ada we were flying students, billeted by our school at the Henry Hudson. She did not for a moment believe this, and insisted we were "into something real odd." But she said if "students" was what we wanted her to

40

believe, she'd go along with the gag. She attached herself to our group, joining us for drinks, dinner, walks in the park, whatever. She was relentlessly curious about our activities, and once cleverly goaded Russell into showing her those famous Star of David wings.

One Saturday afternoon shortly after we had moved to Millville, Russell delivered some spare engine parts to the New Jersey airfield. He invited Ada, who he knew was anxious to visit Moonitz, to drive down with him from New York. They drove directly to the airport just in time to watch Moonitz, flying with Gerson on a check ride, grease a C-46 onto the runway.

Gerson, appalled that Ada had seen the Millville installation, ordered her back to New York within the hour. To go the same way she came, with Russell. But Russell had unloaded the spare parts and was on his way back. Then, dammit, Moonitz would have to drive her back. But only a single car was available, and that was needed for local transportation. No trains, buses, or even taxis. I suggested Gerson ask the T-men to give Ada a lift; he was not amused. He had no choice, then, but allow her to remain overnight. Being Gerson, he quickly cooled off and took us all to dinner. The next morning Moonitz flew Ada back to New York—in one of the C-46s. By then it made no difference. She had already seen the airplanes, all of them.

Security.

(Not long after we left the country for good, Ada White checked out of the Henry Hudson Hotel. No forwarding address. Although to my knowledge none of us ever saw or heard from her again, it was exciting to believe she was a British agent. She might have been.)

Meanwhile, according to the newspapers, things were not going well in Palestine. The Arabs had tightened their blockade of Jerusalem. A number of doctors, nurses, and technicians were killed in the ambush of a convoy attempting to reach the Hadassah Hospital on Mount Scopus. Already, even before the invasion started, the war had cost the lives of more than twelve hundred Jews.

And we were still in Millville, New Jersey.

Work continued on the airplanes. More pilots and crewmen joined us. I brought in an advertising agency friend, Al Raisin, a former B-17 pilot. Someone else found our first "goy," Tryg Maseng, who left his studies at Columbia University to fly with us. And Hal Auerbach, an ex-Navy bomber pilot. Sol Fingerman, a radio operator, also former Naval Air Service. And others, more all the time, but we were still dangerously undercrewed.

What a way to run an airline.

And then one afternoon at Millville, Gerson announced that Swifty was expected to return from Washington that evening with the clearances. These clearances were for the C-46s only, not the remaining two Constellations. Both Connies were now at Newark Airport under U.S. Customs impound, which for some strange, convoluted legal reasoning precluded their transfer to Panamanian registry. The four Millville C-46s were to leave for Panama the next day, April 8, without waiting for the other five C-46s from California; even if those five did arrive, they could not be adequately crewed for an overseas flight.

As for the existing crews, they had been shuffled, reshuffled, and shuffled again. I was no longer with Gerson, who had been ordered to California to pick up one of the C-46s there. But Gerson's replacement unexpectedly quit, and so Bill was to make the Panama flight anyway. I was with Larry Raab now and I decided to stay with him. Our crew consisted only of Larry and me, and Jim Wilson, LAPSA's chief mechanic. Plus a passenger, Milton Lowenstein, a fifty-year-old Jewish Agency executive who would assume administrative duties in Panama.

Swifty brought the clearance papers. We were to leave late the following afternoon, the four airplanes taking off at twenty-minute intervals. We would fly at night down the

Atlantic coast to Kingston, Jamaica, for refueling, then direct to Panama.

At 3:30 P.M., April 8, one hour before the scheduled take-off, the T-men notified Swifty that the airplanes were not permitted to depart. On what basis? We knew the T-men were aware of our State Department clearance.

The T-men quoted a federal statute authorizing them to prevent the departure of any ship or aircraft suspected of carrying contraband.

That again? Weren't they already satisfied we were *not* carrying contraband?

Apparently not, for they now termed "contraband" the two disassembled BT-13 trainer airplanes, one stowed in our C-46, the other in Moonitz's.

Rather than engage the T-men in another interminable debate over the definition of "contraband," Swifty chose instead to remind them that the statutes applied to U.S. registered aircraft only. Our C-46s were foreign flag carriers.

The senior agent, a tall, lean, white-haired man with the somber bearing of a mortician, quietly rebutted the point. "Those planes have U.S. numbers," he said.

"Only because we haven't had time to change them," Swifty said. "We planned to do it in Panama."

"They're U.S. registered," said the agent whose name, according to the embossed business card he had presented—a card Swifty gave me as a souvenir, and which I still possess—was Ralph Fisher. "U.S. registered," he repeated. "I'm sorry, Captain Schindler, but you will not be permitted to leave."

"I'll be back in a second," Swifty said, and vanished into a hangar. Ralph Fisher glanced at his colleagues and shook his head sadly, as though saying "These Jews just don't know how to take no for an answer." It happened that I knew Mr. Fisher—more accurately, knew of him. Not long before this, he had had a conversation with Bill Gerson, the gist of which Bill related to me.

In a moment of pure whimsy, never expecting a serious–if any–response, Gerson had asked Fisher why the Treasury Department was so determined to prevent the airplanes from leaving. Fisher replied that the Department was merely carrying out the policy of the United States government which, after some goading from Gerson, he admitted was to prevent the Jews of Palestine from receiving munitions. Gerson then pointed out to him that the U.S. had voted in favor of the UN resolution that partitioned Palestine into separate Arab and Jewish states; without arms, there could be no Jewish state. So where was the logic of an embargo? Fisher's reply, Gerson told me, sounded like an Egyptian–or British–propaganda leaflet: " . . . the Russians are dying to get into that neck of the woods. That's the last thing we want. We're afraid if the Jews and Arabs fight, the communists will use it as an excuse to go in. To stop the bloodshed, they'll say. If that happens, we'll probably have to go in. Is that what you want, Captain? Us fighting the Russians over Palestine?"

Gerson had said, "So if the Jews don't have guns, they can't fight, which means the U.S. and the Soviets won't get involved, but which also means the Arabs will take over the whole place?"

"I guess that's what it means, yes," Fisher had said.

When Gerson repeated the story to me, I remember saying that if that was U.S. policy, it made no sense. "You're wrong, kid," he had answered. "It makes a lot of sense. If you're sitting in the State Department, that is, and you'll do anything not to offend the British, who are trying like hell to appease the Arabs. Or," he added, "if you're a lobbyist for Standard Oil."

To me, it still made no sense, and I was still trying to reason it out when Swifty emerged from the hangar. He had been gone less than a minute and was flanked by two of our mechanics. One mechanic carried a bucket of blue paint and a brush. The other mechanic carried a ladder, which he propped against the rear fuselage of the nearest C-46. The first mechanic climbed the ladder, dipped brush into bucket, and on the windowless area aft of the C-46's cargo door, began printing a large **R**. Then an **X**, and then the numbers **1 3 5**.

RX-135, the airplane's Panamanian license designator.

The paint, a thin household type, almost immediately began running. From each letter and number little rivulets of blue dripped sloppily down the side of the aluminum fuselage.

The mechanics moved on to the next airplane and repeated the procedure: RX-136. Then RX-137, and RX-138. For 138, my airplane, some paint remained. Just enough for the mechanic-artist to slap the letters L A P S A above the numbers. It reminded you of a child smearing paint on a fence, and looked it, with the paint of those letters bleeding bluely into the numbers and letters directly below.

But that was it. Now it was official. The "transfer" was done. No longer were our aircraft subject to the rules and regulations of the United States of America.

The T-men were unimpressed. They parked their sedan directly in front of RX-135, Auerbach's airplane. Swifty accused them of delaying us on any pretext to insure our presence in the United States on April 15, the date the new embargo—which included foreign flag carriers—became effective. The T-men telephoned their district office in Philadelphia for further instructions. We made phone calls of our own. We were assured that injunctions were en route, and rulings from Federal judges, even policy decisions from the White House itself.

We waited, they waited. Hours passed, night fell. Unless we took off soon we would be unable as per plan to land at Tocumen in daylight. Swifty decided it was now or never. It might be our last chance. He went to the T-men's car.

"Mr. Fisher," he said, "I am ordering my airplanes to take off immediately—"

"—not until we hear," said the T-man.

But Swifty called to Auerbach, "Okay, Hal, get going!"

Auerbach jogged toward his airplane. The T-man shouted after him, "No! By government order, you are prohibited from leaving the United States!"

"Mr. Fisher, these airplanes are going to take off," Swifty said quietly. He turned and started walking toward his own airplane, RX-136, but stopped abruptly and faced the T-men again. "If you want to stop them, you'll have to shoot them down!"

Shoot us down . . . ?

Good old Swifty.

But ten minutes later, Auerbach simply wheeled RX-135 around the black sedan and taxied out to the hold area. He ran up the engines and then, landing lights coming on, moved on to the runway. The lights, cutting horizontally into the darkness, resembled a pair of disembodied white lines, moving forward now as the airplane began rolling. The hornet-buzz of the engines roared louder, shriller. Louder, louder, louder, until the very ground beneath you vibrated; and then, all at once, the two white lines angled upward into the black sky. The roar of the engines quickly receded to a steady, almost quiet purr. And then the lights, retracting, shone straight downward like long, ever lengthening silvery legs. Which then, as the landing lights went off, vanished, and all that was visible now were the engine exhausts glowing red in the night.

Twenty minutes later Gerson in RX-137 followed. We, RX-138, were scheduled next, but Moonitz in RX-136 had somehow taxied out in front of us and blocked our runway access. We had to wait for him to receive a revised air traffic control clearance radioed from New York Center. Anticipating Moonitz's immediate clearance, we did not cut our engines. We waited, engines idling, nearly fifteen minutes for Moonitz to take off. Twenty minutes later, we followed.

A smooth, textbook takeoff. The airplane wanted to lift off halfway down the runway, but with our cargo of spare generators and the dismantled BT-13 we were grossing 53,000 pounds, 5,000 more than the permissible maximum. Raab took no chances; he held her down. The landing lights shone on into the emptiness beyond the runway boundary.

And still Raab waited. Until Wilson, in the right seat, called out, "Ninety . . . !" Raab rolled back the elevator trim. The airplane flew into the air.

I spoke into my microphone, "Millville Radio, one-three-eight off the ground at one-nine-two-seven. Wheels coming up."

Wheels coming up. Little did we know.

3.

Our assigned altitude was 8,000 feet. Climbing out to it we could coax only a top speed of 115 mph from the overloaded airplane. And burned up well over 200 gallons of gasoline getting there. Not until Wilson trained an Aldis lamp on the landing gear did we discover the problem. The right wheel had never retracted. Despite the gear signal lights in the green, the right wheel had been down since takeoff.

Wilson lowered the left wheel, then raised both wheels again. This time both retracted properly. But if our navigation was not pin-point perfect, excessive gasoline consumption from the dragging wheel and from time on the ground awaiting the ATC clearances posed a potential fuel problem.

We carried no navigator. We were relying on the weather–the forecast of clear and unlimited visibility–and the radio compasses. Radio reception was poor, a constant crackle of atmospheric static. From Norfolk to Miami I could obtain only inferior quality radio beacon position fixes. Compounding the problem, I had lost contact with the other airplanes. We were alone.

Despite all this, the first four hours of the flight were fairly routine. We estimated our position slightly south of the Florida keys, perhaps already overflying Cuba. On course, or at worst only a few miles off. It was then I finally transmitted a signal clear enough for Miami Control to plot a triangulated fix.

Not only were we not overflying Cuba—we were 150 miles *west* of the island, somewhere over the Gulf of Mexico. One hundred fifty miles off course! Raab immediately corrected our heading, but now to reach Kingston we needed 450 gallons of fuel. The gauges indicated remaining fuel at slightly less than that amount.

"Hey, buddy," Wilson asked me quietly. "Can you swim?"

"No, but I can float," I said, not yet too concerned. Now, back on course, I was confident we could make Kingston.

Ten minutes later I was not so sure. The needles on the main fuel tank gauges had dipped even further. Wilson and I exchanged some gallows humor, and then he asked, "How long can you stay afloat?"

I framed a tough, wry reply, but the words from my mouth were gibberish. All at once I could not speak. My throat was parchment dry. My temples pounded with each loud beat of my heart.

Wilson smiled thinly, almost sadly. He understood my terror. He was a big, stocky Southerner, a non-Jew receiving a respectable salary, but a thorough professional totally dedicated both to his craft and to Al Schwimmer. I had first met Wilson on that memorable day in March when Raab, Eichel, and I ferried the C-46 to Millville from Teterboro.

He, Wilson, was the first person to greet us. Stepping down to the ramp, we stood shoulder to shoulder facing him. Between us—Raab, Eichel, and me—is a height difference of, at most, two inches. (I, alas, the shortest.) Raab had extended his hand and said, "Hi, I'm Larry Raab."

"Where's the captain?" Wilson asked.

"*I'm* the captain," Larry said.

Wilson's forehead had wrinkled in a narrow, perplexed frown. "Jesus, sweet Jesus!" he said. "An airline with midget crews!"

I remembered that and tried to laugh. It sounded like a hoarse rasp. Larry glanced at me over his shoulder. "Relax," he said. "We're on course."

"Yeah," I said, and concentrated on contacting Miami again. I was receiving bearings from them every fifteen minutes, and we were indeed back on course and had been for the past hour, steering straight for Kingston.

Outside, ahead and below, a thin but solid undercast extended in the dark as far as you could see. It covered the water like an endless blanket of slate gray. The sun would not rise for more than an hour. Not only were we in danger now of running out of fuel before reaching Kingston but, worse, running out of it at sea, in darkness.

"What about air-sea rescue?" I asked Raab. "Shall we alert them?"

"Not yet," he said.

I knew—and agreed with him—that we should not call unnecessary attention to ourselves, but neither did I want us to go down with no one aware of our location. He looked at me again. He read my mind.

"We'll wait," he said.

We flew on. The engines droned evenly, reassuringly, the exhaust flame steady and blue. I exchanged places with Wilson and sat in the right seat while he rested on the floor with his back propped against the bulkhead wall. Every now and then our passenger, Milton Lowenstein, came to the flight deck to glance at the fuel gauges and study our faces. Each time, he asked the same question in the same hopeful voice, "How's it going?"

For some reason he always directed the question to Wilson, and each time Wilson replied with the same answer. "Fifty-fifty."

We drank coffee and smoked cigarettes. We said little. Finally, Wilson rose. He leaned past me over the pedestal and tapped a fingernail on the glass of the main tank gauge.

"Down to two hundred," he said. He looked at Raab. "I

don't think we can make it."

Raab said nothing a moment. He sat, one elbow propped on a chair arm rest, chin cupped comfortably in his palm. He was gazing out the front window, his face tinged an eerie green from the reflection of the fluorescent lights trained on the instrument panel. He remained silent, motionless, another moment. Then he moved his head slightly, his eyes fixed on the instruments, his lips pursed in a tight narrow line. He seemed almost in a trance. Then he turned to me.

"All right, Harold," he said quietly. "Tell Miami to alert air-sea rescue."

"I did," I said. "Ten minutes ago."

He said nothing, only nodded with a grim little smile and turned away. He leaned forward, resting both elbows against the crash pad. He stared out the window. I knew he was planning ahead, each minute detail of the ditching. I also knew he had never ditched before. But then again, ditching was not a certainty. We might make it.

If the gauges were wrong. If the wind was right. If we were lucky. Wrong, Right & Lucky. Incorporated. It sounded like a firm of attorneys.

Or undertakers.

Ironically, now, radio transmissions were five by five, loud and clear. I was in contact with both Miami and Kingston. Their operators were very concerned and solicitous. I pictured them in their warm secure stations, communicating with each other on a different frequency, anticipating my "Mayday" signal. They were safe, and I resented them.

The inflatable life raft was positioned near the airplane's rear door. The Mae Wests were ready, and the hand-cranked emergency radio. And K-Rations, water, shark repellent, survival kit. All this efficiently executed by Milton Lowenstein, and I resented him, too.

I knew we were going in. But I also knew we—I, at least—would survive. Death is not possible. Death happens to others, not you. I wondered if Raab and Wilson were thinking the same. A cigarette dangled from Wilson's lips. His eyes were closed. I wondered if he was praying.

I considered praying. But even as the thought entered my mind I forced it away and asked myself, What the hell is wrong with you?

I'm sorry, I answered myself.

You should be. Everybody knows, rationally, there is no God.

Okay, okay, so lay off.

Lay off? Then why are you even making the gesture?

I'm not, I told myself, and then thought, But everybody makes that kind of gesture at one time or another. Hedging the bet, you could say.

Forget it, I'm not hedging anything. I will not pray now, or ever. I refuse to stoop to such hypocrisy.

Instead, I told myself, think of something pleasant. Girls, the Boston Red Sox, Paris. The Haverhill Country Club, where one year ago almost to the day, I shot 76—and with two double bogies! If only I had bogied those holes, it would have been 74! My best score ever. Let's go before that, to Paris. No, even before Paris, to Stornoway, a desolate USAAF base in the Northern Hebrides where I was stationed once for a few months as a form of reprimand. Punishment for amending an officer's order. I considered the amendment helpful; he disagreed. Stornoway was a WREN training center, with six hundred of those Women's Royal Naval Auxiliary girls stationed on the island—and thirty American GIs.

Some punishment.

Okay, now Paris. I arrived in Paris less than a week after Liberation Day, when an American could not walk ten feet without pretty girls offering him wine, brandy, champagne, cigarettes—or themselves. I spent my first night in the city as the guest of the Madam at a famous *maison d'amour*. The second night I slept with a girl I met in a restaurant. We stayed in a little hotel off Boulevard Montparnasse, and all night long snipers—die-hard *collabos* and even some Ger-

51

No Trophy, No Sword

mans–shot from the rooftops. The girl, who was very pretty, wore a turban which she did not remove even when we went to bed. Later, after we made love, I asked about the turban and she turned away and began crying. I remembered then having heard that the FFI, the French Resistance Forces, shaved the heads of women who had collaborated with the Germans.

I strained to keep my mind on those images but they were continually swept aside by the image of myself in this C-46 cockpit as we ditched. I am staring through the windscreen at the water surging up at us. The landing lights are trained on the water, reflecting back into my eyes as two glaring white blobs. But no, there are no lights, the generators are off because the engines were cut. No, the lights are on, powered by batteries. Or are they? No, the engines are not cut. Raab surely will not wait until all the fuel is gone. He needs power to assist him ditching. Yes, of course. Of course.

My brain whirled with all of that, a dozen different versions, always focusing on the airplane plowing into the water and the whole ocean pouring through the smashed windscreen, sluicing into the cabin like a burst dam. But we are already in the cabin, scrambling out the rear door of the sinking airplane, into the life raft that is inflated now and bobbing wildly on the rough sea. Somehow we board the raft–only to have it capsize! We are all in the water, the swirling waves smashing into us. I can taste the water, a wall of gagging salt hosing up into my nostrils, flushing down my throat.

"–red compass!"

It was Raab, shocking me out of the reverie. "The red compass! Look at that goddam red compass . . . !" He was tapping his finger on the ADF glass, on the red needle pointed rigidly and unerringly almost due east. Toward Cuba, Camaguey, a small airport almost in the center of the island. Only a few minutes before, when I had tuned that red unit to Camaguey's frequency, the station was not transmitting.

"How far away are we?" Wilson asked.

"Forty, forty-five minutes," I said. "Almost the same distance as Kingston." I looked at Raab. He was staring at the ADF needle. "Do we try for it?" I asked him.

"They don't have night landing facilities," he said.

"It'll be light by the time we get there," I said.

Raab glanced at Wilson. "How much fuel is left?"

"Fifty minutes," Wilson said. "Maybe a little more."

"Maybe a little less," said Raab.

"Yeah, buddy," Wilson said. "Maybe a little less."

"We've got this slight south wind," I said. "It might make a difference." In truth, not much of a difference, but even a single gallon saved kept the engines running that much longer.

Raab said nothing. He gazed at the needle another instant and then, unseeingly, through the front window. Ahead and below the thin cloud cover stretched endlessly. Just then, in my earphones:

"One-three-eight from Miami. What is your present position and fuel remaining, please?"

Raab also heard the transmission. He looked at me. I said, "Do we try for Camaguey?"

Raab peered at the instrument panel, the fuel gauges. And then at the ADF, the needle locked, pointing east. The Camaguey beacon's Morse signal, C-M-Y, boomed into our earphones like the beating of a loud, beckoning drum.

"Camaguey," Raab said quietly, and leaned forward to disengage the auto pilot. He gripped the yoke and began turning the airplane.

I slid out of the right seat and gestured Wilson in. I resumed my station and said into the microphone, "Miami, this is LAPSA one-three-eight. We are forty-five minutes southeast of Camaguey, with approximately fifty minutes fuel remaining. Please alert that station for an emergency landing."

Now the airplane's nose was lined precisely with the arrow tip of the radio compass needle. The engines droned steadily, powerfully. Five minutes. Ten. To our right the dark sky lightened with a pale glow that slowly spread across the eastern horizon. It was like a band of gold. The sun.

If we go down at least we'll have light.

Raab sat hunched comfortably forward, eyes straight ahead, face calm and reflective. Wilson also sat hunched forward, his fingers poised over the fuel booster pump switches, prepared to flick them on the instant the pressure needle fluctuated, or at the slightest cough of an engine. His head was bent low over the fuel pressure gauges, his eyes trained on the needles as though willing them to remain steady.

I watched the fuel gauges. I was sure I could actually see each indicator moving slowly, inexorably, toward "E." In my mind I wrote in the journal I always had intended to keep but never did. I regretted not having done it; at least it would have been something to leave behind. My literary legacy. A legacy, to date, consisting of a few dozen high school sports stories I had written when I was the *Haverhill Gazette's* schoolboy correspondent, and some letters home for money. Some legacy. For the grandchildren I will never have.

But how foolish you are, I told myself. You are not going to die, we both know that. "Both," of course, being me and my other half, my alter ego. Which brought to mind a boy whose last name was Alter, whose first name I could not at all recall. I attended high school with him, and saw him clearly: tall, stringbean-thin, acne-faced, very friendly. A pleasant, likable boy. But what was his first name? Lester? Ben? Lew? What the hell was it?

And what did it matter?

What did anything matter? All that mattered was keeping those engines going. Do not stop, I told them in my mind. You bastards, don't stop! And then the faces of my mother and father flashed before me. Her eyes were dry but you knew she was struggling for composure. He, however, wept, his voice rising and falling in that sing-song wail of Jewish grief and pain.

" . . . why did he do it?" my father asked. "Why?"
"He was fighting for the Jews," my mother said.
Wait! I told myself. Your whole life is supposed to pass in front of you. Everything. But nothing was passing in front of me. All I could think of were those engines. Do not stop, do not stop, do not stop.

I was thinking all this, my eyes no longer on the fuel gauges, but fixed straight ahead through the front windscreen. And then all at once through the spinning arc of the right propeller I saw, rising up out of the ocean, mountains. Wilson saw it at the same time. He tapped my knee. "There it is, buddy. The coast."

We all stared at it. The mountains were closer and clearer, although still too distant to discern in detail. Raab said, "The field is nearly forty miles inland."

No one spoke. I wanted to make a tough-guy crack about us now having a choice of getting wet, or running out of fuel in those hills. We flew on, over the coast now, over the hills. No more choice now of wet or dry, perhaps not even of living or dying. Now, if we crashed, we were dead for certain.

Five minutes, eight, twelve. Wilson said he had the engines leaned out so finely they were running on fumes. His fingers rested directly on the booster pump switches. He expected any instant to have to flick them on.

"The field is just over those hills," Raab said. He cleared his throat and repeated it as though to reassure himself. "Just over those hills. Okay, cut it to eighteen inches, twenty-three hundred rpm. Gear up until we're in the pattern." And, never taking his eyes from the approaching hills, he called to me, "Harold, tell them we want to make a straight-in approach!"

Wilson and I exchanged glances, each thinking the same thought: straight in meant *over* the mountains. We were supposed to come in on the other side, the safe side, *away* from the mountains.

I said worriedly, "Larry—"

He knew; he pointed at the main fuel tank gauges. The

white tips of both indicators lay heavily against "E." We probably were on whatever reserve remained in the tanks. It might be fifty gallons, it might be five.

Another remark framed my lips. *These machines don't glide so good!* I did not say it, it did not need to be said.

Camaguey Tower radioed permission for the straight-in approach. They also advised me that crash vehicles were standing by. We were down to 3,000 feet now, lower it seemed than the highest peak. The brush-covered hillsides were plainly visible, and a series of narrow trails snaking up to the summit. Raab turned left a few degrees and steered for an opening between two smaller hills.

Closer, lower, and then we were in the opening. It was like moving into a canyon, walls on both sides rising steeply above us. Now we were committed, trapped inside. I glanced at the Camaguey page of the airways facilities chart book that lay open on Raab's lap. The airport should be just ahead, off to our left.

And all at once there it was. Tucked between small hills, the runway ten miles away. In the early morning sun the black asphalt sparkled invitingly.

From this approach Raab had to line up with the unfamiliar runway and then, from 2,000 feet, drop in on the end of it. He flew on, over the hilltops, both hands lightly gripping the yoke, as though allowing the airplane to feel its way through, like a jockey giving a powerful horse its head.

No one bothered to look at the fuel gauges anymore. Now, for sure, we were on the reserve. But the airport was closer; on one side of the runway you could make out buildings. On the other side, a fire truck. And a crash truck.

Raab misjudges this one, there won't be enough gasoline left for five seconds of power adjustment, let alone enough to go around with.

Just then the fuel pressure warning lights flashed red. Wilson flicked the switches on both pumps to pour in whatever fuel remained. "Boosters on!"

"Gear down!" Raab called. "Hold the flaps! Props full forward!"

The airplane's nose was angled sharply down, almost a shallow dive. Trees, brush, other foliage suddenly sprang from the ground. But just ahead, unwinding like a long black ribbon, the runway.

"Over the fence. Eighty!" Wilson sang out. "Eight-ee miles an hour, buddy! One hundred feet! You are doing just fine!"

The runway slid beneath us. Left hand on the yoke, right hand on the throttles, Raab flew straight onto it with full power. The wheels felt for the surface, touched. A slight, soft crunch, and then they held, rolled smoothly. Behind us, in the cabin, I saw Lowenstein close his eyes and sag wearily against the bulkhead wall.

"You did it!" Wilson shouted. "You marvelous little bastard, Larry, you did it!"

I added my congratulations, pounding him elatedly on the shoulder. An ever-widening splotch of perspiration stained the back of Raab's shirt. Throughout the landing, beyond the quiet, crisp issuance of orders, he had said nothing. Only when we swung off the runway, onto a taxi strip, did Raab even turn his head. He looked at me, then at Wilson, and then he slumped back in his chair.

"I guess it wasn't a bad landing—" he never completed the sentence. At that exact instant the right engine stopped. One instant it was idling smoothly, propeller spinning, the next instant it simply stopped. Not a warning cough, not even a sputter. It went dead.

Raab leaned over to see it. For at least fifteen silent contemplative seconds he studied the frozen propeller. And then, eyes still fixed on that dead engine, he grinned. He began laughing. We all joined in.

We refueled and continued on to Panama, where the other three airplanes—after experiencing their own en route difficulties—had already landed safely. That April week we arrived in Panama was the week Jerusalem was cut off. The same week the British handed over to the Arabs possession of two vitally strategic military bases at Sarafand and Tel Litwinski; and, perhaps most damaging of all, Lydda Airdrome.

The Haganah was suffering these losses even before the real war began: in six weeks, when the five Arab armies invaded Israel. And we—the "saviors" of the Jewish-nation-to-be, we who were to deliver the supplies and airplanes that would help withstand the invasion—we were 6,000 miles away.

THREE

THE BAGEL LANCERS

I think it was in Panama that we first began envisioning ourselves as true life, bigger-than-life, honest to God Yankee adventurers. A latter-day Flying Tigers volunteer group, risking life and limb this time for a noble, glorious Jewish cause. Storybook heroes, seat-of-the-pants aviators defying the most powerful nation on earth to fly their ancient crates by gosh and by golly down into this Central American banana republic.

An undeservedly romantic image, of course, and belied by the fact we were really a scruffy bunch of ex-USAAF airmen working for a phony airline. Of course, you couldn't help but ignore the reality of it, swept into the intrigue, glamour, and excitement of such a clandestine operation as we were. We even relished Hal Auerbach's apt labeling of us as "The Bagel Lancers."

The ambience was itself bigger than life. Panama City, on the Atlantic side of the Canal, a city of 100,000, with good restaurants, an entire street of action-packed nightclubs, girls galore. And a government-operated casino (making it no less dishonest) atop the city's finest hotel. There was even a synagogue.

There were nearly three dozen of us now, living in two leased apartments in a fashionable section of town. One, on Avenida Peru, we called Peru House. The other, on the second floor of a local Packard automobile agency, Packard House. A LAPSA ticket office was opened, an impressive downtown office complete with embossed stationery and a desk-stand plastic model of a LAPSA Connie, and picture postcards of that same Connie flying over the Isthmus. We were issued official LAPSA ID cards with small passport-type photographs of the bearer, and separate Panamanian Ministry of Commerce documents certifying us as rated pilots and aircrew.

Tocumen now, truly, was the bustling modern air terminus Marty Bellefond had promised. The Connie and the C-46s flew continually: training and transition flights, under Hal Auerbach's supervision. There would be no repetition of the sloppy, near-disastrous Millville-Panama flight. The next leg, Panama to Italy, was to be machine-perfect. Every pilot, navigator, and radioman would know his job and be thoroughly familiar with every facet of the flight and the airplane.

The first few weeks were good duty. Moonitz and I bought identical white linen suits. We liked to think we resembled Alan Ladd and William Bendix–I, of course, was Ladd–and swaggered about as though living in one of their movies. We purchased a 1936 Buick Phaeton for $150. We dined each evening at the best restaurants and frequented the most popular night spots.

The money for all this high living came from the casino. Note that I said "came from," not "won." More accurately, *collected*. Initially, Moonitz and I had pooled our money–$50 expense money issued in Millville, plus whatever few dollars we had. Then, as partners, we assaulted the casino.

To be predictably and rapidly wiped out. Flat broke. But only a day later Moonitz insisted we dine at Club Atlas, the city's swankest restaurant. *He* was buying, he said. And he did, with a Ladd-Bendix flourish, nonchalantly plucking from his pocket a $100 bill, waving the bill at the waiter and saying to him, "There you are, my good man!" Imagine someone today displaying a $1,000 bill and you have an idea of the effect.

Although he acknowledged our "partnership," he steadfastly refused to reveal the source of this finance, only that there was more where that came from. And there was. The bonanza continued. We bought the clothes, and the car, and lived like playboys. Ladd and Bendix.

We became regulars at Tierra Feliz ("Happy Land"), a nightclub featuring a raucous floor show whose chorus girls were the prettiest on the Strip. In between numbers the ladies doubled as B-Girls, and after closing hours, pending satisfactory negotiation, invited you home with them for the night.

For nearly two weeks Moonitz maintained his silence concerning the origin of the money providing all this marvelous entertainment. But late one evening at Tierra Feliz I recognized a casino blackjack dealer, a swarthily handsome man whom we called "George" for his striking resemblance to the actor George Raft. He had entered the nightclub, nodded at Moonitz, then vanished into the men's room adjoining the club entrance. Immediately, Moonitz excused himself and strode casually to the men's room. It suddenly occurred to me that this was not the first time I had seen George walk into the club men's room and Moonitz abruptly follow. This time, a few seconds later, so did I. Moonitz and George were closeted in a lavatory stall.

" . . . okay," I heard Moonitz say, "here's your eighty."

"Thank you," George said. "Don't come to the casino tomorrow night. Come the next night. Except if you see Ramon—he's the floor boss, the short ugly one in the tuxedo—don't even sit down. Make believe you're only watching, maybe play some roulette. But leave fast. Too risky with him around."

"Gotcha," said Moonitz.

I hurried back to the bar. I saw George leave the club. A moment later Moonitz rejoined me. I ordered another round of drinks and in the same breath said to Moonitz, "I finally figured it out."

He looked at me blankly.

"The money," I said.

"What money?"

"Our money." I scooped up a handful of bills and change on the bar and let it sift through my fingers. "Where it comes from."

"Oh, you found out about my rich uncle?"

"Yeah," I said. "His name's George."

The hint of a forbearing little grin that had appeared on Moonitz's face vanished. "What George?"

"You're in cahoots, you and Old George," I said, debating whether or not to simply tell him I had eavesdropped on them, deciding not to. "I saw him come in, and you run to meet him. You and him have some kind of deal."

Moonitz reddened. "'Deal?' What deal? You don't know what the hell you're talking about."

"What's the deal, Norman?"

"There is no deal. Now forget it!"

"The deal, Norman, tell me what it is."

He studied me an exasperated moment and then, being Moonitz, wasted no further time parrying. He knew I would never stop nagging for the truth. He admitted to an "arrangement" with George. At the proper signal he sat at George's table. No matter what cards were dealt, George paid off. Three or four hands, followed then by smaller bets, win a few, lose a few, and then George's gesture to quit. Moonitz would leave the table and cash in his chips. Hours later they met at Tierra Feliz for the split. This was certainly no daily occurrence, two or three times a week at best, with modest winnings—no more than fifty or a hundred dollars at a time—not enough to attract attention.

"Fine," I said. "And now that I know about it, I want in."

"You are in," he said. He scooped up all the bar money in one big fist and held it under my nose. "So shut up!"

"Come on," I said, "I want a turn at the table. We can double the winnings!"

Moonitz exploded. The fist enclosing the money smashed down on the bar. "You just can't mind your own business, can you? Goddam fools like you can never let well enough alone! You never know when you're well off!" He had a talent, Moonitz, for slicing straight to the heart of a problem, brushing aside the extraneous. It was black or white, yes or no. That simple. You were a good pilot, or a bad one. You did, or did not do, something. In flying, and in living, Moonitz brooked no nonsense. He evaluated the situation, based his decision upon the existing facts, and acted.

His decision to join Service Airways was reached in precisely that manner. Married, father of a five-year-old son, he held a secure, well-paying job with the New York City Fire Department. But flying for Israel was something that needed to be done, something he needed to do.

Moonitz and I appreciated and respected each other's directness. It was the basis of our friendship, so in the end he agreed to ring me in. What the hell, I was sharing the money, I might as well share the risk. Looking back, I shudder at our naïveté. While it was a time long before closed-circuit television in casinos—and the Hotel Internationale casino employed no "eye-in-the-sky"—the danger should still have been obvious. It was so foolish. But not to us, not then. Then it was high adventure, great fun.

Ladd and Bendix.

But with all the fun and games, we were working hard. As a result of our "escape" from Millville, the North Atlantic route to Europe was closed to us. We were unable, as per original plan, to fly back up the Atlantic coast, refuel in Boston and in Labrador, and then continue over the water to Ireland, and then on to Italy. By order of the U.S. State

Department, LAPSA aircraft were prohibited from entering the continental United States. So now, from Panama, we had no choice but fly to Brazil, then over the South Atlantic to Africa, and from there to Italy.

To accommodate this inconveniently longer flight, 400-gallon auxiliary fuselage fuel tanks were installed in the C-46s, and new crewmen checked out. Eleven new men had arrived. Three pilots, three navigators, five radio operators. All had flown from New York via Peruvian International Airways with whom Bellefond had negotiated an RTA, a Reciprocal Travel Agreement. This was an accepted industry practice whereby airline employees traveled on each other's systems on a gratis, quid pro quo fare basis. Fortunately, during our stay in Panama, PIA never requested LAPSA space for any of its people.

In Newark, the two Connies remained impounded; we had already resigned ourselves to their loss. But the California C-46s, all five, finally were ready to fly to Panama. Auerbach and Gerson joined Sam Lewis, Si Sorge, and Marty Ribakoff in Burbank for a mass flight to Panama. All nine C-46s and the Connie would then depart for Natal, Brazil. From Natal, over the South Atlantic to Dakar, French Senegal. Then to Casablanca, and on to the Italian base.

The timetable for this schedule called for the delivery to Palestine of the first arms shipments no later than May 15. May 15, when the British mandate officially terminated. May 15, the day the Arab invasion would begin.

Clearly, then, the May 15 date depended upon how soon we left Panama. It was equally clear that while we remained here at Tocumen the LAPSA façade must be maintained. And much of that was dependent on the forthcoming Panamanian national elections. If the incumbent party lost, the new government would almost surely take a close, hard look at the "airline." But then even with the present Panamanian government, LAPSA's status was precarious. More than a few curious people were asking impatient questions about the date of LAPSA's first scheduled flight.

We assured the Panamanians that we were on the verge of commencing operations (not at all untrue), and that we had already obtained a few cargo contracts. Accordingly, we began flying occasional flights across the Isthmus supposedly shuttling milk and beef. At least so the invoices stated. It appeared to satisfy the skeptics.

The day before the elections, the five California C-46s departed Burbank for Panama via Mexico City. That same afternoon Marty Bellefond summoned me to his office at Packard House. The Panamanian Transportation Ministry, Marty informed me, had requested copies of the aircraft radio licenses.

"We don't have any radio licenses," I said.

"I know we don't," Bellefond said. "Why not?"

A perfectly reasonable question, for which I had a perfectly reasonable answer. "Nobody ever thought about it."

"Well, start thinking about it," Bellefond said. "And then do something about it."

"Do what?"

"Get the licenses."

"How?"

"Harold, I don't care how," he said. "Just do it!"

After the close call at Camaguey I had decided to keep, if not a journal, at least some notes. My notes regarding the radio license incident, although fairly detailed, begin only with: " . . . *found Comm. Minister.*" It means that I somehow located the deputy in charge of communications at the Panamanian Ministry of Transportation. How or why I made contact with that particular functionary I do not recall, but he was obviously the right person.

He was an American, a retired U.S. Army Signal Corps major. A balding, amiable, almost femininely delicate man in suit and tie (with a celluloid collar) and pince-nez glasses. He could have come straight out of Central Casting as the archetypical small town civil servant.

65

I presented my LAPSA identity card and introduced myself as the airline's "Caribbean Regional Supervisor of Communications." I apologized for the lack of a proper business card, explaining that a typographical error on new cards just recently printed had rendered the whole damn batch useless.

I stated my business. Radio licenses for the aircraft.

"Ah, yes," he said. "Radio licenses."

"Yes sir," I said. "We need them as soon as possible."

"Of course," he said, and smiled politely. For a moment we regarded each other in solemn silence. He smiled again. "Radio licenses, eh?"

"Yes sir," I said.

"I'm afraid this might be a bit of a problem for me," he said. "I deal in ships, not planes." And once again, that polite little smile. "Also, I'm aware of no provisions for aircraft radio licenses. Frankly, I wouldn't even know where to start. Or how."

I suppose it was his appearance and manner—so meek, almost self-effacing—that filled me with bravado. The words flowed confidently from me. I sympathized with his position, I said, but a start had to be made somewhere. This was the dawn of a new era for Panama. The country was assuming its destined place in the family of nations. I talked fast, but carefully, articulately. All with absolute spontaneity, totally impromptu and unrehearsed. I was playing a role whose very unreality plunged me into it deeper and deeper. And the more involved I became, the better I performed.

I spoke at least ten minutes, so pumped up I think I could have gone on indefinitely and well might have, had not the major raised one hand, palm up like a traffic cop. It was more a gesture of surrender than a signal to stop.

"Excuse me," he said abruptly. Without another word, he rose and left the room. I had no idea where he went, or why. To the bathroom to vomit? To call the police and have me arrested?

I cursed Marty Bellefond for sending me on this fool's errand. We didn't need the damned licenses, no one from here to Italy was about to board an airplane demanding to see a radio license. I had opened a Pandora's Box that could only close with me trapped inside. Suppose this Major—or the Minister himself—began asking pertinent questions? For example, as a certificated government airline, what wages were being paid? And when they learned that the average monthly salary, from Captains on down, was *$100*, would they then not realize something was drastically wrong? After that, truth upon truth would be revealed. I began feeling the dankness of a Panama jail cell. Jail? I would be lucky if jail was all that happened. This was Central America: they shot you for jaywalking!

I waited in that office more than ten minutes, literally forcing myself with each passing minute not to flee. But when the major returned, he carried a large manila envelope. In the envelope were the licenses. Maritime radio licenses, the aircraft numbers substituted for "name of vessel."

The major escorted me from the office. At the door he clapped me lightly on the back and said, "Young man, you're doing a fine job for this country. Keep up the good work."

"Thank you very much, sir," I said. We shook hands and I left. I had all I could do not to burst into semi-hysterical laughter. Triumph, and relief. A marvelous moment, I remember thinking, of an even more marvelous adventure. Fun and games. Glamour, excitement, intrigue. Looking back on it, reconstructing the scene from my notes, it all sounds so almost farcical now.

In light of what immediately followed, a tragic farce.

2.

I sauntered into Bellefond's office at the Packard House and tossed the licenses smugly onto his desk. "I sold him the bridge," I said.

Bellefond swept the documents into a desk drawer with hardly a second glance at them, or me. I waited for him to congratulate me. But he said nothing. He stared grimly at his hands.

"Who do we scam next, boss?" I said.

Now Bellefond looked at me. Silently, he handed me a cablegram. I read it. And then again, and then once more. I could not believe what I read. I did not want to believe it.

GERSON CRASHED MEXICO CITY STOP
CO-PILOT KING KILLED STOP PILOTS
REFUSE TAKEOFF UNLESS OVERLOADS
REMOVED STOP SEND EMPTY SHIP STOP
SEND LOWENSTEIN SUPERVISE FUNERAL
ARRANGEMENTS STOP SIGNED SCHWIMMER

"Gerson's dead, too," Bellefond said.

I said nothing. I stared dumbly at him, at his forehead which in my mind became a backdrop for the first two words of the cablegram flashing on and off. GERSON CRASHED GERSON CRASHED GERSON CRASHED.

I said, "It says King was killed, not Gerson." Glenn King was a mechanic pressed into last-minute service as Gerson's co-pilot.

"Rothman called from Mexico City a few minutes ago," Bellefond said. "Bill died on the way to the hospital."

I said nothing. I did not know what to say. No wise-guy remark on my lips now. Again, as in the major's office less than an hour ago, I wanted to run away. I could feel myself turning and walking to the door and rushing out, but I did not move. I could not move.

"The other planes got off okay," Bellefond said. "They off-loaded their overages and left the stuff at the Mexico City airport with Rothman. I'm sending Moonitz over there to pick it up. You go with him."

I nodded. I had heard the words but they did not register. I was suddenly overwhelmed with a feeling of abject, total relief. The thought had just then flashed through my mind that had I remained with Gerson—and knowing him, and he knowing how much it meant to me, I'd have been checked out as his co-pilot—instead of Glenn King in that airplane, it would have been me. I tried to wipe it from my mind; it filled me with remorse and guilt. I felt disloyal.

" . . . you leave first thing in the morning," Bellefond was saying.

"Leave for where?"

"I just told you, Mexico City."

"When?" I asked, knowing he had just told me that, too. It was as though by continuing the conversation I might somehow erase the picture of Gerson's C-46 smashing into the ground. But the picture remained and, with each passing instant, in ever more vivid detail. I could actually hear the dying scream of the engines and the abrupt, heavy, ominous silence that followed.

Bellefond felt equally helpless. "Look, these things happen," he said.

These things happen. During the Big War my singular experience with the death of a friend was when a Sergeant named Jack Webber was struck and killed by a truck on a blacked-out London street. I had not experienced it even in Normandy, on Omaha Beach, at the auxiliary airstrip we set up, although in truth the possibility of combat death or injury was by then quite remote: we came ashore nearly a full week after D-Day. The beachhead was already secure; the only real danger was the nightly Luftwaffe strafing and bombing.

Prior to that my closest encounter with personal wartime death or injury was the terror and defenselessness (shared with millions of civilians) of the "Little Blitz," in the winter of 1943, in London. And, six months later, also in London, during the V-1 and V-2 buzz-bomb terror raids. Once a V-1 demolished a building a block from a hotel I was in.

I was with a girl I had picked up in a Piccadilly bar the previous evening. We heard the V-1's unique buzzing sound, louder and louder until it seemed almost overhead. And then its motor stopped. The silence you dreaded, for you knew this was when the missile started down. That morning in bed in the hotel, the girl and I waited, staring helplessly at each other, counting the seconds. The V-1 plunged into a nearby building. The concussion rocked our hotel room and rattled the windows.

I remember that after one of them hit close to you, you always released your breath and smiled with self-conscious relief, knowing that a short distance away people lay dead, and you had to wonder why them, not you, for which there was no answer, and which only reinforced your feeling of immortality.

But that was the Big War, not this war, this nice little war. The nice little war that all at once had turned very real, and very deadly. Gerson dead. I could not imagine it. I could still feel his fingers ruffling my hair that day at Teterboro when I nearly botched the Ercoupe flight. And his voice: " . . . Mr. Livingston, I will make a pilot out of you—even if it kills me!"

Something killed him.

And killed, too, any illusion, or delusion, of immortality. It was like removing a blindfold. Now, suddenly, everything was frighteningly clear. Including mortality and the unarguable fact that you simply could not cram cargo into an airplane, get in, and casually fly away. That was how we had operated during the fun and games period. It was the cause of Gerson's crash.

He had taken off from Mexico City carrying communications equipment, 4,000 pounds overloaded. He was third in line to take off, preceded by Sam Lewis and Marty Ribakoff. Sam needed every inch of the 8,400 foot runway to wrestle his C-46 into the air. Ribakoff also barely staggered into the air. Gerson used the whole length of the runway also, but could not attain flying speed. At the very last instant, at the runway boundary, he lowered his flaps. It provided sufficient lift. The heavy airplane began climbing. He nursed it up to 150 feet and, I am sure, breathed a sigh of relief.

And then he lost an engine. Not nearly enough altitude to feather the propeller and compensate. No chance to regain control. In an instant the C-46 had turned nose down into the dead engine and plummeted to the ground. Glenn King was killed on impact. Gerson, pinned under the left engine, badly burned, died shortly thereafter.

Moonitz and I flew to Mexico City. From the air we saw the wreck, the bits and pieces strewn about just off the end of the runway, glinting brightly in the late afternoon sun. We landed and were driven immediately to the crash site. The entire area was covered with charred, metallic debris. It was like walking through a junkyard. The fuselage lay on its side, broken in two at the nose. From the cockpit, wiring, tubing, and control cables dangled uselessly like obscenely exposed intestines of a huge stricken animal whose head had been severed from its body.

Thirty feet away, the top half of the right engine and propeller lay partially buried in the ground. A wheel and still inflated tire rested against the two protruding blades of the four-bladed propeller. Nearby was Glenn King's chair, upright, safety belt with almost mocking neatness fastened across the seat, eloquent in its emptiness. A few feet away was the smashed and twisted instrument panel, the left engine, and the pilot's chair. The impact had torn the engine loose and driven it backwards into the cockpit where it bent the chair in half like a flattened beer can. With Gerson still strapped into it.

We shuffled aimlessly about, Moonitz and I, each carefully avoiding the other's eyes. It was as though we were determined to continue playing our Ladd-Bendix roles. Hardened, sophisticated, cynical soldiers of fortune displaying no emotion. In truth, as we both later admitted, our thoughts at the time were focused elsewhere. My mind, again, filled with more of that guilty relief. His, Moonitz's, occupied far more pragmatically: how to avoid a repetition of this disaster. He had already decided that Gerson exercised poor judgment. You do not take off with an overload in 100-degree temperatures from an airfield 7,500 feet above sea level. Yes, the situation demanded urgency, and two others had already managed to take off successfully, but that did not reduce the overall risk. It was an accident waiting to happen.

But our whole operation was an accident waiting to happen. And yet, melodramatic as it might sound, upon that operation could well depend the fate of a nation. Long afterward, when the nation was proclaimed and the war decisively won, it was sometimes said—and not entirely in jest—that Israel's victory resulted more from the ineptness of its enemies than from its own military prowess. It is perhaps more generous to say we were luckier than they, the Arabs. Either luckier, or if we—the progenitors of today's vaunted Israeli Air Force—are any example, Jews really are the Chosen.

More than Chosen. Blessed. Divinely Protected.

Makers of Miracles.

3.

During our flight from Panama to Mexico City, forced by weather to fly over a 17,000-foot mountain range on no oxygen, Moonitz and I had both suffered anoxia. Landing, Moonitz was still slightly disoriented, and while flaring out at twenty-five feet he cut both engines. We slammed like a rock down onto the runway. The impact cracked an oleo strut. We had to wait three days in Mexico City for a replacement part.

Three educational days.

Haganah's Mexico City representative, Herbert Rothman,

an American attorney, entertained us lavishly. Moonitz, me, and our navigator, Buddy Rosensen. A three-room suite at the Hotel Reforma, dinners at Maxim's and at Longchamps Grille, playtime at the city's poshest nightclubs. Whatever we wanted—from newspapers to the girl at the Les Ambassadeurs bar who claimed to be a former mistress of the Duke of Windsor—was ours for the asking. For the taking. Nothing was too good for our boys in the trenches.

At the airport Rothman showed us two rows of P-47 fighters, twenty-four of them, bought and paid for by the new Jewish state, not a single one of which would ever see action. The Mexican government, pressured by the United States and Great Britain, had embargoed the aircraft. Millions down the drain, said Rothman. Along with another million for ammunition that was the wrong caliber for Haganah rifles.

But Rothman appeared surprisingly sanguine about it. More where that came from, he said. The dollars were pouring in. Enjoy yourselves. Marvelous therapy for dealing with the grief of Bill Gerson's death.

On our very first evening in Mexico City, Rothman introduced us to an articulate man named Wilson Brown. Claiming to be a retired U.S. Marine Corps colonel, Wilson Brown certainly looked the part: trim, middle-aged, lantern-jawed, salt-and-pepper hair crew cut militarily perfect. In the posh bar at Longchamps, over forty-year-old Fundador brandy, Wilson Brown made a most astounding proposal.

He offered us jobs.

He said he was forming a new cargo airline. He sought experienced personnel whose pay would be commensurate with their skill. In other words, real salaries, not the $25 weekly expense allowances doled us by Haganah. Fair enough, but then came the bombshell.

The aircraft to be flown by this new airline were our own C-46s.

According to Colonel Wilson Brown, our C-46s were

already consigned to his new enterprise. Oh, to be sure, we would fly the airplanes to Italy and then, with munitions and supplies, to Palestine. But those same airplanes eventually would return to Mexico for Wilson Brown's use. A kind of lend-lease arrangement, Wilson Brown's reward for providing Haganah this invaluable Mexican connection.

If true, it meant we had been suckered into literally donating our time and talent to Service Airways and LAPSA. For the benefit of Panamanian politicians and then, later, Colonel Wilson Brown. Further, if such sums of money were available, why, we asked ourselves, were they skimping with us? $25 weekly expenses? Why couldn't we share in the bonanza now? Why shouldn't we?

Numbed with brandy and rich food and the luxurious, all-expenses paid surroundings, anything and everything made sense. We were dizzy from Colonel Brown's facts and figures. We had seen with our own eyes the evidence of big-time corruption and chicanery. These people, Wilson Brown, Herbert Rothman, and their associates—or, more accurately, accomplices—indulged themselves in a lifestyle apparently financed with the dimes and dollars collected by the Jewish Agency to purchase airplanes and guns.

And for this Bill Gerson died?

Put it all together and add the Panamanian elections—the incumbent government had been voted back into office—this Mexico City business painted an ugly picture that made considerable sense. And more so when we returned to Panama and compared notes with the other crews who had encountered Wilson Brown.

The same story. A new airline, a commercial enterprise, flying the same airplanes we had smuggled out of the United States at great risk to life and limb.

What the hell was going on?

Swifty Schindler had by now assumed command in Panama, and it was from him we demanded answers. Poor Swifty. He had himself posed those very questions to the "wheels," to Al Schwimmer and the appropriate Haganah representatives, and been assured of an investigation into the allegations of Mexico City high living. More important, Wilson Brown was an infamous Central American con man and entrepreneur. Pay no attention.

Pay no attention.

Three days and nights in Mexico City, in a Hotel Reforma luxury suite. Maxims, Longchamps, Les Ambassadeurs. English showgirls and $50-per-night American call girls. All on the house.

Pay no attention?

This advice from Swifty came with his announcement that the date for our Panama departure was now May 8. Preparing for the long, circuitous flight to Italy should be our prime concern, not wasting time, energy, and emotion on wild rumors.

It turned out that Wilson Brown was indeed nothing more than a con man-entrepeneur. A kind of "futures" broker. Should our plan to fly supplies to Israel for any reason fail, Wilson Brown had a project to immediately replace it. And there were several hundred reasons why our plan might fail. At the time, however, we might have accepted Swifty's vague assurances that "nothing underhanded was going on." If the issue had not been unwittingly resurrected by Martin Ribakoff.

A short, wiry, hawknosed man in his early thirties, perennially in need of a shave, Marty Ribakoff was one of those journeymen pilots who had learned to fly hanging around airports. Before the war he logged thousands of hours in aircraft of all types. He flew in Spain with the Loyalists, and then in the Big War with the USAAF ATC—including eight hundred C-46 hours flying the Hump—and after the war with a half dozen non-skeds. He was a "Midnighter," that legion of superb pilots unable for one reason or another—personality, religion, age—to find employment as scheduled airline captains.

His experience could not be purchased or taught. He was a pilot you wanted to fly with because, as we all liked to say, he got you there and got you back. Which made him a good pilot, the best. Jewish, but married to a gentile who was raising their three young children in her faith, he purported no real interest in Jews or Jewishness. And while he chronically griped and continually threatened to quit, he did admit that here, now, in this "Jewish Airline," he felt comfortable. What he meant was that he, like me and almost everyone else, felt he belonged.

Bill Gerson and Marty Ribakoff had been close friends. Bill's death had left a lasting mark on Marty; he said it never should have happened. Bill should never have been allowed to take off with a 4,000-pound overload. The fact that all five airplanes were overloaded did not lessen Ribakoff's bitterness. Or ease his pain.

Ribakoff had taken off from Mexico City just prior to Gerson and witnessed the crash from the air. He said it so unnerved him that he had to hand the controls over to his co-pilot. The day after our return from Mexico City we sat on the Peru House veranda, Ribakoff, Buddy Rosensen, Moonitz, and me. Ribakoff had just confirmed the Wilson Brown "airline" story, having himself been offered a captain's job by Brown. He was convinced Wilson Brown's money came from the same sources financing LAPSA.

The Haganah.

" . . . you saw how they're living like kings down there," Ribakoff was saying. "What more proof do you need?"

"Marty, what the hell point are you trying to make?" Moonitz said. "Are you saying we should ask for more money?"

"How much do you think those P-47s cost?" Ribakoff said. "The ones that aren't going anywhere? Bought with Haganah money that's just been flushed down the toilet. If they can afford that, why can't they afford to pay you guys a decent salary?"

"You guys?" I asked. "Aren't you included?"

Ribakoff shrugged. "Look, as far as I'm concerned I happen to have a decent allotment sent home for me. I mean, I'm satisfied."

"But you're worried about us?" Moonitz asked dryly. "That's real thoughtful of you."

"I'm worried about what we're doing here," Ribakoff said. "Flying these crates that should have been junked years ago, and putting guys like Bill Gerson six feet under. What are we doing it for? For some smart businessmen to line their pockets?"

"That might be true, and it might not be," Buddy said. He was a strikingly handsome New Yorker who had left his own printing business to join us. During the Big War he was a lead navigator in a B-17 group. "But even if it is true, how the hell does it affect what we're supposed to do? How does it interfere with what we came here to do?"

"You came here to be played for a sucker?" Ribakoff asked.

"Nobody's being played for a sucker," Moonitz said, and added uncertainly, "Yet."

"Bill Gerson was," Ribakoff said.

"Bill was played for a sucker?" I asked.

"You bet," said Marty. He nodded tightly and then, almost casually, added, "There's no insurance for Bill's family."

Upon joining Service Airways, each of us had been issued $10,000 life insurance policies. We had elected not to inform the beneficiaries of the existence of these policies, but instead file them in Service Airways' New York office, thereby sparing our families any undue concern over the potential dangers of our mission. In our absence, Service Airways could easily have canceled the policies.

" . . . last week, just before we left for Panama, I found out there's no insurance," Ribakoff was continuing now. "There aren't any policies."

"You found out?" Buddy asked. "How?"

"I phoned the insurance company," Ribakoff said. "They

said they didn't have a record of any policies."

That broke it. If they were capable of canceling insurance behind our backs, they were capable of anything. We called a meeting of all personnel. This, and several other meetings, did little to clarify the insurance situation but did reveal a Service Airways pay scale of astonishing variance. Some men received as much as $800 monthly, and one navigator with no dependents was being paid $250. These salaries, in addition to the famous $100 monthly expense allowance, were negotiated individually during each man's recruiting phase, after which he was sworn to secrecy.

Now it was out in the open and there was hell to pay. We drew up a list of grievances, including a demand for proof of insurance and a guaranteed $100 monthly additional allotment banked for anyone with no dependents. The petition, signed by all crewmen who had not previously negotiated an individual pay scale, was presented to Swifty.

What a way to run an airline.

What a way to fight a war.

Swifty called it Blackmail. We called it Justice. Whatever it was, in response to Swifty's urgent summons, the very next day Al Schwimmer arrived in Panama. Schwimmer, he who had convinced Haganah of the feasibility of an air force, was Chairman of the Board, Chief Executive Officer, Commanding General.

Service Airways, LAPSA, the Israeli Air Force Air Transport Command—call it what you will—it was, all of it, from conception to inception, Al Schwimmer's creation. He was the driving force, and the last word.

Physically unimposing—tall, solid, with thinning sandy hair and a broad, bland, Slavic face—he might initially impress you as an unassuming, perhaps diffident man. But almost immediately you sensed within him a certain confidence, a strength. A kind of fire really, evident in his eyes, but conveyed in the mildest manner. In all the time I knew him I never once recall him raising his voice or even speaking sharply. He never had to. He was a born leader. He was the Boss.

We crowded into the largest room of Packard House, sitting on cots, chairs, the floor. Schwimmer faced us, his quiet voice perfectly modulated, articulately clear.

"I'm told you guys are blaming me for Gerson's death."

No one replied. Schwimmer glanced around, his gaze falling on one man, then another, and another. Each man looked away as though ashamed.

Schwimmer went on, "Well, I personally supervised the loading of his airplane, and I okayed his flying with that load. Sure, he was overloaded. All the airplanes were." Another pause. I thought he was looking straight at me. I looked away. He said, "If overloading caused his death, then I murdered him. I'm a murderer."

The room was silent but for some throat-clearing, shifting about of chairs, matches struck for cigarettes. No one seemed to know what to say. But then again, of course, Schwimmer had said it for us.

"I personally tested each airplane before it left California," Schwimmer continued. "I tested them with the same load they would carry to Panama. Not only was Bill satisfied his airplane was safe, his was the lightest load of all five."

He went on to say that while no one knew the precise cause of the accident, it appeared to have been the engine failing at that critical moment of climb out–and, Schwimmer emphasized, lowering flaps. A trick that sometimes worked, but more often proved lethal.

In any event, he said, never again would an airplane be permitted to fly under similar conditions. He also gave us his word that the $10,000 life insurance policies were valid, and would remain so, a commitment that most definitely included Bill Gerson's survivors. He further agreed that single crewmen should, and would, receive $100 monthly allotments deposited in their names in a New York bank.

But Al Schwimmer was too shrewd to simply let it go at

that. He had not come alone to Panama. He had brought with him two other men, Hank Greenspun and Hy Marcus. Hank, who had abandoned his embryonic Las Vegas publicity agency to join us, was a former infantry major and ordnance expert. Only a month before, he had convinced a recalcitrant barge captain to deliver a cargo of six hundred machine guns from a Vera Cruz, Mexico, warehouse to a waiting freighter. Hank's .45 pressed into the captain's forehead had done the "convincing." Hank, in charge of Schwimmer's Mexican operations, put to rest the Wilson Brown story. Brown, I later heard, was himself subsequently "put to rest." Years afterward, when I asked Hank about this, he denied any knowledge of it. I never believed him.

Schwimmer's other companion was a slender, soft-spoken young man in his late twenties who introduced himself as Hy Marcus. A U.S. citizen, American-born, Hy Marcus had emigrated to Palestine as a young boy. In World War II he came back to America to serve in the USAAF as a B-25 navigator. After the war he returned to Palestine. His real name was Hyman Sheckman, which would be changed to Haman Shamir when he became Deputy Chief of Staff of the Israeli Air Force.

But that day at Packard House, as Hy Marcus, he said he was speaking on behalf of Jews fighting for their lives in Palestine. Palestine, where the Arabs were massing their British-trained and supplied armies. Palestine, where they said the gutters of Jerusalem ran red with the blood of Jews defending the city. Jews awaiting our help. Jews, whose clandestine air unit was known as the "Primus Air Force" because the pitifully few Haganah airplanes sputtered and banged like hand-pumped Primus field kitchen stoves.

Airplanes?

A few dozen, if that many. Taylor Cubs and Austers. Tiny, two-place, forty horsepower aerial flivvers, hardly worthy of the name "airplane." Hardly more than toys. Flown by members of an aero club: kibbutzniks, students, office clerks. In the whole country, even for the Primus Air Force, there probably were not three dozen qualified pilots.

If that many.

We Americans in that room, said Hy Marcus, were the nucleus of the new Jewish state's air force. Every screwdriver, can opener, and rifle cartridge brought into the country had to be flown in.

By us.

We, he said, were the Air Force.

He went on, more eloquent, more convincing, but also cautioning us not to overestimate our importance, for even without us the new nation would come into being. Rest assured, he said, Israel would survive without us American Jews. Nothing on earth could stop it now. But our presence would help. Oh, so much. So much.

Although later—under circumstances far less amenable or inspiring—I would come to know him better, I was aware then only that what he said was all too true, and made me and everyone else ashamed of our momentary mistrust. Then, in Panama, Hy Marcus was a man pleading for his people. Pleading for our help.

For my help.

A week later, on May 6, five LAPSA C-46s took off from Tocumen. Destination: Natal, Brazil. The Panamanians were told that the mass departure was a "route survey flight" to evaluate the most practical routes to Europe for LAPSA cargo and passenger service. Although route surveys are seldom, if ever, conducted by more than a single aircraft, no one questioned LAPSA's use of *five*. Conversely, no one was informed that these five proud bearers of the Panamanian flag had embarked upon what would be a strictly one-way journey.

It was a gala event, this inaugural LAPSA flight. Representatives of the Panamanian government came to wish us good luck, Godspeed, and bon voyage. Newspaper photographers snapped pictures of the big transports. All that was missing was the brass band.

One after another the airplanes roared down the long concrete runway and flew gracefully into the air. Hal Auerbach in the lead C-46 circled the airport and waggled his wings. The dignitaries on the ground waved and cheered.

FOUR

"... HOW ARE THINGS IN PALESTINE?"

... Panama to Zandery, to Natal. Uneventful except Andes electrical storm & brief argument w/Raisin.

These are my notes, torn and tattered now, so old that when touched they literally crumble. Translated, we flew from Panama down the eastern coast of South America, landed for refueling at Zandery Field in Paramaribo, Dutch Guiana, then continued south around the hump of Brazil, to Natal, 1,300 miles north of Rio.

I was in RX-133, captained by Swifty, who after the Panamanian "trouble" had asked to be relieved of his executive position and assigned as a line captain. I suppose my note-comment "uneventful" means we landed in one piece, with only the routine problems—hydraulic leaks, runaway props, excessive fuel consumption, faulty navigation. As for *brief argument w/Raisin,* instead of "brief" I should have written "violent."

Al Raisin, a former USAAF 8th AF B-17 commander, was our co-pilot. Al and I had known each other more than a year, having met through a mutual friend in the advertising business. In 1947–shortly before we met and long before Service Airways–Al left his family's dairy business to join with an iconoclastic Rabbi named Baruch Korff in a wild, fanciful scheme to fly Jewish refugees from European DP camps to Palestine. (The hapless passengers were to be ferried across the Mediterranean in PBY Catalinas, and then *parachuted* into the country!) Understandably, the project never progressed beyond the planning stage.

We were an hour out of Zandery, at night, flying low over the jungle under a heavy overcast that rose more than 15,000 feet. Swifty had gone into the cabin for a sandwich and coffee, leaving Raisin in the left seat, me in the right. Suddenly, ahead, was an ominous-looking front with some foreboding black clouds. Raisin debated disengaging the autopilot, but this was his first flying time since the war. He was rusty. And not overwhelmed with confidence.

I said, "Why don't I go get Swifty?" I started unbuckling my safety belt.

"No!" Raisin gestured me back into the seat. "He'll think I'm some hot pilot, I have to ask his permission to hand-fly through a front. Sit still," he said, and reached for the autopilot switch.

"Maybe you shouldn't, Al," I said. His own obvious uncertainty troubled me. And so did the weather. The air was increasingly turbulent. Flashes of lightning brightened the sky.

"What the hell do you mean, 'maybe I shouldn't'?" he said. "What do you know about it? You're only a goddam radio operator!"

We had been feuding, good-naturedly, since the day after his arrival in Panama when I made the mistake of introducing him to a Tierra Feliz bar girl I cockily considered my special friend. A relationship that once Raisin entered the picture was promptly terminated. A turn of events I accepted graciously. She preferred him, so big deal, good luck to them both. But now, the "you're only a goddam radio operator" remark all at once filled me with delayed resentment and indignation.

"Yeah, and what the hell are you?" I said. "A broken-down co-pilot!"

Ah, *that* stung him good. He leaned forward and prepared to disengage the autopilot. He asked me the time.

"Twenty three oh seven," I replied.

"What are you talking about?" he shouted. "We took off less than an hour ago. At six-ten!"

"You mean eighteen-ten," I said.

"Okay, eighteen-ten. So what time is it now?"

"Twenty-three oh seven. Coming up on oh-eight."

"It can't be!"

"It is," I said. "Greenwich time."

"Give it to me in local time."

"What's the difference?" I asked, trying to be clever, knowing from long experience it annoyed him.

"The difference," he said, "is I want it in local time."

"So figure it out," I said. "Subtract five hours. No, four."

"Well, how much?"

The commanding tone of voice made me resent him even more. "Figure it out yourself!" I said.

"I'll ask you just once more," he said. "What time is it in local time?"

"And I'll tell you just once more," I said. "Figure it out yourself!"

It was like pulling the bottom card out of a house of cards. All the pent-up pressure and frustration of the past months burst free.

Somehow, suddenly, Raisin and I were leaning across the control pedestal grappling with each other, our fingers around each other's throats. The airplane, on automatic pilot, flew on into the storm, bucking and heaving. And entirely unattended.

Ahead, in the windscreen, flashes of lightning zig-zagged through the darkness. The rain beat like a jackhammer on the airplane's aluminum skin, and she kept yawing to the right. Raisin leaned slightly forward, one hand stretched out to the autopilot knob to correct the drift, the other hand fending me off. Then, course corrected, he immediately resumed choking me. He was determined to force me to reveal the time in local. I was equally determined not to. It was like a Laurel & Hardy routine. It continued at least ten seconds, ending mercifully when Swifty, alarmed by the turbulence, rushed back to the flight deck.

What a way to fight a war.

"Personality problems" were not confined to our crew. On this same Zandery-Natal leg, Moonitz, in RX-137, became so exasperated with his co-pilot, Sheldon Eichel, he demanded that a curtain be erected between the two seats so he would not have to look at Eichel! He was utterly serious. They had argued over a course correction.

Moonitz grudgingly conceded the impracticality of such a curtain, but for the remainder of that flight and several afterward, he refused to address Eichel directly. He issued orders either by hand signal or through the radio operator. On takeoff, for example, he would call to the radio operator, "Please ask the first officer to reduce power . . . " or, " . . . tell the co-pilot I want half flap!"

Despite the eccentricities—or perhaps thanks to them!—all five of our C-46 captains landed safely at Panamarim Field, Natal. We checked into the town's best hotel, El Grande, where the local BSAA complement, British South American Airways, also resided. The Englishmen were delighted to see us and welcomed our company in the dining room and at the bar.

The evening of our arrival Auerbach received a cable from Schwimmer in Rome. The runway at Castiglione Del Lago was unsafe for the C-46s. We were to proceed therefore not to Perugia, but to Catania, Sicily.

Catania would be our European terminus.

We set to work repairing minor damage from the Andes storm and preparing for the long overwater journey. Our airplane, RX-133, needed new slip rings for the right engine propeller governor. Moonitz's airplane required a new oil pump. We would have to wait for these parts to be shipped in from Panama.

Two days later, Ribakoff, Raab, and Auerbach took off at night for Dakar. Auerbach returned almost immediately with a faulty propeller governor. The others landed in Dakar the following morning, refueled, and continued on to Catania.

The next day the local Natal newspaper ran a three-column front-page headline.

PANAMANIAN FLYERS VANGUARD
OF ZIONIST AIR FORCE!

The story described the presence in Natal of five "Curtiss airliners," and the subsequent departure of three (the newspaper was unaware of Auerbach's return) to an unknown destination, and " . . . if the pilots' visages are examined closely, it is easily determined that many are of the Hebrew persuasion. Their presence here and the events now unfolding in Palestine can hardly be considered a coincidence."

Auerbach composed a denial, translated into Portuguese by a friendly Brazilian Air Force officer. The "Curtiss airliners," wrote Auerbach, were Panamanian flag carriers conducting route-survey evaluation tests for scheduled transatlantic operations. He went on to say that, yes, some of the pilots did happen to be Jewish, which he considered graphic testimony of the democratic ideals and policies of the Panamanian government and the airline's management. As for the other crewmen, the majority were Quakers and Annemites. The newspaper printed the denial without comment.

If the unneeded publicity made any impression on our new BSAA friends, they were too reserved to show it. They now not only included us in their social circle, they also made available their airways radio facilities. But, as Swifty put it, we were walking on razor blades. It was imperative that we leave Natal as soon as possible. He briefly considered taking off without a propeller governor, gambling on flying with the propeller in fixed pitch. Thankfully, he decided against it.

Another C-46 arrived. RX-136, piloted by an experienced former airline captain, Don Kosteff, with Milton Russell, my old TWA colleague, as radio operator. They remained in Natal only long enough for an eight-hour daytime sleep and, at 2:00 A.M., left for Dakar.

A day later two more C-46s came in. RX-131, Elliot Polansky the pilot, and RX-134, co-captained by Art Yadvin and Tryg Maseng, our only non-Jewish captain. Both airplanes departed for Dakar, landed without incident, and flew on to Catania.

These names–Kosteff, Russell, Polansky, Yadvin, Maseng–tumble onto the page. And the dozens of other names. Some, after all these years, faceless; some, still vivid in my memory. Each one, unique unto himself, with his own unique motive for volunteering to fly with us.

Exchanging such information, our motives, was almost a ritual. You felt compelled to share the secret. A kind of initiation rite, after which you were accepted into the club. The majority of us, as Jews, were of course accepted unquestioningly, and that included even those now suspected of receiving generous salaries. There was always a justification: a wife and four children, an aging parent, college educations.

To the best of my recollection, at that early period, only two of us were non-Jews. They, like me and some of the other unmarried volunteers, earned the lowest pay, $100 monthly. It followed therefore that these "Goys" were the true idealists. Certainly, more idealistic than any of us Jews whose "duty" it was to serve in this war.

Moonitz's radio operator, for example. Big, blunt, twenty-five-year-old Ed Styrak, the "Polack." A former Merchant

Marine radio officer, Styrak had fought for a Jewish cause long before any of us. He was the radio operator on *The Ben Hecht,* a ship packed with European refugees, captured by the British in 1947 attempting to run the blockade. Styrak spent six miserable weeks in a damp, dank cell in Acre Prison (released only after providing proof positive of his non-Jewishness, which he accomplished by the simple expedient of showing his jailers that he was uncircumcised!).

Ed Styrak's Polish-born parents had brought with them to America that particularly virulent Polish anti-Semitism. He was weaned on it, he said. Only after leaving home for college and then the Merchant Marine did he realize that none of it made any sense.

Tryg Maseng was another. I liked Maseng, a tall, almost anemically thin twenty-six-year-old former USAAF captain. Like me, he was an aspiring writer, and in Panama—when not occupied with Tierra Feliz bar girls or devising ingenious schemes to break the casino's bank—I enjoyed talking books and writing with him. Of Norse extraction, he grew up in Chicago where, as he said, "The Polish kids didn't make me feel too welcome."

One day a Jewish boy moved into Tryg's neighborhood. The Poles made the little Jew's life miserable; a pogrom in microcosm. Tryg "sold out." To gain acceptance, he said he became the worst Jew-baiter of all. I remember him asking, "Can you top that one?"

Yes I could, but was not honest enough to say so. I could top it easily by confiding in him my once almost-overt shame of Jewishness, and my almost inordinate pride in it now. And that this newly discovered Jewish pride was a great paradox I could not come to terms with because I insisted on thinking of myself not as an American Jew or even an American of Jewish descent, but as a plain old American. A Yankee, helping Jews build their new land.

"Their" new land.

Not mine, not ours, theirs.

2.

. . . 12 May. Auerbach repairs plane, finally takes off. Now only us & Moonitz in Natal. Waiting spare parts to fix. War starts in three days . . .

Three days, and no realistic chance of leaving Natal in less than a week, if then. Two airplanes and crews, stranded in Brazil.

We spent our days at the airport or lounging on the hotel veranda. At night we amused ourselves at the town's swankest bordello, which offered a surprisingly good cabaret show. The ladies of the establishment never pushed their services. If your pleasure was to sit innocently at a courtyard patio table and sip strong Brazilian beer or nurse fine Portuguese wine, the management was happy to accommodate you.

Moonitz outfitted himself in an Anzac hat, British officer's bush jacket, khaki shorts, tooled-leather boots, and a swagger stick. He strolled the Natal streets, trailed by hordes of adoring shoe-shine boys onto whose heads he flicked ashes from an ornate ivory cigarette holder, as the boys cried, "El Capitano Mooney! El Capitano Mooney!"

El Capitano enhanced the image a few days later with the addition of a marmoset, a small monkey-type animal. Now he strode about with the marmoset perched on his shoulder. He claimed he was teaching it to fly so it could replace Eichel as his co-pilot.

. . . May 14. Moonitz takes off. No marmoset. Arrives okay Dakar. Raisin back to N.Y. for sick mother.

Raisin's unexpected departure left Swifty and me as the entire crew for the one remaining C-46, still awaiting delivery of a new propeller governor from Panama. Now there was no chance of reaching Israel on or before the 15th, the momentous date.

At the airport that afternoon of the 15th, Swifty and I sought out the friendly Brazilian Air Force officer. A seemingly routine request: I wanted to check airways frequencies on one of the high frequency control tower receivers. The officer obliged. I tuned in the BBC South American service.

There, huddled in a corner of the busy control tower, Swifty Schindler and I listened to a BBC radio announcer's bland description of the birth of the State of Israel. And the simultaneous invasion of the new state by five Arab armies. I hated the BBC announcer for his calm indifference. It was late evening in Israel, mid-afternoon in Brazil. Radio reception was poor, with heavy static and intermittent fading. But we clearly heard the roar of the crowd gathered in front of the Tel Aviv Museum as David Ben-Gurion appeared on an arc-lighted balcony to proclaim the existence of the State of Israel. The Prime Minister spoke in Hebrew, which we could not understand but required no translation. I remember the tingling sensation at the back of my neck, and the rapid beating of my heart, and the glow of pride when Ben-Gurion finished speaking and the crowd began singing the *Hatikva*.

Three days later, entering the hotel dining room, Swifty and I walked casually to the table we had been sharing with our BSAA friends. There were no empty chairs.

"Good evening," Swifty said to the BSAA station manager, a middle-aged Scot who in the past had been most convivial and cooperative.

The manager, whose name was Ian Trippett, nodded coldly and turned away. He began chatting with a tablemate, pointedly ignoring us.

Swifty said, "Well, it was a good evening."

We sat elsewhere, alone. We were finishing coffee when Ian Trippett, leaving, stopped at our table. "I think you might find this interesting," he said, placing a newspaper down on the tablecloth, a *Manchester Guardian*. He indicated a small front-page item.

> Rome, 15 May (Reuters)—Two transport air-
> craft flying the Panamanian flag were reported
> to have arrived today in Catania, Sicily, from
> Palestine. The same two planes landed in
> Catania last Sunday with two collapsible
> fighter planes on board. When they returned
> this morning the fighter planes were gone. It
> is believed they were delivered to Jewish
> elements now fighting in the Holy Land.

Ian Trippett waited patiently for us to read the story.
Swifty and I looked at each other and then, helplessly, at the
Scotsman. I remember an image flashing in my mind just
then: a building exploding, sending tons of debris showering
down on the heads of passersby. Before anyone could speak,
Ian Trippett snatched up the newspaper and said, "Those
would not, by chance, be *your* aircraft, would they?" He did
not wait for an answer. He turned and strode off. That same
evening I received a note:

> To: Communications Supervisor, LAPSA
> From: Station Manager, BSAA Natal
>
> Effective immediately all communications
> facilities previously extended LAPSA are with-
> drawn.

As I told Swifty, borrowing Ed Styrak's favorite line,
" . . . I guess they can't take a joke."

Two days later, on May 20, a LAPSA mechanic arrived
from Burbank with the propeller governor slip ring. An hour
after it was installed we were rolling out for takeoff. A daylight departure, bringing us into Dakar at night, but Swifty
was so anxious to leave he chose not to wait. With Raisin
absent, I would fly co-pilot. I like to think this was an indi-
cation of Swifty's confidence in me, but I have always feared

it was more a measure of his desperation.

It was probably a little of both, for shortly after reaching cruising altitude, Swifty slid back his seat, rose, and announced he was going into the cabin for a nap. "Keep it on this heading," he said, "Make sure the power settings stay exactly where they are. You need me, ring the alarm bell." And he left.

I slipped elatedly into the left seat, strapped in, and flew the airplane. On autopilot, to be sure, but for more than two glorious hours I was the captain.

3.

Swifty's navigation was so flawless that he split Dakar straight down the middle and landed with nearly 400 gallons of reserve fuel. We remained in Dakar only long enough to refuel and eat. Next stop, Casablanca. There, at Cazes Air-drome, we had hardly parked in the transient area when the customs inspector boarded the airplane. A cheerful man, white-uniformed with a "Douane Francais" badge on the crown of his pith helmet, his first words were, "How are things in Palestine?"

I do not recall my answer, if indeed I answered at all, but remember that Swifty hastily decided to forego the planned six-hour layover for rest and food. We filed for an immediate departure to Catania. At the Flight Operations office, a clerk, a Moroccan, casually mentioned that one of our airplanes was en route to Cazes.

"RX-135," said the clerk. He waved the teletyped aircraft-destination message at us. Swifty snatched the paper from him. He read it, then handed it to me.

LAPSA RX-135 DEP AJACCIO 1100. ETA CAZES 1730.

"Ajaccio?" I asked. "Corsica? What the hell is he doing in Corsica?"

"What do you mean, 'what's he doing there?'" Swifty said

quickly, and almost too loud, but for the clerk's benefit. "That's where he's supposed to be, isn't it, Corsica?"

I got the message. "Oh sure, Corsica," I said, as though I'd known it all along.

"He's only an hour and a half out," Swifty said. "We'll wait around for him." He gestured me to gather the clearance papers. We hurried outside.

"135 is Ribakoff's airplane," I said. "And I'll ask you again: what the hell is he doing in *Corsica*? And why is he coming *here*?"

"Maybe to tell us something," Swifty said. "I'll go out and preflight the airplane. You nose around and see what you can find out."

It did not take me long. In the airport radio room I struck up a conversation with the shift supervisor, a retired Air France flight radio officer. He told me that for the past week LAPSA C-46s had been arriving and departing daily from Corsica.

Daily flights? Casablanca and Corsica?

An hour and a half later, with no sign of RX-135, I returned to the Cazes radio room. On the Flight Information Board was a notation: RX-135 Arr 1725.

RX-135 had landed ten minutes ago.

But not here, not at Casablanca, and not that day or any other day. The flight information messages were obviously phony. We would learn the details later. We wasted no more time. We refiled for an immediate departure to Catania and in less than ten minutes were in the air.

Over Tunis, I received a revised weather report. Catania was closed. Tunis Radio suggested we land there, at Tunis, and wait for the Italian weather to clear.

Swifty thought about it a moment. "Tell them that if Catania is still closed when we get there, we'll go on to Rome."

I relayed the information. Tunis Radio replied that Rome was also closed. For our safety, they again advised us to land in Tunis.

"They seem pretty anxious for us to land," I said to Swifty.

"They're that worried about us, eh?" he said.

I read his mind: no one had interfered with us in Casablanca where bogus LAPSA arrival and departure messages were filed daily, and where a Moroccan customs inspector greeted us with, "How are things in Palestine?" So why tempt fate further?

I said, "I'll say, 'Thanks, but we're staying on course and trying for Catania.'"

"And tell them we appreciate their concern."

I relayed the message and switched off the receiver before they could reply. We flew on, over the Mediterranean now, the sky above and ahead a dull slate gray, and the water below choppy and white-waked. Not a pleasant day.

Approaching the Italian coast Naples Radio informed me that Catania remained closed and was not expected to open for at least six hours. Rome, however, was open; contrary to the Tunis radio advice, it never had been closed. We received permission to continue on to Rome, but to preclude that airport suddenly declaring itself closed (to us) I called into Ciampino airfield that we were coming in for an emergency landing. Mechanical problems.

We had hardly turned off the engines in the transient aircraft area when a battered old Fiat sedan raced up. The car circled tire-screechingly around the airplane, then pulled to a stop under the left wing. A man vaulted from the car and pounded on the cabin door demanding entrance. A tall, slender, bespectacled man of thirty, Danny Agronsky. A sabra, the son of *Palestine Post* publisher Gershon Agronsky, Danny was the erstwhile manager of LAPSA's "Rome office." In other words, Haganah's man in Italy.

Danny Agronsky was a world-class troubleshooter. He could fix anything. From arranging for airport customs officials to blithely overlook an arriving C-46 or C-54 loaded with munitions, to successfully pacifying an irate hotel manager who had discovered two of his rooms completely stripped of furniture. The rooms were occupied by a half-dozen of our fighter pilots, Americans and Canadians on their way to Israel, who had turned up in Rome purely by mistake, and very broke. Which did not dissuade them from inviting three prostitutes to dinner and drinks, charged of course to Danny. The furniture—beds, bureaus, chairs, lamps, even bedding—was presented to the girls in lieu of cash, payment for services rendered.

After giving us hell for landing here (yes, but with Catania closed, where in the hell were we supposed to land?), Danny said it was a good thing we hadn't landed in Catania after all. Catania, thanks to British and American pressure on the Italian government, was now closed permanently to LAPSA. Luckily, however, the French had agreed to allow our airplanes en route to Israel to stop for refueling in Corsica, at Ajaccio.

Refueling from where?

From the main supply base in, of all places, Czechoslovakia.

Czechoslovakia? Behind the Iron Curtain?

Yes, said Danny, Czechoslovakia. The Israelis had struck a deal with the Czechs for the purchase of guns and ammunition and, more importantly, Messerschmitt ME-109 fighter airplanes.

Messerschmitts?

More accurately, Avia S-199s, the Czech-built version of the ME-109. From an airfield near Prague the fighters, dismantled, were loaded into the C-46s and flown over the Alps to Ajaccio. There, Danny explained, the C-46s refueled and continued on to Israel. Returning, they refueled again in Ajaccio for the return flight to the Czech base.

While we struggled to digest all this, Danny shepherded us through customs and immigration and drove us into the city. He checked us into the Hotel Mediterraneo (not the same establishment frequented by the fighter pilots!), bought us dinner, and explained the nature of the Ajaccio-Casablanca "daily flights."

Flight plans, cleared through European Air Traffic Control, correctly reported the aircraft's point of departure as Ajaccio. This airplane's destination, however, was listed as Casablanca. Shortly after LAPSA Flight 25's ETA at Cazes Airdrome—or Flight 27, or 35, or whatever westbound flight number sounded good—someone in Casablanca reported its arrival there. That same someone, shortly afterward, filed a return flight plan for Ajaccio.

This, remember, in an era when radar-controlled flight control and computers were yet to be invented. All communication was by radio or radio-teletype. Controllers never saw aircraft as moving objects projected with all pertinent data onto a screened display. An aircraft, then, was a chalked symbol on a board. There was no way to track it electronically.

In reality, of course, all these Ajaccio departures and arrivals were to and from Israel, where the C-46 had delivered its cargo of guns and a Messerschmitt fighter.

Messerschmitts.

Jewish Messerschmitts.

After Danny left, Swifty and I fell exhausted onto our hotel beds and were immediately asleep. In the morning we would leave for the Czechoslovak base. I might not have slept so soundly had I known that in less than six hours I would be awakened with grievous news.

Moonitz, on his first flight into Israel, had crashed.

FIVE

ZEBRA

" . . . over the coast, Skipper, at twenty-three ten," said Moe Rosenbaum, the navigator. A pleasant, soft-spoken young man, an ex-USAAF 8th Air Force captain, just three weeks ago he had been attending classes at Cornell University.

"Yeah," Moonitz said glumly. "But where the hell is it?" He was staring through his side window down at where the landmark on the beach should be, but was not. The entire coastal area was shrouded in thick green-gray fog extending inland as far as the eye could see.

"What do you think the ceiling is?" the co-pilot, Sheldon Eichel, asked.

"Five hundred feet," Rosenbaum said. "If that much."

"No, no, no," said Ed Styrak, the radio operator. "A half hour ago Aquir reported ceiling and visibility unlimited!" He spoke sarcastically, for it was already a standard joke that all weather reports from the airdrome at Aquir, the final destination—a former RAF station twenty-two miles southeast of

Tel Aviv–advised unlimited ceilings and visibility.

Moonitz laughed dryly. He was thinking, sure, why not say ceiling unlimited? It made no difference. Whatever the weather, you had no other place to land. Although that was not technically true: there was an alternate field.

Cairo.

He studied the altimeter. Two thousand feet. He was silent a moment, deciding. Then, "Okay, we'll head out to sea and let down over the water." He glanced over his shoulder at Styrak. "Find out where Auerbach is!" Hal Auerbach, in another C-46, was also due in at that same time.

"I heard them give him the 'clear-to-land' signal," Styrak said. "That was more than ten minutes ago. He's got to be down by now."

"Yeah," Moonitz said. "But where, I wonder?"

Moonitz had already swung the airplane around and was out over the water now, in the clear, beyond the fog. The moon was still low but bright enough so that to the east, at the coast, you could actually see where the fog began. It resembled a solid gray fence at the water's edge.

"It looks almost down to the ground," Rosenbaum said.

"Can you raise the beacon?" Moonitz asked Styrak.

"They told me it's on, but I can't hear it," Styrak said. He rose from his chair, stepped to the pedestal, and reached up to the ADF units on the overhead instrument panel. He clamped one earphone to his ear and manipulated the ADF tuning knobs. First the red unit, then the green. He shook his head. "Not a bloody fucking peep!"

"We'll fly out three minutes, then come back in again," Moonitz said. "Maybe by then we'll find a hole in it."

"Good luck," said Styrak. He stuck an unlighted cigar in his mouth and, sprawling in his chair, resumed reading the paperback book he had placed face down on his desk. A collection of William Faulkner short stories. He was particularly fond of *The Bear*. He said it reminded him of Moonitz.

They flew on, out over the water, and then turned to come

back in, descending now at three hundred feet per minute. Moonitz estimated this would bring him over Aquir just under the ceiling. If there was a ceiling.

"Four fifty!" Eichel called. "Better pull up!"

But Moonitz continued descending another few seconds, straining desperately for a glimpse of the runway lights. He thought he was almost exactly over the field, or at least close enough to see lights. He went down to three hundred, then pulled up. He climbed back to twelve hundred and began cruising in a wide circle.

Suddenly Eichel shouted, "There's a break!"

Sure enough, just ahead, a jagged opening in the clouds. And, shining beckoningly, the single row of runway lights. Moonitz nosed the C-46 down toward the hole. But just as unexpectedly as it had opened it all at once closed. Moonitz racked the big airplane around like a fighter. He pulled up and climbed back to six hundred.

"I can hear Auerbach!" Styrak shouted. "They just landed!"

"All right, then ask the tower what they want us to do," Moonitz said to Styrak. "And tell them if the beacon isn't working, I'm gonna play hell lining up with a runway I can't see!"

There was no time to encode a message. Styrak spoke to the field in clear language. He relayed the reply to Moonitz: "They don't know what the ceiling is—listen, be grateful for small favors, at least they're not saying it's 'unlimited'—and they don't know how long the weather will last. They want to know how much fuel we have—"

"—not enough to stay up here and wait!" Moonitz said.

"Maybe thirty minutes," Eichel said. "*Maybe!*"

Styrak conveyed that information to the field. He listened to their response and laughed unhumorously. "Stay up as long as we can, and keep looking for a break!"

Eichel looked at Moonitz. "Norm, how do you say 'Go fuck yourself' in Hebrew?"

Moonitz did not reply. He was staring straight ahead at

the fog swirling in and around the airplane. It was so heavy that at times it even obscured the blinking green navigational wingtip lights.

Eichel said to Moonitz, "What do you want to do?"

Moonitz whirled to him. "Do? I want to have a game of Parcheesi! What the hell can we do?" Immediately, he regretted the harsh tone; this was not the time for it. The idea of apologizing flitted through his mind, but this was not the time for that, either. Besides, despite the fact he had begun to grow genuinely fond of Eichel, he really felt like punching him. What do you want to do? What a dumb question! Dumb, because it was the same question he had been asking himself.

Moonitz glanced around the flight deck. "Where's Moe?"

"Back at his desk," said Styrak. The navigator's station was in the cabin, the drop-down table and chair squeezed snug against the bulkhead to accommodate the Messerschmitt fuselage that occupied the entire cabin from cockpit door to tail.

"Get him up here," Moonitz said. "I don't want him back there with that cargo when we land."

Styrak opened the cockpit door and called Rosenbaum to come forward. Rosenbaum said he'd be there in a minute, he was plotting their fuel reserve.

"We'll have to try to get in," Moonitz said quietly, really thinking aloud. "That, or put her down in the water."

"Forget it," Styrak said immediately. "Not with four thousand pounds of fighter plane in the cabin behind us."

"Hey, don't knock it," Eichel said. "It's not everyday you can get an ME-109 stuck up your ass!"

"What about you?" Moonitz asked Eichel.

Eichel shrugged. "I can't swim."

Moonitz was silent another moment. Then he pointed to the landing facilities chart on Eichel's lap. "Obstructions?"

Eichel said, "According to this, the highest hill is two hundred feet. It's a little to the left of the runway. But where's the runway?"

Moonitz rolled his seat forward. He gripped the yoke with his left hand, throttles with his right. "We'll make a normal approach and see what happens. Okay, gear down!"

Eichel lowered the gear.

"Half flap."

Eichel lowered the flaps to half.

"Call out altitude and airspeed," Moonitz said.

"Seven hundr—" Eichel began, and then his voice rose with shrill excitement. "Hey, there's the flashing beacon! I can see the field—what luck!" And then, in the same breath, "Oh, shit!"

Again, the break in the undercast had abruptly closed. They were blind again. Eichel continued, "Four hundred, one-twenty. Three fifty, one-twenty. Three hundred, one—"

Eichel never completed the sentence.

The airplane stopped. Everything stopped.

2.

All this—those details, and what went through Moonitz's mind—I learned days later in Tel Aviv. It was in Rome that I learned of the crash itself, and as though in a dream. From voices in my sleep.

" . . . who checked Moonitz out?"

"Gerson, I think."

The voices came from the other bed, Swifty's, in this pleasant room at the Hotel Mediterraneo. Swifty was sitting up. I remember thinking that his bright red and white striped pajamas blended perfectly with the black tufted leather headboard. Two men sat on the bed edge talking with him.

One was Danny Agronsky. The other was Arnold Ilowite, a twenty-seven-year-old former USAAF ATC pilot, another of Schwimmer's original volunteers. Ilowite apologized for waking me and suggested I go back to sleep. But now I was wide awake.

"What's all this about Moonitz?" I asked, and instantly regretted the question. I already knew the answer. Something had happened to Moonitz. I sat up. "What happened?"

"He had an accident," Swifty said.

"Moe Rosenbaum was killed," Danny said.

"Oh, Jesus!" I said, but at the same time felt a flush of relief. Moonitz was alive. Danny would have mentioned his name first otherwise. But with the relief came guilt. I hardly knew Moe Rosenbaum, he had joined LAPSA only a few days before we left Panama. Now he was dead.

" . . . Styrak and Eichel are okay," Danny was saying. "Both badly burned. Styrak's leg is broken. They'll be okay, though."

"Moonitz is fine," Ilowite said, answering my unasked question. He went on then to describe the circumstances. Groping blindly for the field, the C-46 struck a hill just off the end of the runway. Moe Rosenbaum was in the cabin during the landing. The Messerschmitt had torn loose and crushed him against the bulkhead. Killed instantly. In my mind I envisioned the scene. I wondered if Moonitz saw the hill in the split-instant before hitting it. I would have to ask him.

Danny said, "They gave Rosenbaum a military funeral."

"Where are they now?" I asked. "Moonitz and the others?"

"They're in the hospital," Danny said. "They should be out in a few days. Moonitz and Eichel saved Styrak's life: they pulled him out of the burning plane."

All two hundred pounds of him, I thought, wondering how they managed to squeeze Styrak's huge bulk through the cockpit window, which had to be the only avenue of escape. "By now that Polack bastard should know what happens to goys who fight for Jews," I said. "I hope this taught him a good lesson."

"Yeah," said Ilowite. "He got a good lesson."

Arnie Ilowite had learned some "lessons" of his own, commencing two months before, in March, when he and

Leo Gardner flew that very first C-46 to Italy. A flight beset with problems, jinxed from beginning to end. The airplane, forced down with engine trouble in Geneva, then impounded in Rome where it required all Danny Agronsky's skill (spelled bribery) to secure the C-46's release.

But that was only for starters. From Rome, early in May while we were still in Panama, Ilowite flew that same C-46 to Israel, to Aquir. There, with a pick-up crew, he immediately began flying supply missions to several northern kibbutzim under siege. For two days, back and forth from Aquir, they dropped food, medicine, ammunition. With both approaches to the Aquir runway in Arab Legion hands, every landing and takeoff was directly over enemy guns.

On the third day their luck ran out. The C-46 was peppered by .50-caliber machine gun fire. One shell smashed into the cockpit. Ilowite and Jack Goldstein, his Canadian navigator, escaped with superficial but painful facial wounds. The airplane, this ill-starred C-46, was extensively damaged; as a final affront it was strafed on the ground by an Egyptian Spitfire. Scratch one C-46. Of the original ten, two now were gone.

Twenty percent of our total strength.

3.

We took off from Rome early the next morning for the Czechoslovak base. We filed for Ruzyne Airfield, Prague, but with no intention to land there. At the approximate time of our scheduled arrival, "someone" in Ruzyne would close the flight plan. Our actual destination was thirty miles north of Prague.

An airstrip code named "Zebra," a former Luftwaffe auxiliary field twenty miles south of the German border, five miles east of the Sudeten town of Zatec (pronounced *Jhaa-tets*).

From the air the town Zatec resembled a movie set. Almost Graustarkian, with its quaint cobblestoned, clock-towered town square, and *lederhosen*-attired old men guiding horse-drawn wagons through narrow twisting streets lined with gingerbread buildings.

Less Graustarkian was the huge red star stanchioned to the facade of one large brick building, and the hammer-and-sickle banner draped above the entrance of another. We were low enough to clearly see these, although unaware yet that the town square once was called Adolf Hitlerplatz, and the best hotel, formerly the Kaiserhof, was now the Stalingrad.

(In 1981, Barbra Streisand chose Zatec as the location for the film *Yentl*. The entire film company was housed in the same hotel, by then no longer called the Stalingrad. I doubt that Ms. Streisand realized that some thirty-three years earlier that very hotel had been crowded with dozens of young American fliers, and that the airfield outside the city was the European terminus for the Israeli Air Force Air Transport Command.)

Zebra from the air resembled a narrow white ribbon haphazardly dropped into the center of vast green fields of hay and hops. Closer, you saw it was a single concrete landing strip. No hangars, no control tower, only a smattering of flimsy wood sheds located just off the halfway point of the runway. Trucks and a few automobiles were parked near the sheds. And, parked on a small asphalt hardstand not far from the sheds, its Panamanian registration numbers glistening blue in the afternoon sun, was a LAPSA C-46.

A long flatbed truck was backed to the C-46's open cargo doors. Men were maneuvering the wingless fuselage of a Messerschmitt fighter airplane from the truck into the transport's cabin. Other men removed smaller crates and boxes from a GI six-by-six truck, stacking them outside the airplane, obviously to be stowed later in the cabin. A third truck, a fuel carrier, was positioned directly behind the C-46's left wing. Two more men, steadying a fuel hose into the wing tank receptacle, crouched atop the wing. Some of the men wore coveralls. But others were in uniform, the brown coarse wool uniforms of the Czech Army.

Swifty made one pass over the field. The coverall-clad men waved. Swifty glanced at me and shrugged. "I guess that means we can land," he said, and did.

The first person to greet us was Sam Pomerance, a slight, balding man in his late thirties. An American Jew, a pilot and near-genius of an aeronautical engineer, Sam Pomerance supervised all maintenance operations at Zebra. It was a job demanding more than genius; it required magical skills.

And luck. All that could be found, bought, or borrowed.

Accompanying Sam was a short, almost cadaverous man of indeterminate age. He wore an ill-fitting threadbare suit, a fraying food-stained shirt, and a carelessly knotted, wrinkled tie. His eyes—the most prominent feature of his haggard face—seemed to glow.

This man, I would quickly learn, was known as a Little Man. One of two Little Men who seemed to be constantly present and who functioned as a liaison between the Czechs and ourselves. The other Little Man, whom I met later, was known simply as "Levy," and bore such a remarkable resemblance to his colleague they could have been brothers, although they were not.

"*Ich heisse Meyer,*" the man said, and extended his hand.

We shook hands. His was very dry and calloused; and as he withdrew it I saw on his forearm a blue-tattooed number, M-19563.

In Yiddish, Meyer asked us for our passports.

Sam translated, then said, "It's all right. Meyer's one of us."

Meyer, understanding, smiled self-consciously. He glanced at three grim-looking young Czech soldiers standing nearby, then spoke again in Yiddish.

Sam also glanced at the soldiers. He explained, "They don't want anybody traipsing around the countryside with American passports."

Meyer nodded and smiled again.

Sam said, "You'll be able to move around in town without

a passport, and even in Prague. Just try to behave yourselves. And, for Christ's sake, never, but *never*, get into political discussions with any Czechs. That is strictly *verboten*. No politics! Tomorrow, before you take off, they'll give you back the passports."

I heard "tomorrow," and "take off" with mingled relief and disappointment. What I wanted most—what I needed most—was sleep. In Rome, after our brief rest, we had spent the remainder of that day and almost the entire night eating and drinking. But I also did not want to delay, even by another hour, going to Israel.

We gave Meyer the passports. He presented them to a soldier. The soldier slipped the documents into his breast pocket. By now we had been greeted by several of the coveralled men, Americans, Al Schwimmer's mechanics. Some two dozen of them were here, all non-Jews, working round the clock. They were themselves geniuses. Somehow, with little or no spare parts available, they kept the C-46s flying.

The C-46s that brought the Messerschmitts to Israel.

The Messerschmitts that already had challenged, and chased away, the previously unopposed Egyptian Air Force. In the war's first week, although you could hardly call them mass raids, the Egyptians had bombed Tel Aviv daily. Two or three Spitfires indiscriminately dropping small bombs, or a Dakota with heavier ordnance. But it did cause damage and casualties. And a Dakota once put a hundred pounder directly into the Central Bus Station on Allenby Street and killed forty-one civilians.

But now the picnic was over. Now the Egyptians faced real combat aircraft flown by experienced American pilots. The days of young Israeli student pilots of the "Primus Air Force" flying near-suicide missions were over. No longer, as point blank targets for small arms fire, would they hurl gasoline-filled bottles down at enemy columns. Or, as once actually happened, a dozen cases of empty seltzer water bottles: the shrill whistle of the wind rushing past the bottles supposedly simulated the sound of bombs, supposedly panicking the Egyptian soldiers.

The Messerschmitts were here. The irony–or, if you will, poetic justice–of Jews flying Nazi aircraft was obvious. It was also an act of desperation.

The Avia S-199, the Czech-manufactured Messerschmitt, was a far cry from the fabled and reliable ME-109. The S-199 lacked the powerful Mercedes DB-600 engine that had made the Luftwaffe fighter so deadly, and its landing gear was considerably narrower than the original, thereby endowing it with an alarming tendency to ground loop. In the end, for this and a myriad of other faults, the S-199 was a total disaster. But in those early days it flew, and fought.

For each S-199, the Israeli government paid the Czechs $40,000 cash, American. Plus an additional $10,000 to train each volunteer pilot to fly these troublesome, unforgiving machines. The arrangement benefited both parties. The new Czech communist government needed our hard currency. We needed their aircraft.

4.

Meyer drove us into town in an automobile of uncertain vintage and dependability. He and Swifty carried on an animated conversation in Yiddish. Surprisingly, with Swifty's occasional assistance, I understood much of it. A Pole, Meyer had been smuggled into Palestine shortly after his liberation from Mauthausen. Now he functioned in a liaison capacity between the Provisional Israeli government and the Czechs. The point man.

The money man.

This Little Man had access to an apparently unlimited supply of American cash. The purchasing power of an American dollar–at unofficial rates or, more accurately, black market exchange–was ten times that of the local currency.

The $100 bill Meyer presented us as payment for our monthly salary, which he promptly exchanged for Czech kroner–at the unofficial rate, of course–would therefore provide us with $1,000 worth of anything we wished.

Whiskey to women.

Neither of which, I quickly discovered, was readily available in Zatec. Certainly not at the Stalingrad Hotel where we were billeted. This hotel, a stolid foreboding building in the town square directly opposite the hammer-and-sickle-flagged City Hall, had been entirely requisitioned for our aircrews and mechanics. Two other hotels, the Zlaty Lev ("Golden Lion") and the Zlaty Andel ("Golden Angel") also housed our personnel.

I never did learn what explanation was offered the townspeople for the presence of so many young, casually dressed Americans. Perhaps the Czech government believed no explanation necessary; after all, many of these people had themselves only recently arrived in Zatec, Czech citizens now living in homes formerly owned by Sudeten Germans who had fled the country after the Nazi defeat. They simply seemed to accept the fact we were there, period. Another, but less unpleasant, foreign invasion.

Hal Auerbach and his radioman, Eddie Chinsky, awaited us in the hotel courtyard. Meyer was to drive them to the airstrip. Auerbach and his crew were scheduled out in RX-135 the following morning. Hal wanted Eddie to check out a newly installed radio transmitter.

Auerbach said, "Gentlemen, how nice to see you! Things have never looked brighter!"

This was his signature. No matter what the situation, no matter how bleak or critical, to Hal Auerbach it was invariably, "Things have never looked brighter!" It became a battle cry.

Auerbach's next words were less inspiring, at least for Swifty. Swifty would not fly to Israel in the morning. He was being sent back to New York on a "special mission."

Auerbach did not know the nature of the assignment, only that Schwimmer had cabled instructions for Swifty's immediate return.

Things have never looked brighter.

Although you might not think so from Eddie Chinsky's bedraggled appearance. Eddie, whom I had not seen since Natal, wore a grease-mottled jacket that fell almost below his knees. And trousers in similar disrepair, their cuffs rolled up three or four times to accommodate his height. I liked to believe Eddie was the only man shorter than me. (This, however, occasionally varied: Eddie owned a pair of shoes with two-inch heels.) A Canadian, a wartime RCAF flight radio officer, Chinsky had already made several flights to and from Israel; he was a veteran.

I asked him where in the hell he found that outlandish outfit. Where was the dapper, suave, ladies man I knew and admired? My drinking, dining, gambling, and girl-chasing companion? Where was his pride? How did he expect to make his mark on the women of Prague?

"You look like a fucking refugee!" I said.

"I feel like one," he said, and explained that the jacket and trousers belonged to Steve Schwartz. Pure doeskin, of which I remembered Steve was excessively proud, and that now resembled a discarded chamois rag you cleaned your car with.

Eddie had inherited the suit a week before on his first flight into Israel. It seemed that somewhere between Natal and Catania, he lost all his clothes and personal possessions. Fortunately for Eddie, and to Steve Schwartz's subsequent dismay, Steve had stowed his B-4 bag–containing among other items the handsome doeskin suit–aboard RX-135 for delivery to Tel Aviv.

"Gentlemen," Hal Auerbach said to us, "I want you to meet 'bomb-chucker first class,' Edward Chinsky!"

"What," I asked accommodatingly, "is a 'bomb-chucker'?"

Eddie, although Canadian born, spoke English in the careful, clipped, cryptic cadences of one whose first language was other than English. In his case, Polish, with the second language French. The ensuing result, accompanied by appropriate facial contortions and arm-flailing gestures, was an indefinable accent, a melodic combination of English, Quebec French, and Middle European.

"Last trip in, we are just leaving T.A. when a guy runs up," Eddie said. "He asks if we want to do a great thing for Israel. 'We have already done great things,' I tell him. 'Do you want us to bomb Cairo?' I say this as a joke, you understand. But the schmuck is serious. 'Not Cairo,' he says. 'Someplace else.' Hal here, he says to the guy, 'Surely, sir, you are joshing: bomb with a C-46?'"

Eddie paused to light a cigarette, a procedure that required no more than three seconds and hardly interfered with his soliloquy. "'No,' says the guy, 'I am not joshing. There is a large enemy concentration below Ishdud. Our soldiers have destroyed a bridge, but the Egyptians are still moving toward this bridge. Now they are piled up in a traffic jam of armored vehicles and troops strung out a mile in front of the bridge, waiting to cross. They cannot move.'"

Eddie paused again now for a deep drag. He exhaled impatiently, waggled the cigarette, and continued. "Hal asks us if we want to do it. We say okay. So they load ten fifty pound bombs on the airplane. And you know how they load them? In little wood crates like eggs! Eggs, for Christ's sake! Okay, so away we go. We come over the bridge. Sure enough, there is the whole goddam Egyptian army! We are less than a thousand feet and the dumb shits are standing there, waving hello at us. Hal says, 'Mr. Chinsky, sir, you are the bombardier. Chuck them out!'"

So Eddie, along with the navigator and the co-pilot, Bob Luery (a former U.S. Army captain, who also happened to be Auerbach's first cousin), rushed into the cabin and opened the cargo door. Luery pulled the pins from the bombs and handed them one at a time to Eddie. Eddie, standing in the open doorway, simply heaved them down on the Egyptian column. It was, said Auerbach, a reasonably successful raid.

"Yeah, but only because I didn't fall out with the fucking bombs!" said Eddie. "And do you know how I get to stay inside the plane? The navigator is standing behind me, one of his hands grabbing on to the back of my belt, his other hand grabbing the door handle so *he* won't fall out!"

What a way to fight a war.

5.

The high-ceilinged Stalingrad Hotel lobby could have been the bar and lounge of any USAAF Officer's or NCO club in World War II England. Wherever you looked were khaki-clad young Americans. Drinking, smoking, talking, laughing, playing cards. I recognized four of the six players engrossed in a poker game as some of the fighter pilots whose wild antics in Rome had brought Danny Agronsky one of his many headaches.

Seated before the huge, roaring fireplace were Phil Schild and his co-pilot, Ted Applebaum. In the morning I would fly with them into Israel. Phil, who had flown B-29s in the Pacific, sacrificed a long-sought opportunity for medical school to volunteer his services with LAPSA. Ted, after flying C-46s in a USAAF Troop Carrier Command squadron, worked at his father's Washington, D.C. jewelry store. One day, leaving for lunch, he told his father he might be a little late. He neglected to say that by "late" he meant ten months.

Near the ornately carved double-doored kitchen entrance, kibbitzing a gin game, was Willie Sosnow. Willie, the jolly, rotund master aircraft mechanic, the archetypical Jewish Brooklynite. Built like a beer barrel, with rapidly vanishing red hair and concrete-mixer voice, he was the mechanical genius of geniuses. Willie not only helped Sam Pomerance maintain our airplanes, he scoured the war surplus depots and junkyards of Europe for engines, parts, guns, airplanes. And he found them, from Mosquito bombers in England to Spitfires in Yugoslavia. Willie Sosnow was the only man I ever knew whom it was impossible to dislike.

Willie and the others—some just returned from flights or preparing to leave—brought Swifty and me up to date. Our C-46s were in continual operation, which Marty Ribakoff said was a kind of aerial Russian roulette. The airplanes stayed in the air only through the expertise of Willie Sosnow and Sam Pomerance, along with gum, spit, innovation, and considerable prayer.

But more than prayer was needed for the aircrews; they, said Larry Raab, needed whole new bodies. We were averaging two and one half round trips weekly. You flew to "Jockstrap" (Ajaccio), then to "Oklahoma" (Israel), laying over only long enough for a night's—or day's—sleep, then flew back to Jockstrap and then on to Zebra. You slept, then got up and flew again.

Welcome aboard, pal. Welcome to the Israeli Air Force.

I was assigned a room on the hotel's second floor. On my way upstairs I passed the dining room. A familiar, high-pitched voice called out.

"Hey, you lousy poker player!"

It was Sol Fingerman, another radioman. He sat at a communal table in the huge dimly lit room with the other two members of his crew. Ray Kurtz, the one-time Brooklyn cop, ex B-17 squadron commander, and Jules Cubernik, the B-17 navigator turned Chicago druggist, turned Israeli Air Force navigator. All three were happily munching thick slices of black bread heaped with butter brought in from Ajaccio. Bread and butter, they explained, was the main luncheon course this particular day, Tuesday. Tuesday was the kitchen staff's day off, hence the short rations. But no one, they assured me, went hungry. Although under the new communist regime such staples as meat, eggs, butter, and fresh fruit were tightly rationed, we flew in our own provisions from

Ajaccio. Supplemented by an abundant supply of local potatoes and cabbage.

Fingerman asked me to lend him some money. He had busted out of the poker game and wanted to get back in. I said all I had were the Czech kroner given me by Meyer, and $30, American.

"Let me have the thirty," Fingerman said. "We'll be partners. I'll do the playing. You need to get some sleep for the flight tomorrow."

"You're going out tomorrow, too," I said. "When do you sleep?" The notion of Fingerman playing with my money was terrifying. He and I were the most inept poker players in the outfit, he slightly worse.

"I never sleep," he said, which I knew to be almost true. Somehow he managed on three or four hours. He held out his hand. "Come on, give me the money."

Just then to my relief I noticed the poker game in the lobby was breaking up. "The game's over," I said.

"Only for now," he said. "We're taking those fighter jocks in with us tomorrow. The minute we're off the ground, the cards'll be dealt. A sixteen-hour flight. Plenty of time for me to get even, and us to win."

The marathon poker game. Like a floating crap game, this one moved from hotel to airplane, back to hotel, back to airplane. A Flying Poker Game. It had started on the very first flight from Millville to Panama, continued throughout our stay in Panama City, and never stopped. Panama to Natal, in Natal, then Natal to Zebra. And now Zebra to Oklahoma.

Fingerman always found players: passengers, mechanics, once even a high-ranking Israeli diplomat. For the airborne portion of the game Fingerman rigged a seventy-foot extension cord from his station on the flight deck to the rear of the C-46's cabin. There, earphones fastened to his head, cramped between the Messerschmitt's empenage and the cargo door, he and the others sat on the floor around a blanket-topped ammunition crate (labeled *Fragile–Glass!*), and played.

"Come on," he said, his hand impatiently extended palm up. "Let's have the money."

"You'll only lose it."

"No," he said. "No chance. It's in the bag." He glanced around to make sure we weren't overheard. "On the Zebra-Jockstrap leg, we go over the Alps. Fifteen, sometimes seventeen thousand feet. No oxygen." He glanced around again, now at the poker-playing fighter pilots. "No oxygen. Those hot-shots'll never know what's happening to them. It'll be like they're drunk." He smiled triumphantly. "The altitude won't bother me."

"They'll sober up when you get past the mountains," I said.

"Yeah, but by then I'll have their dough," he said. I knew it was a hopeless cause, but gave him the money anyway. I was too tired to argue. And too excited, looking forward to tomorrow, to Israel.

SIX

OKLAHOMA

Approaching Klagenfurt at the foothills of the Austrian Alps we had begun climbing. The steady, reassuring drone of the engines changed to a labored, almost asthmatic whine as the carburetors struggled for oxygen in the ever-thinning atmosphere and the propellers found increasingly less air to bite into.

Ahead, in the bright cloudless sky, the morning sun flashed down on the snow-covered peaks and reflected glaringly back into our eyes. The mountains on the Italian side rose up against the horizon like an ominous white barrier.

A 15,000-foot barrier.

Fifteen thousand feet over the Austrian Alps, a flight I was to make some two dozen times, and each time unfailingly rendered me helpless. At that altitude with no oxygen, erratic cabin heaters, and a throbbing headache, I could do little more than lay my head on the radio table and gasp for breath. And listen to the hypnotic beat of the engines and the metallic slamming of small chunks of ice, flung loose from the propellers, ricocheting off the airplane's aluminum fuselage.

And with yet still another, but hardly so esoteric inconvenience. Box lunches packed in Zebra consisted of the famous black bread, and hard-boiled eggs, which we devoured shortly after takeoff. By the time we reached the mountains the food was digested. High altitude pressure distends your abdomen. The body expels its natural gases—in genteel vernacular, breaks wind. Hard-boiled eggs, digested, emit a potent sulfur-like odor. At 15,000 feet the flight deck was a blue haze of sulfuric stench. You were almost afraid to light a cigarette.

The mountain flight was thankfully brief and soon we were down to 8,000 feet, over Trieste. Past Trieste, we turned west over the Adriatic Sea and the marshy Venetian flatlands. Then south again across the green belt of central Italy. And then more water—the Tyrrhenian Sea, with Napoleon's Elba off to our left like a drab brown stain on a carpet of glittering blue—to Corsica, and the red tiled roofs of the whitewashed buildings of Ajaccio.

After a series of hasty, albeit expensive "arrangements," the French government had granted LAPSA landing rights at Ajaccio and agreed to look the other way. Or, more accurately, not look, period. A glimpse at any map tells you that on a flight from Central Europe to Israel, you are traveling almost prohibitively out of your way stopping for fuel in Corsica.

A detour of four hundred and fifty miles.

We had no choice. With Catania unavailable—and permission to refuel at a Yugoslavian Adriatic airstrip still being negotiated—impractical as it was, we were lucky to have Ajaccio as a refueling point for the long, nonstop Mediterranean flight.

The Ajaccio airdrome was controlled by the French military, *L'Armee de l'Air*, under the command of an overage, overweight, but extremely cooperative French Air Force major, Commandant Latour. Each time a C-46 landed, Commandant Latour personally greeted the aircraft captain who, as standard equipment, carried with him a briefcase containing $10,000 cash, American. The captain responded to the major's comradely greeting by withdrawing from the briefcase a neatly bound packet of fifty $100 bills: $5,000, cash, which he presented to Commandant Latour. This transaction paid the "landing fee," but did not include payment for gasoline—at that time selling for ten cents per gallon—the price to us, a flat $1.00 per gallon. Cash.

The ritual, which never varied, was completed within ten minutes of the airplane's arrival. The portly major, a Malacca cane supporting his sloppily bandaged gouty leg, hobbled to the C-46 cargo door and waited for us to climb down to the tarmac. Then, after shaking hands—in proper command sequence, captain, co-pilot, navigator, radio operator—Commandant Latour addressed us as a group:

"Have you any firearms on your person?"

"No sir."

"Are there any weapons aboard your aircraft?"

"No sir."

"Very well," Commandant Latour would say, whereupon he stepped to the left to glance past the captain's shoulder into the C-46's open doorway. On Israel-bound flights the cabin was of course entirely occupied by a Messerschmitt fuselage. This Commandant Latour blandly but silently regarded. Then he moved even closer to peer into the cabin itself and tapped the steel tip of his cane against a wooden crate. Those ubiquitous crates, packed with machine guns or ammunition, all bearing the black-stenciled legend: *Fragile—Glass!*

Commandant Latour would then nod gravely and, facing us again, lean on the cane. "Welcome to Ajaccio," he would say, and walk off, accompanied into his office by the C-46 captain. While the captain and Commandant Latour transacted their business, we other crew members visited the restaurant.

On that first flight, exactly sixty-five minutes—and $6,400—after landing, we taxied out for takeoff. Engines were run-up, takeoff checklist completed, and Phil Schild nodded at the co-pilot, Ted Applebaum. Ted eased the throttles forward. With our heavy load—Messerschmitt and guns— we needed every foot of runway and flew into the air almost at the runway boundary, which itself uncomfortably abutted the beach and ocean.

We climbed to 6,000 and recrossed the southern tip of the island and the Tyrrhenian Sea, then turned southeast over the instep of the Italian boot. Over Bari, the navigator, Julie Cubernik, plotted a new course heading. We flew due east, on out over the Mediterranean.

A twelve-hour flight, no electronic navigational aids save an occasional and seldom reliable ADF fix obtained from homing in on various land radio stations. (The clear channel 50,000-watt Radio Tunis station was generally helpful; and, later in the flight, Cairo Radio!) Beyond that, other than a combination of our navigator's skill and good old-fashioned dead reckoning, we were absolutely blind.

And unknown.

Since we still employed the Ajaccio-Casablanca-Ajaccio ruse of departure and arrival messages, the appropriate Mediterranean Control Area stations were unaware of our presence. On paper, or on an aircraft control area location chart, we did not exist. We were phantoms, our airplanes moving unseen and unacknowledged through the night. Should we go down and our distress call be unheard, we would never be found. We could not even be declared missing, for no one knew we were there.

At a specified time, approximately three hundred miles off the Palestine coast, I began listening for the feeble signal from Aquir. In International Morse, it would be transmitted precisely thirty seconds, then terminate until the next specified time. When you finally heard them, you replied on a different frequency, exchanging a further series of authenticating signals. Then, in that day's code, Aquir transmitted weather information and landing instructions. In return, you informed them of your fuel requirements. You might, for example, tap out on your key the numerals 9-1-0. The number "9" indicated a fuel message, "1-0" that 1,000 gallons was needed.

Now, closer in, we watched for the landmark, the two egg-shaped patches of sand on the Tel Aviv beach. We notified Aquir of the sighting and they radioed a "proceed" signal. We flew inland—hopefully toward the field—until receipt of the "engines heard" signal, and then commenced the let-down procedure.

Fifteen seconds before touchdown, Aquir switched on its single row of runway lights. We in turn switched on the airplane's landing lights. In those early days, on descent, sometimes a string of yellow, arcing lines trailed directly behind the airplane, and you did not use your landing lights. The yellow lines came from the tracers of Arab Legion guns at nearby Lydda.

That night, my first flight in, the Lydda guns were silent. The instant we touched down, the runway lights went out. In total darkness we rolled along the strip until the "Follow-Me" jeep appeared to guide us onto a taxiway and into the parking area. By then, my eyes accustomed to the dark, I could discern the looming outlines of several large hangars and other, smaller buildings, and many vehicles, and the shadowed figures of people.

Israelis.

I remember trying to be blasé, urbane, worldly. I remember telling myself again that this was just another flight. Routine, simply because we had gotten here in one piece; anytime you get where you are going it is routine.

I knew better.

I knew it was not routine and never would be. I knew it was the most important achievement of my life. Especially when I opened the airplane's door and replied "shalom" to the soldier who greeted me.

The Jewish soldier.

There were dozens of them, swarming all over the C-46, transferring the *Fragile–Glass!* crates to a waiting truck, and then manhandling the Messerschmitt out of the cabin and into a larger flatbed truck. Simultaneously, a fuel carrier had pulled up alongside the C-46; other uniformed figures clambered up on the wing to refuel the airplane. In a few hours, before dawn to protect the airplane from the daily Egyptian air attack on the field, a different crew would fly that same C-46 back to Zebra. To pick up another Messerschmitt, and more guns and ammunition.

I saw all this from the doorway of a small hangar that had been converted into a combination dining hall and operations room. The noise was deafening, but not at all unpleasant. A kind of exotic, almost soothing music all its own. The heavy trucks trundling back and forth, the mechanical rasp of the block and tackle device hauling the Messerschmitt fuselage out of the C-46, the tinny putt-putt-putt of the fuel carrier's single cylinder gasoline pump, the constant buzz of sing-song, guttural, Hebrew-speaking voices. Male, female.

Israeli voices.

Inside the hangar, before a communal platter piled high with sandwiches and fruit, Phil Schild, Julie Cubernik, and Ted Applebaum sat at a long trestled table chatting with the outgoing crew and drinking tea or coffee, or soft drinks from bottles with Hebrew labels. Khaki-uniformed men and women rushed about, although their uniforms were not so uniform, varying from wool sweaters and tattered shorts to tailored jackets. A surprising number of the women were young and attractive. Most of the men were older, many grizzled and wrinkled; younger men, obviously, were fighting at the front. Most of the older women were civilians, graying and motherly. They had shaken our hands and thanked us for coming and all, one after another, insisted that we sit down and eat. Surely we were exhausted after the long trip.

Talk about Jewish mothers.

Phil called me to join him at the table. I said I'd be there in a minute. I wanted to watch the Messerschmitt being unloaded. Even today, forty-five years later, the scene remains fixed in my mind as almost otherworldly. Surrealistic. The warm night, the gentle breeze, the air heavy with the fragrance of nearby citrus groves, while off in the distance the sky was opaque with occasional artillery flashes followed immediately by the dull rumble of the shells, and the earth shaking under your feet. All this like a second orchestra performing a slightly different rendition of that same, strange music created by the din of activities from the field, blended now with the sporadic crackle of small arms fire a few miles away, from Lydda, where a battle still raged.

I watched the soldiers load the Messerschmitt, this most precious of cargo, and drive away. I knew that within twenty-four hours the fighter would be assembled, flying, bearing on its wings and fuselage the Star of David. That same Star of David many of those same people once wore as a Badge of Shame. And I, I told myself, had helped make it possible. It filled me with an extraordinary—and, I must admit, unfamiliar—sense of accomplishment.

And, again, pride.

And proud of them, too.

"Them." It seemed imperative at that particular moment for me to reaffirm my American identity. To, as it were, reassure myself. I was Jewish, yes, but also, first and foremost, American. A Yankee, head to toe, through and through.

Red white and blue.

2.

We went into the city in a battered old Plymouth sedan, a taxi whose middle-aged Rumanian-born driver had been drafted into the army along with his vehicle. We drove through a deserted Arab village. Every building had been razed to the ground. Only the crumbling shells of larger houses still stood. The moonlight cast jagged ghostly shadows over the empty ruins. Between the airfield and this village much of the land consisted of orange groves and open farmland. The driver, in British-accented English, explained that the farms and citrus trees had all been planted and were owned by Jews. Arabs and Jews worked the fields together. All had prospered until the war started and the Arab Legion destroyed the village and forced the people to leave. In the same cheerfully informative tone he told us that small bands of renegade Arabs sometimes hid in the groves to ambush passing cars.

I withdrew my little Skoda pistol and cocked it. Julie Cubernik told me to put it away: the highway was well secured and heavily patrolled. Besides, he said, all I could do with that capgun was shoot off my own balls. Or, worse, his.

For all of that, it was not an unpleasant ride, although no one really relaxed until we passed the third roadblock and the dusty, rutted narrow road unexpectedly became a broad smoothly paved tree-lined boulevard. And then, all at once, we were in Tel Aviv.

The city was blacked-out, but on either side of the boulevard were modern high-rise buildings and wide sidewalks crowded with people. And a constant flow of vehicles, all with headlamps painted over to only emit pinpoints of light that in the dark resembled glowing white fireflies.

We approached a small park where some half dozen soldiers appeared to be confronting a lone, white-armbanded policeman. A soldier just then pushed the policeman. He retreated a few steps, brandishing a phosphorescent traffic baton.

I craned my neck to peer through the rear window but we were already beyond the park. I asked the driver what in the hell that was all about.

He shrugged. "Probably some drunken *Palmachnicks.*"

The Palmach, I knew, was Haganah's elite striking force. Composed of native-born Israelis, sabras, they were rough, tough, and unrelenting. They gave no quarter and expected none, a characteristic not confined to the battlefield as more than one of our intrepid birdmen discovered when he became imprudent enough to engage a *Palmachnick* in a barroom or street brawl.

"Jewish soldiers fight with the police?" I asked.

The driver shrugged again. "Why not? The police are Jewish, too, aren't they? And so is the jail!"

Jewish police, Jewish jails.

We continued through the darkened city onto a winding four-lane Esplanade that paralleled the beachfront. Now, framed like solid black blocks against the sky, were the silhouetted outlines of the large hotels. It reminded me of Miami Beach, which was also blacked-out when I did my army basic training there. Except that in Miami Beach you had a sense of restful quiet, a tranquility that here would be almost alien. Here, the very air throbbed with energy. Here, you not only felt the movement, it became part of you. Everything seemed in motion. Nothing and no one ever seemed to stop. And you sensed, too, this was not from the war but the natural way of things here.

True then and, forty-five years later, now.

We were billeted at the Park Hotel, then the *Fountainbleu* of Tel Aviv, the poshest of the posh, a favorite haunt of war correspondents and foreign diplomats. Even at that 2:00 A.M. time of our arrival, although well past the designated closing hour, the bar and lounge was busy. Crowded with combat-weary Israeli Army officers, some wearing smartly tailored British-style uniforms, others in more functional but no less correct military garb. To them, we, in our rumpled suntans and grease-streaked wartime GI flying jackets, must have looked like the survivors of a defeated *Afrika Korps* regiment.

I shared a beer with Julie Cubernik and then went to bed.

I was too tired and too exhilarated to sleep. I turned off the room lights and opened the terrace doors and stepped out on the balcony. I stood gazing down at the beach directly below, at the surf foaming white up on the sand, and out at the ocean. The blackness of the water, now and then mirroring the artillery flashes to the north, then black once again, extended as far as the eye could see, all the way to the rim of the night horizon.

A Jewish ocean, a Jewish horizon.

3.

I slept late, awakened finally by the noonday sun streaming into the room through the open terrace doors. I went out on the balcony. Now, in daylight, the whole ocean seemed empty. No small freighters or tankers anchored off shore. No fishing trawlers, and certainly no pleasure craft. The only vessel in sight was a large civilian speedboat with a .50-caliber machine gun mounted on the bow, thereby converting it into an Israeli Navy patrol boat.

The beach, too, was empty. No swimmers, no couples strolling the beach or sunning themselves on the sand. No children playing in the surf. On either side of my Park Hotel balcony other hotels lined the beach, their beachfronts also deserted. This was a nation at war.

A war that once again resembled a Good Little War when I entered the hotel dining room and saw the melange of uniforms. There was Johnny Donovan, a CBS war correspondent, always accompanied by a huge boxer dog named Timoshenko. And white-bearded Tom Van Dyke, another correspondent whose snow-white hair flowed down past his shoulders and who drank his scotch with a milk chaser.

There were freelance writers and photographers, and mercenary guns-for-hire of every nationality. Women of all sizes, shapes, persuasions, and professions. There was even a

Nicaraguan soldier of fortune, a stout, aging, mustachioed man in a sweat-stained Anzac campaign hat, khaki bush jacket, khaki twill riding breeches, gleaming leather cavalry boots, and a pair of pearl-handled revolvers in silver-studded holsters. He insisted on being addressed as "Colonel," and said he had come in search of one final, "good" war.

That morning after breakfast I took a walk with Julie Cubernik. We strolled down Hyarkon Street to Allenby Road, which was then the main shopping district. There were department stores and fashionable boutiques, canopied sidewalk cafes and restaurants. The sidewalks were crowded and the streets were filled with vehicles, buses, trucks, taxis, even a few civilian automobiles. People surged back and forth past us, many of course in uniform. An equal number wore civilian clothes, many women in chic summer dresses, men in business suits and ties. Others in more casual attire of open-collared shirts and shorts.

We went on to Dizengoff Square which was even busier with its cafes and theaters. I remember Julie stopping suddenly in front of an ice cream parlor and peering at me. "What the hell's the matter with you?"

"What are you talking about?"

"Look at you," he said. "The way you're gawking at everything."

"Gawking?"

"Yes, gawking," he said. "You look like a hillbilly on his first visit to the big city!"

"Maybe I didn't know what to expect."

He laughed. "What the hell did you expect? Camels, and tents pitched on sand dunes?"

No, camels and tents I had not expected, but it was also true that I was somewhat overwhelmed by what I did see, and too embarrassed to tell Julie why. What had gone through my mind, I remember, was that this sparkling white city, this cosmopolitan metropolis, was—like the ocean and the horizon of the previous night—wholly and totally Jewish.

Later the same day I visited Moonitz, Eichel, and Styrak in the hospital. Except for two blackened eyes and a broken nose, Moonitz appeared none the worse. Eichel was still heavily bandaged from his burns. Styrak, also burned, and with a fractured leg the most seriously injured, told me how Eichel and Moonitz saved his life by pulling him from the burning airplane—through the cockpit window as I had envisioned—and about Moe Rosenbaum's military funeral.

Maybe it wasn't such a good war, after all.

4.

Early the following morning, just after dawn—and escorted out now by a Messerschmitt—we took off for Zebra. We carried a package of ten fifty-pound bombs, "presents" for an Egyptian truck convoy reportedly moving north from Ishdud, a few miles south of our flight path. The convoy was there, all right: some two dozen trucks and jeeps.

Although they had seen us, or at least heard our engines, they continued blithely on, ignoring us, it seemed. I remember thinking, Those stupid bastards don't know what's in store for them! I also remember feeling not the slightest discomfort knowing that some of them might soon be dead. And feeling, too, an almost smug sense of superiority: our Messerschmitt escort guaranteed no interference from Gyppo Spitfires.

Low-level bombing was not possible—not unless you wanted to be an inviting target for enemy rifle fire—so we would drop from 3,000 feet. Since we had no bomb-chucker, that job was consigned to Julie Cubernik and me. By the time Julie and I concluded a brief but heated discussion about angles of attack, wind drift, deflection, and forward velocity, we were already nearly over the target.

"Shit!" Julie cried. "We'll never hit anything now!"

"Get rid of the goddam things!" I said.

Julie and I rolled the bombs, one after another, across the C-46's floor to the door, grasped the door frame for support (praying that Phil Schild held the airplane straight and level), pulled the pins, and kicked the bombs out the door. We succeeded in plowing up a lot of dirt in the fields near the road, and knocking down a few trees. The convoy drove on, undisturbed.

The Messerschmitt stayed with us another few minutes, then waggled his wings, banked around and headed home. We turned north and flew out to sea. We arrived on schedule at Ajaccio, refueled, and landed at Zebra before nightfall.

And then began the long endless routine of flying the Zebra-Oklahoma Airlift. Back and forth, day after day, week after week. We brought guns, ammunition, spare parts, tools, medical supplies, lumber, food, people.

And the Messerschmitts, and the pilots to fly the Messerschmitts.

Although the C-46s still bore Panamanian markings, and would for several more months, we were now, officially, a unit of the Israeli Defense Force, the Air Transport Command. Only six of the original ten C-46s remained serviceable, and the one Constellation that Sam Lewis had smuggled, literally, out of Panama. The remaining two Connies, impounded at Newark, were permanently lost to us.

In the meantime, the war raged. Certainly not a "good war" for the soldiers on land with whom we had little, if any, contact. Indeed, we paid only cursory attention to the war's progress. For one thing, we were too busy flying; for another, we simply assumed that the Israelis would win.

Thinking about it now, however, those assumptions might have been considerably shaken had we had the time to sit in the hotel lounges and bars and cafes of Tel Aviv, listening to our fighter pilots relate their experiences. It seemed that every one of those fighter pilots had an exciting story to tell.

Exciting might be too benign a description. Harrowing is perhaps more accurate. To begin with, in those early days, only once—in its very first sortie—did the fighter squadron ever manage to put as many as four airplanes in the air at one time. More often, it was two; and, frequently, only one. And on those occasions, the pilots flipped coins to determine who would fly that lone operational fighter.

The ersatz Messerschmitts, the S-199s, could well be called the Nazi's Revenge. Those not grounded for mechanical repairs or lack of spare parts, were grounded, period. Pieces of scrap. When they flew, as noted, they proved to be flying booby traps. All too frequently, if their guns did not jam—which was all too frequent—the guns went out of synchronization and shot off the airplane's propellers. In effect, shot themselves down.

But until better equipment would arrive the MEs, like us, were all they had.

On that initial combat mission—flown by an American, a South African, and two Israelis—the four MEs attacked a troop concentration at Ishdud, only twelve miles south of Aquir. The American, Lou Lenart, hit the target and then, on his second pass, his guns jammed. Both Israelis, Ezer Weizman and Modi Alon, had no better luck: their guns also jammed and, on landing, Alon's landing gear collapsed, causing him to nose over. The airplane was totaled. The South African, Eddie Cohen, was shot down by ground fire and killed. In the space of ten minutes, the IAF's fighter force of four airplanes and four pilots was reduced to two airplanes and three pilots.

But, miracle of miracles, the psychological effect on the enemy was such that the Egyptian armored column at Ishdud abruptly halted its advance. So that first near-calamitous mission ended up not the failure it presaged, but a resounding victory.

A few days later, two new Messerschmitts and two new pilots were in action. Immediately, one of the pilots, American Milton Rubenfeld, was hit by anti-aircraft fire. Rubenfeld bailed out safely but was nearly skewered by the pitchforks of irate Jewish kibbutzniks who believed him to be an Egyptian pilot. Only Rubenfeld's rudimentary Yiddish saved him: he started shouting " . . . *gefilte fish, shabbes, gefilte fish!"* The kibbutzniks thankfully understood.

Scratch another Messerschmitt.

But, again, the effect on the Egyptians was devastating, for that same week one of the only two Israeli pilots, Modi Alon, shot down *two* Dakota bombers over Tel Aviv. The effect on the Israeli populace was equally impressive. Unhappily, later in the year, in October, Modi Alon who by then had been appointed commander of the fighter squadron, became another victim of the Nazi's Revenge. Returning from a mission, attempting to land one of the disreputable Messerschmitts, Alon crashed and burned.

And others, before and after, paid the price. Of some thirty-three aircrew members killed in action throughout the war, eight were fighter pilots.

For all that, however, the fighter pilots were a typically zany lot. The incident in Rome where they stripped their hotel rooms of furniture, which they magnanimously presented to their girlfriends, was only a sample of what would follow. Lenart invented a squadron insignia: a winged skull emblazoned on red baseball caps, and whenever the red caps appeared in a Tel Aviv bar, the proprietors had learned from hard experience to instantly notify the MPs. And, usually, too late.

For a time, the fighter base was the envy of all army units for the abundance of jeeps parked everywhere in sight. Until someone deduced that this abundance always matched the shortage of similar vehicles elsewhere. The fighter pilots, it seemed, had been expertly tutored by an unnamed American in the art of hot-wiring.

And then there was another unnamed American fighter pilot, who brazenly drove an empty truck into the courtyard of the American embassy in Tel Aviv and produced impeccable U.S. State Department documents requesting delivery of fifty pounds of choice steaks and two cases of Johnny Walker Scotch from the embassy commissary. The pilots dined and drank well that entire week.

One evening, in the town of Ramat David, near the fighter base, people were startled to see one pilot–quite naturally, an American–astride a white horse. Which might or not have been considered unusual, except that the pilot was stark naked.

Over the years, of course, these exploits became legend– legends that undoubtedly were repeatedly embellished. But they really did correctly epitomize those young men, and no embellishment was required for the events of a single day in January. That January day, technically after the war–with the fighter squadron now a truly formidable combat unit, now equipped with Spitfires and P-51s–five British Spitfires arrogantly appeared over Israel. Three IAF 51s, led by non-Jewish American volunteer Wayne Peake, confronted the Spitfires, who ignored orders to withdraw. The 51s shot down all five RAF aircraft. It was the last time the RAF, or any other hostile entity, attempted to enter Israeli air space.

5.

On June 11, a UN-supervised truce was imposed. By then, we had flown in one hundred tons of munitions, including an entire plane load of heavy machine guns that were ultimately instrumental in breaking the siege of Jerusalem.

Under the truce terms all combatants were to cease supply operations. Neither side honored the agreement. Our ATC efforts continued, and in fact–with the addition of several new volunteer crews–increased. For their part, our main adversaries, the Egyptians, also utilized the truce period to reinforce, reorganize, and resupply. For both Israelis and Arabs, the truce was a mutually agreed respite, to be disavowed by one or the other parties at its earliest convenience.

Or earliest advantage.

The new crews provided us some brief rest time, allowing us to finally visit Prague. Visit? We *invaded* the city. We stayed either at the stately old Hotel Flora, or at Prague's newest and most modern hotel, the Alcron. I preferred the Alcron whose architecture and furnishings seemed straight out of a 1930's Hollywood movie. Classic art deco.

The Alcron's illuminated glass brick bar became our unofficial hangout, along with a popular downtown nightclub that featured a telephone on each table. Each table was identified by a number printed on the table's lampshade. To converse with the interesting-looking lady at table 12, for example, you merely dialed 12 on your own telephone. It was very convenient, particularly if the girls spoke English. It was convenient even when they did not.

Standing orders from the Little Men were no political discussions with anyone, adult or child, male or female. This was specifically directed to the young attractive English-speaking women who magically began to appear wherever we went. Such as the lady Eddie Chinsky and I met at the Alcron on our very first evening in Prague.

A tall bosomy redhead who towered over both of us, she readily accepted our invitation for a drink. She asked what we were doing in Prague. "Tourists," I said, and before the word was out of my mouth, Eddie said, "Students." Yes, of course, student-tourists.

She said she worked as a salesgirl in a large department store and then, in the same breath said, "As tourists, I am sure you have already visited a charming little town called Zatec?"

"Zatec?" Eddie looked at me. "I've heard of the place."

"Sounds familiar," I said.

"Tell us about it," Eddie said to the girl.

She smiled invitingly. "I thought *you* might tell *me* about it."

Again, Eddie and I looked at each other. I said to him, "I don't think we should talk about it here, do you?"

"Oh, no, definitely not. Not here, that's a very bad idea,"

he said, and to the girl, "Why don't we all go upstairs to my room where we can talk in privacy?"

"All *three* of us?" she asked. She seemed intrigued with the idea. So was I.

So was Eddie. "Sure, all three of us," he said. "One for all, all for one."

No sooner were we in the room, and even before the big redhead suggested Eddie and I take turns unbuttoning her blouse, one button at a time, she announced that she had decided to be honest with us. She knew we weren't stupid. She knew we had immediately recognized her as an intelligence agent. But she worked for no particular government, she said. She was a free-lancer, seeking information she might then sell to the highest bidder: British MI5, American CIA, or even the newspapers.

"I admire honesty," I said. "Don't you, Ed?"

"I do," he said, and to the girl, "If we give you the information, what do we get for it?"

"Whatever you want," she said, and to make certain we understood, added, "Anything you want." By now the blouse was off, and the skirt, and we had progressed to the brassiere.

"Shall we tell her?" I asked Eddie.

"Definitely," he said.

"Okay, here it is," I said to her. "We're working for the Egyptian Army. For King Farouk himself. We're supposed to infiltrate the Jewish Air Force." I paused and said to Eddie, "Shall I tell her the rest?"

"Definitely," he said, as the brassiere fell to the floor.

They were everywhere in Prague, these information-hungry ladies, and all seemed as charmingly inept as "Mata," the name Eddie and I gave to the redhead. Larry Raab encountered a lovely young woman claiming to be a genuine Hungarian baroness down on her luck. Larry said she initiated the conversation by offering him a cigarette from the package of a well-known Palestinian brand.

Not all the girls were spies. Al Raisin met a woman who offered him an interesting business proposition. If Al brought in perfumes and cosmetics from Tel Aviv, the lady would pay for these with Skoda pistols, which Al could then sell in Israel to the dissident political party, the Irgun. Al demurred, but only after an English navigator, Cyril Cohen, described the unpleasantness of Prague jail cells.

Cyril, arriving in Prague from an emergency London furlough, had neglected to declare the foreign currency on his person, English pound notes. Czech customs officials promptly accused Cyril of bringing in the money for black market resale, and clamped him into Prague Central Prison. It took three days for the Little Men to clear the matter and free Cyril. Cyril said what impressed him most was the efficiency of Czech customs, and the jail food, which consisted solely of black bread and herring, and which he at first disdained. By the third day, however, Cyril said he was snapping his teeth for the herring like a trained seal.

Another pilot, Bud Skolnick, was involved in a more romantic endeavor. Bud dressed his Prague girlfriend in coveralls and an oversized fedora and, under the very eyes of the Czech security guards at Zebra, smuggled her aboard an Israel-bound C-46. A rabbi married them shortly after their arrival in Tel Aviv. A storybook romance, if Bud's wife had not divorced him a year later when they were back in the States.

The truce continued and so did our supply flights. Haganah representatives scoured the world for surplus airplanes, engines, guns. Aircraft spare parts were salvaged from entire junkyards purchased in Italy and in Belgium. Israel came within a single telephone call of acquiring a surplus U.S. Navy aircraft carrier, the *Attu*. Negotiations were underway with the Czechs for the purchase of forty British-manufactured Spitfires.

In England, Willie Sosnow bought three Bristol Beaufighters. Formidable warplanes, and in mint condition, but prohibited for export by British law. No manner of false papers or dummy corporate ownership succeeded in obtaining the necessary export licenses.

Willie "sold" the airplanes to a motion-picture company. Production immediately commenced on an epic World War II flying film. Aerial scenes were shot at a small private airfield in the south of England, in Kent. On the second day of filming the three Beaufighters took off in formation. The cameras followed their graceful flight. East, they flew, over the channel, and vanished, all three. The evening of that same day three mint-condition Bristol Beaufighters landed in Israel.

Willie Sosnow left England hurriedly. A few weeks later he was to make an equally hasty departure from Fort Lauderdale, Florida. This time, after relaxing on the beach one afternoon, he luckily happened to glance at the headline of an evening edition of the *Miami Herald:*

FBI SEIZES FOUR BOMBERS
BELIEVED HEADED FOR PALESTINE!

The four airplanes were Douglas A-20 attack bombers and indeed headed for Palestine. They had been purchased by Willie through a third party, a Miami aircraft broker, Charles Winters. It was never determined how the FBI learned of the transaction. The prime suspect was a novice pilot, disgruntled at Willie's refusal to hire him for the A-20 ferry flight. This pilot, ironically, was Jewish.

Charlie Winters stalled and otherwise evaded FBI agents long enough for Willie Sosnow to leave the country, but was himself arrested and a year later convicted by a Miami jury of violating various sections of various neutrality acts. He was sentenced to, and served, eighteen months in a federal penitentiary. Charlie Winters, a gentile, was the only "criminal" ever sent to prison for his activities on behalf of the State of Israel. Decades later, the Israeli government granted Charlie Winters's dying request for burial in Israel.

The A-20 incident, however, was not the only service rendered by Charles Winters to Israel. Charlie, this righteous gentile, helped conceive and execute the top-secret mission for which Swifty Schindler had earlier returned to New York. A mission, carried out in the same July week the first truce ended, that would provide the Israeli Air Force with a weapon it desperately sought.

A squadron of heavy bombers.

SEVEN

"BLESSED BE THE GUN"

It was warm and slightly humid, typical for July in lower New York state. The fine weather this Sunday morning had drawn people from miles away, from all over Westchester County, to see the giant wartime bomber that the previous evening had landed at Purchase Airport.

Of course, she was no longer a fighting machine. To qualify her for commercial licensing her gun turrets had been removed, replaced with patches of sheet metal that resembled small squares of tissue paper you slap on your face to cover razor nicks. Her bomb racks were gone. The bombardier's Plexiglas "office" in the nose was boarded over with plywood.

In her shabby flaking olive drab paint she was like a demobilized GI, still in uniform but stripped of all insignia, the faded outlines of chevrons and unit badges a proud reminder of the distant, valiant past.

But despite the civilian registration, NL7712M, now on

her wings and rudder, she was still a B-17, and always would be a B-17, the legendary Flying Fortress.

In the Purchase Airport manager's cramped office, the pilot of this defrocked B-17 filed a flight plan. It was to be a local training and transition flight for himself and his five-man crew. The airplane, as the pilot explained, was owned by a wealthy Manhattan realtor who planned to convert it into a personal luxury liner.

"He's closely connected to the government," the pilot added.

The young airport manager, an ex-GI himself, was elated at the choice of his facility for the B-17's home base. It would bring in other business.

"Yes sir, captain," he told the B-17 pilot. "Anything you need, just ask."

"You bet," said Swifty Schindler, thinking that what he needed was sleep. He had spent the entire previous day, evening, and half the night studying the B-17 manual. This would be his first flight ever in that particular airplane. He also needed more than the four hours of fuel he had taken on board, much more, but could not risk arousing the manager's suspicion by requesting a full fuel load for a training flight.

"Then I guess you're all set," said the manager.

"If we're not, we never will be," Swifty said. He glanced impatiently at his watch. Any minute now he anticipated the arrival of U.S. Government agents. He knew they were closing in. They knew where he was going.

To Zebra, and then Israel.

This, flying the B-17 across the Atlantic to Zebra, was why Swifty had been sent back to New York six weeks before. He had waited all that time for the airplane to be prepared and an experienced volunteer crew assembled.

Swifty's B-17 was one of four acquired for Al Schwimmer by Charlie Winters. By the time U.S. Treasury Department and FBI agents had unraveled the layers of documentation concealing the four airplanes' true ownership, three of the bombers had already slipped out of the country and were safely on their way to Zebra.

But the U.S. Government was determined to stop this fourth B-17, which Al Schwimmer had personally flown into the tiny Westchester County airfield the night before. Al turned the airplane's keys over to Swifty and left. Early the following morning, with only enough fuel for a four-hour flight, Swifty took off for Zebra.

Exactly forty minutes ahead of two carloads of FBI and T-men.

Swifty's first stop—a declared emergency: he claimed to be running low on fuel, a declaration uncomfortably not untrue—was at an RCAF base at Halifax, Nova Scotia.

Swifty apologized for a clumsy amateurish navigational error and explained that the airplane was being delivered to a wealthy London realtor who planned to convert it into a luxury liner. He asked to be refueled, 3,600 gallons this time—for which he would pay in cash—so he might continue on his way to the Azores.

A reasonable request, to which the Deputy Base Commander responded favorably and escorted Swifty to the operations office. An Ops Officer and a Sergeant sat reading the *Halifax Post*, and listening to Lowell Thomas's evening radio news. Enjoying a lazy Sunday.

"Captain Schindler is to have our full assistance," the Deputy Commander said to the Ops Officer. "Whatever he needs."

"My pleasure, sir," the Ops Officer replied.

The Deputy Commander shook Swifty's hand and started out. From the radio came Lowell Thomas's melodious voice: " . . . from Purchase, New York, we have word of FBI agents attempting to trace the flight of a war surplus bomber that took off from the airport there this morning. The plane, a B-17 Flying Fortress, last reported headed north toward Canada, is believed to be en route to the new Jewish state of Israel . . . "

The Deputy Commander, at the door, appeared to falter an instant. He continued out, hesitated again, then left. The Ops Officer and the Sergeant stared curiously at Swifty. He smiled lamely at them.

"About the fuel . . . " Swifty said.

"Yes, of course," said the Ops Officer, and immediately set about preparing the invoices.

It took only a few minutes, but to Swifty it seemed forever. Lowell Thomas signed off, replaced by a variety show. Swifty lit a cigarette and watched the men work on the invoices. Finally they were ready. Swifty pocketed the papers and hurried out.

To nearly collide with the Deputy Commander. And two very tall, very husky young Mounties, each impeccably uniformed, and each holding a revolver, one leveled at Swifty's stomach, the other at his head.

Ordinarily, the story would have ended there: B-17 impounded, crew arrested and turned over to the nearest U.S. Government representative. Crew returned to United States to face criminal charges. Ordinarily, and with someone less inventive or resolute than Swifty Schindler. Swifty had brought his B-17 this far. He had no intention of losing it now.

He convinced the RCAF Base Commander to provide him just enough gasoline to reach New York. He took off, headed due south a few minutes, then turned east.

East?

Yes, east. Toward the Azores.

The Azores? A 2,000-mile flight with only enough fuel for 1,500 miles?

Swifty had successfully stretched his fuel coming north from New York. With proper power settings and flawless navigation, and a little luck, he could do it again. He could make it into the Azores, refuel, and continue on to Zebra.

Some ten hours after leaving Halifax, Swifty taxied the B-17 into the transient parking area at the Portuguese Air

142

Force base in Santa Maria, the Azores.

And saw awaiting him, to his chagrin, the base commander and a contingent of smartly uniformed Portuguese Air Force MPs. The game was over. Swifty was stoical: he had tried, he lost. On the intercom he instructed the crew to remain inside the airplane; things might get ugly. He shut down the engines, walked through the cabin, and opened the door.

A band struck up, " . . . *off we go into the wild blue yonder . . . "* A smiling base commander extended his hand.

"Welcome to Santa Maria!"

Welcome, indeed; so they had not lost after all. Swifty and his crew were wined, dined, and ushered into the deluxe suite at the Officer's Club. Obviously, the Little Men in New York or Lisbon had put in the fix. He idly wondered how much it had cost. Whatever the price, it was worth it. The Israeli Air Force would soon have its fourth B-17.

With the situation so clearly under control, Swifty changed his mind about immediately taking off for Zebra. He and the crew needed sleep. The base commander's kind invitation to rest overnight was gratefully accepted.

Swifty fell into a deep, relaxing, and very gratifying sleep. He described it as a Sweet Sleep, the kind you might enjoy in Las Vegas, going to bed after a spectacular comeback that made you into a comfortable winner instead of a dejected loser.

Two hours later it turned sour.

Another B-17 arrived. The personal airplane of a four-star USAF general. The Portuguese had mistaken Swifty for this visiting American general. They quickly set matters straight.

Swifty and his crew were shackled in handcuffs and hustled to the base stockade. A day later all were placed aboard a Pan Am Constellation and under armed escort returned to the United States.

The B-17 never reached Israel, nor did Swifty. Arrested, charged with illegal export of warplanes, he was prohibited by court order from leaving the United States. A year later he was tried by a jury and found guilty. But Swifty, unlike Charlie Winters, faced a New York jury and a New York judge. Sentence: one year in prison—sentence suspended.

All right, so we lost one fourth of our bomber strength. But the three other B-17s more than made up for the loss. They had made their presence known even before they arrived in Israel.

They had been flown uneventfully to Zebra by Charlie Winters's hired hands. "Uneventfully," that word again. In our case it usually meant without total disaster, or at the very least with only some minor catastrophe. In the B-17s' case it meant that all three aircraft—after filing flight plans from Miami, Florida to Ontario, California—somehow found their way to San Juan, Puerto Rico. And then, somehow, across the ocean to Zebra.

Another "navigational error."

There, at Zebra, the B-17s were delivered to Sam Pomerance for instant "decommercialization." No small task, for although the bomb bay doors of the three airplanes had fortunately not been sealed, bomb racks needed to be reinstalled, and the bombardier's station rebuilt. And new gun turrets, with .30-caliber Skoda machine guns replacing the original, heavier armament.

Moonitz, Ray Kurtz, and soft-spoken Bill Katz whose easy manner belied his unqualified commitment to Israel, were appointed aircraft commanders. World War II B-17 pilots, all three possessed extensive combat experience. Other crew members, ex-USAAF 8th Air Force crewmen and RCAF and RAF Bomber Command veterans, transferred out of ATC into the newly activated B-17 unit. Ray Kurtz was appointed squadron leader. He immediately christened his new command the "69th Heavy Bombardment Squadron."

The 69th's first mission was to ferry the airplanes—with full bomb loads—from Zebra to Israel. The three set out in loose formation, crossed the Alps, and headed south along the Adriatic. They cut briefly over the Balkan land mass, then turned east on the by now familiar route over the Mediterranean. Abeam Crete, they separated. Two, Moonitz and Katz, continued east. Moonitz to Damascus, Katz to Gaza. Moonitz plastered Damascus Airport. Katz hit a huge Egyptian armored column. And where was Kurtz?

Over Cairo.

Where, from 25,000 feet, he had planned to hit King Farouk's palace. But a malfunctioning oxygen system forced Kurtz to descend to 15,000, an altitude that left him vulnerable to antiaircraft fire. With no time to search for the palace, he made one pass over the city and dropped his bombs where he thought the palace should be. He saved three five hundred pounders for the Egyptian Air Force base at Fayid, where he dropped all three on the main runway, that famed "TWA" attack.

The strike at Cairo was not much of an air raid as air raids went, but the Egyptians obligingly denounced it as a "mass terror raid." Hospitals and schools the main targets, hundreds of casualties. In Israel, while the magnitude of the raids deceived no one, it did wonders for civilian morale. The Egyptian military was impressed, too.

I was not involved in any of this; I was still busy flying the Zebra-Oklahoma run. By now, with many ATC crew members assigned to the 69th—or, as they preferred to be called, "Hammers"—we were so short of qualified people we had to hire several non-volunteer Swedish crews.

Expert airmen, these Swedes, and likable. But they were $1,000-per-month mercenaries. It caused considerable grumbling. But then there was always grumbling. Someone was always bitching about something.

The food, the hazardous work, the lack of money, the women, the arrogant Israelis, the ungrateful Israelis, the inexperienced Israelis, the uncooperative Israelis.

We resented, for example, the appointment of an Israeli as titular head of ATC. A pleasant and almost self-effacing man, a bone fide Haganah hero, Munya Mardor was by his own admission an aviation neophyte. He asked us to be patient, to give him a chance. He would learn. At the same time, however, he placed his own people, Israelis, in key administrative positions. These subordinates of Munya's, equally inexperienced, seemed to take themselves and their new jobs quite seriously. They became instant experts in air transport operations.

Inevitably, there were incidents. Ridiculous to just plain dumb, with an occasional touch of the sublime. From a directive—instantly, unhesitatingly, and disdainfully ignored—ordering all air-ground communications to be conducted in Hebrew, to a nonflying Israeli flight dispatcher refusing an ATC pilot's request for a 1:100,000 scale map because the dispatcher considered a smaller scale map adequate. The pilot, Ray Foster, told the dispatcher that unless he produced the proper map the dispatcher could fly the mission himself. Ray got the map.

And more of the same, and more. Including the infamous episode of what became known as "The Move," when a certain Air Force HQ staff officer, whose girlfriend had become involved with one of our pilots, attempted to move all ATC crewmen out of the Park Hotel into far more Spartan quarters at Aquir. For "morale purposes," supposedly, although the rejected boyfriend was obviously the only one with a morale problem.

Most of these confrontations were probably unwarranted; and, for sure, in the hindsight and wisdom of nearly a half century, unimportant. But they seemed important at the time because I think that we Americans believed ourselves above reproach. We, after all, were the veterans, the professionals, selflessly contributing our expertise to the struggling new nation. We had come here to help these people win a war. To create a land. Without us, it would not have been possible, would it? Without us American Jews? So we expected, I suppose, to be treated accordingly.

As saviors.

Come from the new world to save the old.

Our mistake, our misconception, our misperception.

But we—no, I; I, singular, for on this issue I can speak only for myself—I wanted it both ways. I wanted the recognition and respect of being an American, and the pride of being a Jew. I wanted it acknowledged that this, Israel, was not my land, that I was here only to perform a service.

Do a favor.

I understood intellectually but was emotionally unable to accept my Israeli counterpart—be he sabra or blue-tattooed Auschwitz survivor—as also a man with pride. A man who did not appreciate brash young Americans who had never known persecution constantly reminding him that their presence here guaranteed his future.

I understood, too, that but for the most fortuitous and gratuitous of events—my grandparents emigrating to America—I might well have perished in one of those death camps, or in some other anti-Semitic pogrom. This accident of birth should have shown me humility. It did not, and instead only fortified my feeling of superiority, which in turn only further confused my search for identity.

To be sure, the Israelis were not blameless. They believed that we did not appreciate them, did not appreciate the fact that here, now, they were providing all Jews the homeland denied them after two thousand years.

I met a girl, a very pretty girl with long luxurious red hair and deep green eyes and a silken complexion. She was a nurse at a hospital in the Tel Aviv suburb of Hakirya. Her name was Ziporah. She was a second-generation sabra, the daughter of a physician. So we had something in common.

I met her during the first truce. We had lost an engine on takeoff that morning and had to return to Aquir. By the time the engine was repaired it was too late in the day to leave. It gave us a free evening. Ziporah was at the Park Hotel with a friend, another nurse. I bought them both drinks, and then someone came along and asked the friend to dance. Ziporah and I watched them dance off.

"Aren't you going to invite me to dance?" she said.

"I thought we'd sit here a while and enjoy our drinks," I said. "I feel like just relaxing."

Obviously, she sensed my discomfort, for she laughed gently and said, "It doesn't matter that I'm taller. It doesn't bother me at all."

"The truth is, I don't dance," I said. "I never learned how."

"I'll make a confession," she said. "I really don't like dancing. Honestly."

I knew she was only trying to ease my embarrassment, and I loved her for it. We chatted briefly, small talk, which was when we discussed our respective physician-fathers. This led to her telling me about some of the cruel casualties at the hospital. Israeli boys without arms or legs, paraplegics, quadriplegics. Boys unable to perform for themselves even the most rudimentary bodily functions. Not a day passed, she said, when she did not find herself weeping over the condition of one or another patient.

"I know," I said lamely.

"Why aren't more American Jews coming to help us?" she asked. It was an accusation, not a question.

"More Americans?" I said. "There are lots of us." I pointed at the dancers, the crowded lounge tables, the bar. "I'll bet half of them here are American."

"We need more of you," she said. "In America, there are six million Jews. Six *million!*"

"More will come," I said.

"Yes, someday all Jews will come here to *Eretz*," she said. "From America, from everywhere. All of them."

"I doubt that," I said. "Not all."

"You?" she said. "You won't come?"

"I'm here," I said.

"I mean afterward," she said. "To settle."

"I don't think so, no."

She peered at me narrowly, her eyes suddenly hard and

impatient. But almost immediately she relaxed. She smiled. A kind of apology. I offered her a cigarette and a light. She admired my lighter, a Zippo in a sterling silver case with my name engraved on the cover. I had had the case made for me by the old White Russian émigré at Shepheard's Hotel, in Cairo.

"A 'Zippo,' you call it?" she asked, and laughed. "It must be named after me. Everyone calls me 'Zippy.'" And then she noticed the inscription on the cover. "'Harold Livingston, Cairo, 1946,'" she read. "What were you doing in Cairo?"

I told her. She asked if I had enjoyed myself there. Again, it was more an accusation than a question. I said, "Yes, I did. I enjoyed it very much." I knew exactly how she would respond.

"More than you enjoy Israel?"

"No, of course not," I said, and immediately regretted saying it. I knew how she would respond to that, too.

"Then why won't you come here to live?"

"I'm an American," I said.

"You are a Jew," she said quietly, almost sadly.

I said, "Look, I'm here to help do a job. When it's finished, I'm going home. This is not my home."

"But don't you understand?" she said. "Your job will not be finished, it will never be finished. Here, in this country, is where your 'job' is. Not in America."

"Isn't what I'm doing enough?" I asked. "Why must I live here?"

At that moment her friend returned to the table. We all had another drink, chatted a few more moments and then they said they were on duty at the hospital that night and had to leave. I asked Ziporah for her phone number.

She smiled. She had a very nice smile that crinkled up the corners of her mouth. "Aren't you afraid we'll argue?"

"You'll have to promise that we won't," I said.

She smiled again. "I promise," she said, and wrote the number on a paper napkin.

I never did call her, and never saw her again. Once, drunk, I almost called. Almost, and only because I was drunk, but not drunk enough. I told myself she would turn me down and I would feel like a fool. But girls who intend to turn you down do not write their phone numbers on cocktail napkins which they carefully fold and meaningfully tuck into your shirt pocket. So I knew that was not the reason. I then told myself that what I wanted was to get her into a bed, not subject myself to a sales pitch. But I knew she had already given up on me as a potential Israeli citizen and girls like her do not waste their precious spare time proselytizing lost causes. So this was not the reason, either.

Years later, in my novel *The Coasts of the Earth*, I drew upon that incident to dramatize a similar confusion in the mind of the story's protagonist, an American Jew fighting for Israel. But even then I still did not know why I had lacked the courage to follow up with the red-headed nurse named Ziporah who liked to be called Zippy.

It would be decades later—and a thousand more experiences, and dozens of failures and successes, tragedies and triumphs—before I finally found the answer. More accurately, before I finally *admitted* it.

She had shamed me.

She made me feel I was betraying my heritage.

I was aware of this, but only in the most abstract fashion. I did not want to, nor at the time could I, cope with it. Moreover, quite coincidentally, an event was at that very moment unfolding that would then, and for long afterward, confirm the belief of many American volunteers that no matter how unreasonable, illogical, whimsical, or impulsive an order seemed, because we were Jews, we were expected to unquestioningly and unhesitatingly obey that order.

It was called the *Altalena*.

2.

"Blessed be the gun which set the ship on fire," said David Ben-Gurion. *"That gun shall have its place in Israel's war museum."*

The ship was the *Altalena.*

The gun was a Haganah mortar.

Before the war Irgun Zvai Leumi, now Israel's second largest political party, had functioned as a separate underground military force apart from Haganah. While Haganah's operations in the struggle to drive the British from Palestine were conducted in a sophisticated, almost civilized manner, the Irgun fought in a fashion considerably more extreme and violent. Outright terrorism to deadly guerrilla warfare, often in direct opposition to Haganah political policy and objectives. But now, with the state established, the Irgun had pledged its loyalty to the Ben-Gurion government and was allowed to maintain its own armed units.

The Irgun had purchased six hundred tons of munitions from the French government. The munitions were transported from Marseilles to Kfar Vitkin, a small port north of Tel Aviv, in a World War II LST, the *Altalena.* An agreement was reached with Ben-Gurion whereby Irgun retained twenty percent of the *Altalena's* cargo. The remaining eighty percent would be consigned to the government. But at Kfar Vitkin, when the *Altalena* arrived, Haganah troops were ordered to seize the ship.

Altalena's American captain refused to surrender the vessel and took her out to sea. Pursued by Haganah naval units, he raced *Altalena* south toward Tel Aviv and, one hundred yards off the beach, ran her aground. Haganah troops were rushed to the scene. The Haganah commander on shore radioed another surrender demand. *Altalena's* captain replied that he had no intention of surrendering his ship or cargo, or any of its personnel.

The Haganah commander cordoned off the area near the

Kaete Dan Hotel and set up mortars and heavy machine guns on the beach. He then sent the *Altalena* an ultimatum, which was ignored.

The soldiers opened fire. One or more mortar shells struck boxes of small arms ammunition stacked on the ship's deck. The ensuing explosions and fire ignited more ammunition below deck, and destroyed an entire cargo hold containing Bofors antiaircraft guns, antitank weapons, five thousand rifles, and six armored cars. Huge clouds of thick black smoke enveloped the ship. She started listing to her starboard side. Crewmen began sliding down that side, hurling themselves into the water. Some were pulled aboard life rafts, others swam for shore.

The men in the water, like the soldiers firing on them, were Jews.

I saw it all from the terrace of my Park Hotel room. A center aisle, front row seat. I was with Al Raisin. We had been here the better part of several hours. It was like watching a movie whose heroes and villains could not be told apart. You did not know who to root for.

"It's a civil war," Al said. "A fucking civil war!" He was repeating himself. At least twice in the past hour he had uttered that same sentence, and with the same disbelief. He, as most of us, had regarded the endless Haganah-Irgun bickering and infighting with almost amused indulgence. It was so typical: show me two Jews, I'll show you five political parties.

Not so amusing now.

We continued watching the spectacle until, after one particularly violent eruption from the ship, Al said bitterly, "There goes another night's flight! It takes us four weeks to fly in what they're blowing up in ten minutes! Come on, I've seen enough."

We went downstairs to the lounge. Hal Auerbach and Tryg Maseng were there, the room's only occupants. Everyone else was outside on the beachfront veranda or up on the roof. We helped ourselves to drinks from the bar and joined Hal and Tryg at their table. Now and then ammunition exploding on the ship rattled the lounge windows and shook glasses on the bar.

"Things have never looked brighter," I said to Hal.

He said nothing.

Al said, "It's a civil war."

"No, not yet," Hal said.

"But it could be," I said.

"Yes," said Hal. "It could be."

Just then a fighter pilot, Stanley Andrews, entered. He looked disheveled and tired. He pulled a chair from another table and sat with us. "They're out to finish the Irgun," he said. "Once and for all, they're out to finish them!"

"That's okay by me," Tryg said.

"They asked us to bomb that thing, you know," Stan said.

"We heard," said Al.

"Then why the hell didn't you?" Tryg said to Stan.

Stan peered incredulously at Tryg. "My God, do you think we'd go out and bomb other Jews?"

"There's a slight difference between people who jeopardize a whole bloody cause, and 'other Jews,'" Tryg said.

"I came here to kill Arabs, not Jews," Stan said. He was an ex-USAAF B-25 pilot, one of our first Messerschmitt pilots. Twenty-six, dark haired, matinee-idol handsome, he was also an avid Zionist. One of the few, true idealists.

"You came here for Israel," Tryg said. "Whatever it takes to make Israel happen, you do it."

Stan's face tightened. His eyes flashed angrily. "That's fine for *you* to say!"

"Why?" Tryg asked. "Because I'm a goy? You know better!"

Yes, Stan Andrews knew better; we all did. Tryg Maseng was as dedicated to the Israeli cause as any Jew. Probably, because of his very non-Jewishness, more so.

Stan acknowledged this with a curt nod, and as a form of apology to Tryg spoke in a friendlier voice. "Everybody in the fighter squadron feels the same way. We all refused."

"What about Weizman and Alon?" I asked, referring to the two Israeli fighter pilots. "Did they refuse, too?"

"The refusal was unanimous," Stan said.

"They ordered you, and you 'refused'?"

"We weren't ordered, we were asked to *volunteer*," Stan said. "It wasn't an order. Yet," he added grimly.

"The Haganah soldiers didn't refuse," Tryg said. "They knew what they had to do and they did it."

"Yes," said Hal Auerbach. "And let's us stop fighting with each other. The question is, what do we do? Where do we stand?"

The question was rhetorical, but I had an answer. I, the American Jew, who read in this *Altalena* incident only further evidence that our heroic services on behalf of our beleaguered Israeli brethren were improperly acknowledged, let alone appreciated. Now I saw an opportunity to prove to the Israelis how truly indispensable we Americans were. I knew how to wake them up.

I said, "Hal, you're ATC Operations Chief. You should write a letter to our guys at Zebra about what just happened here. You should ask everybody to sign a petition that we won't fly until this thing straightens out."

"And if it doesn't straighten out, what do we do then?" Al Raisin asked.

"We'll request that we be allowed to return to the States," I said.

"You're crazy!" Tryg shouted.

"And you're blind!" I shouted back. "Look, if the government sees that they might lose their air force, they might decide to handle all this a little different. A little more intelligently, maybe."

"How do you handle a revolt intelligently?" Tryg said. "And who the hell are we, any of us, who are we to tell the government they're not acting intelligently?"

"Hold it!" Hal said. "Tryg, I think the people at Zebra

should know what's going on—"

"*—your* version, you mean," Tryg said. "Why don't you ask Haman Shamir what's going on?"

Haman Shamir, aka Hyman Sheckman, was the American-born Deputy Chief of Staff of the Israeli Air Force. The same man who in April, after Bill Gerson's fatal crash, had rushed to Panama to help dispel our discontent and impatience.

Hal agreed to do exactly that—to demand an explanation from Haman Shamir—and to not send any letters until we heard the Air Force's side of it.

Haman's response was immediate. He asked all foreign volunteers to attend a meeting the very next morning.

3.

From the Park Hotel, Air Force HQ was a five-minute walk down Hyarkon Street to the Yarkon Hotel. The Yarkon, a four-story building enclosed on all sides by rolled barbed wire, bustled with arriving and departing vehicles and a constant stream of visitors. Couriers, Israeli WACS, soldiers, civilians. Armed sentries at the single wire-gated entrance carefully examined the identity papers of all who sought entry, from postmen to staff officers.

I had been here for the first time several weeks before to discuss radio codes with an intelligence officer. The bathtub in the bathroom of his office—a former hotel room—was piled high with correspondence, directives, and other papers. The bathroom door had been removed from its hinges and placed over two wood sawhorses, now to serve as a desk for two WACS seated side by side, typing. On typewriters whose carriages moved backward, right to left.

At 9:00 A.M. on the day following the *Altalena* sinking every Air Force foreign volunteer present in the city, more than fifty of us, crowded into a small auditorium in the

Yarkon basement. The morning was already quite warm, and although the horizontal sidelight windows were open wide, the room was thick with cigarette smoke and stuffy with the uniquely masculine smell of aftershave lotion, leather, and tobacco.

The room was also heavy with displeasure. During the night Haganah and Irgun units had continued skirmishing. There were casualties. Jewish blood spilled by Jews. The Irgun briefly had controlled nearly the entire Esplanade, an area that included the Park Hotel and this very Air Force HQ. A small stone wall fronting a residence less than fifty feet from the Yarkon was freshly pocked with bullet holes. We had been ordered not to venture into the streets. Only at dawn, when the last Irgun elements were driven off, was the order rescinded.

Haman Shamir stepped to the front of the room and raised his arms for quiet. He wore a neat khaki uniform, crisp and well-tailored, devoid of any insignia other than his black epaulet overlays, each containing the embroidered twin silver leaf insignia of an IDF lieutenant colonel. He impressed you as a simple, almost uncomplicated man, but I remembered him well from Panama, especially his quiet ability to command respect.

After a brief exchange of friendly greetings with some of the group, Haman gestured for silence again and said, "Aharon couldn't make it. He sends his apologies."

Although Aharon Remez, an Israeli with RAF wartime flying experience, was nominal Air Force Chief of Staff, the volunteer air crews came under Haman Shamir's direct supervision. Haman understood not only the idiom, but our psychology as well. He could deal with us on our own level.

Wherever and whatever that was.

The Deputy Chief of Staff patted down his thinning sandy hair, a nervous habit, then continued speaking. "All right, now let me talk a few minutes without questions or interruptions. I'm sure you'll be able to see our side of the picture."

He went on to describe the government's negotiations with Irgun regarding the *Altalena's* cargo: Haganah had agreed that one hundred and twenty tons of the munitions would be allocated to Irgunist forces fighting in Jerusalem. But the Irgun, he claimed, reneged on that agreement and demanded a greater share.

"We have absolute knowledge that Irgun planned to cache those arms. For what? Why would they need more guns? Well, we believe it might have been for an uprising after the war, to take over the government. If you don't know what Irgun is and what it stands for, come up after and I'll tell you." He paused to light a cigarette. "The fighter squadron was called out yesterday to attack that ship. They said they didn't want to kill other Jews. I say they should have gone out and accomplished the mission. I'll tell you why–"

Someone in the audience shouted, "No, Haman, you *can't* tell us why! You can't, because there's no good reason for it!" This was followed by shouts of approval from some, and from others to shut up and let Haman talk. He patted down his hair again and waited for the room to quiet.

"You men came here to help establish a Jewish state, the State of Israel. Anything or anyone that interferes or otherwise obstructs the realization of that objective . . . must be eliminated. We fight the Arabs because they threaten our survival. The Irgun poses the same threat.

"The Irgun, as you all know, was an army within an army. We could tolerate that as long as they obeyed government orders and promised, at the appropriate time, to allow themselves to become absorbed into the main army. They broke those promises."

He paused for breath, started speaking, then stopped. He smiled self-consciously. "That's it, I guess. Now, are there questions?"

Stan Andrews raised his hand and stood. "Haman, I understand your point, but I could never bring myself to go out and kill other Jews."

"Suppose civil war breaks out?" Haman asked. "Will you protect Israeli government aircraft and installations, or will you allow the Irgun to take them over?"

Stan Andrews said, "Excuse me, but I think that's a foolish question. Without us, those airplanes can't be flown. And nobody can make us fly them. I for one refuse to participate in a civil war, and I refuse to lift a finger against other Jews!"

A chorus of voices seconded this, some shouting they were willing to go on record, in writing, as refusing to even step into a cockpit until the internecine fighting stopped.

Listening, watching, I remember feeling a little glow of justification: my suggestion that we threaten to stop flying was not so "crazy" as Tryg Maseng had implied. I also remember glancing at Tryg. He looked at me, then shook his head in disgust and turned away.

But now, in a single succinct sentence, Haman silenced and pacified the dissenters. "I understand how you feel. So you have my word that if you feel that strongly about not taking part in operations against the Irgun, you will not be required to do so."

At once, he and the government were back in our good graces. What he carefully failed to tell us was that his assurance of our not being asked to fight fellow Jews was academic. More accurately, deceptive, for at the very moment Haman Shamir spoke, Irgun forces throughout the city were surrendering, their commanders arrested, their soldiers dispersed and absorbed into Haganah battalions. As an autonomous armed organization Irgun no longer existed.

The incident left a lasting mark on men like Stanley Andrews, who believed nothing could justify asking foreign Jews to take sides in an Israeli civil war, which itself was beyond his comprehension. As it turned out, for Stan Andrews the question became truly academic. Three months later, in the Battle of the Negev, his Beaufighter was hit by Egyptian ground fire. He crashed and was killed.

As for me, I left the Yarkon that day in high spirits. I felt we had won a victory, made a point. The Yarkon had heard and taken note of our foreign voices.

I remember having dinner with Steve Schwartz the same evening at a small Viennese restaurant on Allenby Road, The Rishon Cellar, an establishment famous—or, depending on your digestion, infamous—for its *Wiener Schnitzel*. I had eaten only half my cutlet when the proprietor received a telephoned warning of a possible attempt by obdurate Irgun soldiers to seize control of the area. Although it never happened, the proprietor immediately shuttered the restaurant and asked us to leave.

It is worth mentioning that in 1979, thirty-one years later, The Rishon Cellar still existed, at the same location, and I dined there once again with Steve. When I ordered the Schnitzel, Steve said it was probably the same one I'd left behind that night.

We laughed, but it reminded me of the other time, and that the *Altalena* had continued burning through the night.

EIGHT

"THINGS HAVE NEVER LOOKED BRIGHTER"

Don Kosteff was missing.

En route to Ajaccio from Zebra, the cabin packed nose to tail with a ceiling-high cargo of rifles, machine guns, and ammunition, plus two fighter pilot passengers, Kosteff's C-46 was last reported climbing for the Alps crossing. No further word in a day and a half.

We learned of this late one evening at Aquir. I was with Auerbach preparing to take off for Zebra. Larry Raab had just arrived from Ajaccio and Auerbach asked him why Kosteff in RX-138 was delayed there. Larry replied that he had not seen RX-138 in Ajaccio, he had assumed Kosteff to be here in Tel Aviv. And Larry continued with the obvious question:

" . . . if he's not here, and not in Ajaccio, where the hell is he?"

"If he never got to Ajaccio, he couldn't have taken off from there," someone said. "At least we know he's not down in the water."

I was thinking of Kosteff's crew: Julie Swing, the co-pilot; Bob Luttrell, the navigator; Sol Fingerman, the radio operator. Names instantly bringing faces and voices to mind. Kosteff, the craggy ex-airline captain. Swing, mild-mannered, almost diffident, the former Douglas Aircraft test pilot. Luttrell, the lanky always-cheerful non-Jew, former Merchant Marine navigator. And Fingerman, undoubtedly having inveigled the two passengers, American fighter pilots Aaron ("Red") Finkel and Sid Antin, into a poker game.

"He probably had to land somewhere for repairs," Auerbach said with confidence, too much confidence. "I'll bet by the time we get to Ajaccio, he'll have already been there and gone."

But Auerbach's face betrayed him; he did not for one instant believe it. And I knew, as we all knew, that sooner or later the odds had to catch up with us. I could read their minds, Auerbach's and Raab's: sixteen thousand feet with no oxygen, no de-icing equipment, engines falling apart. We were more than ever an accident waiting to happen.

For all that, there was still a chance that Kosteff had indeed put down for repairs, and was unable or did not wish to make contact with Zebra. So we took off, and not a word further about it was said during the entire twelve-hour flight to Ajaccio.

A conspiracy of silence.

Which ended when we made the landfall, Corsica, and followed the long gentle curve of the coastline around to the airdrome, all eyes now straining for the sight of a C-46 parked on the hardstand in front of the terminal.

The only large airplane visible was a clumsy four-engined twin-ruddered Air France Languedoc lumbering out to take off on the daily Paris flight. We swung in behind the Languedoc and landed. The moment we touched down I asked the control tower for any word on RX-138.

None.

When this happens, when someone is lost but whose fate is as yet undetermined, you do not allow yourself to dwell upon the obvious, that the downed airplane lies in a tangle of charred wreckage on some unknown mountainside. That the crew is dead. Your friends and comrades are dead.

No, you insist that while they might be down, they are alive, uninjured. Or if injured, not seriously. They will be found and rescued. This is a reflex, a phenomenon well known to that elite company of men who are bonded together by their facility to control machines that defy all the accepted laws of nature. And their willingness—or, if you prefer, arrogance—to challenge the dangers inherent in such defiance. But it is a marvelous arrogance, and spells the difference between success and failure, life and death.

It is that same arrogance that allows you the conviction, no matter how irrational or unrealistic, that all aboard the downed airplane have survived. Indeed, until it has been proven otherwise, you must steadfastly maintain a belief in their survival, for to believe differently is an abandonment of your own omnipotence, an acknowledgement of your own mortality. This, acknowledging your own mortality, you fear might somehow make you vulnerable. Somehow create situations affecting your own good judgment, your better judgment. You will repeat their mistake, or be victimized by the same bad luck.

We took on a full fuel load at Ajaccio, and despite warnings of a storm front moving westward from central Europe, departed immediately. Auerbach wanted to reach the Italian-Austrian Alps with enough gasoline and enough daylight for a thorough search. By now we were resigned to it: Kosteff was down in the mountains.

As soon as we were in the air I went into the cabin for a nap. We would be at 16,000 feet over the mountains and I thought some rest, if not sleep, might somehow prevent—or at least ease—my usual anoxia. My passing out at altitude meant one less pair of eyes for the search.

I slept. A deep, gratifying two-hour sleep, abruptly interrupted by Auerbach shaking me awake. "Come on, son, up and at 'em! You have to call Treviso and tell them we're making an emergency landing! We're icing badly and we're only at nine thousand!"

"Why Treviso?" I asked.

Auerbach, already halfway back to the flight deck, shouted, "We'll never get over the mountains until this front passes!"

Which really did not answer my question, why Treviso?

The only airfield there was an Italian Air Force fighter base. Why a military station instead of a civil airdrome? But then I remembered that on a Zebra-Ajaccio flight several weeks earlier, Auerbach had landed at this same field. Not by choice, but forced down by an Italian Spitfire.

The fighter base commandant had taken one look at the Messerschmitt in the cabin of this "Panamanian" cargo carrier and placed Auerbach and his crew under guard. But after telephoning Rome for instructions, the commandant extended his apologies and treated the men with utmost courtesy. He fed them, refueled them, wished them good luck, and sent them on their way. All this obviously the result of Danny Agronsky's knowledge of who to talk to, and their price. Therefore, now, faced with an emergency, Treviso was the logical place for Auerbach to land.

Treviso tower granted us permission to land. We homed in on the beacon and broke into the clear at 2,000 feet, twenty miles south of the field. Eight minutes later the runway was in sight.

And on the tarmac, like a little silver toy, was a C-46. RX-138.

Just as Auerbach's face had earlier betrayed his anxiety, now it mirrored his relief. You could literally feel him relax. His eyes were all at once alive. Thankfully, for once, he omitted a "Things-have-never-looked-brighter!" recital.

He said, "Thank God!"

Which said it all.

The commandant himself met us, Colonel Auturo Bracci, a handsome man with thick immaculately coiffed graying hair and a heavy ink-black mustache. He spoke excellent English, which he said he had learned while a POW in the United States, in the beautiful state of Michigan. Listening to him, that booming basso voice, you could well imagine him on the La Scala stage, delivering a Verdi aria.

And it was like a scene from an Italian opera. Colonel Bracci ushered us into his office, one arm draped fraternally over Hal Auerbach's shoulder, the other arm over mine, and in a classic Italian accent described Kosteff's misadventure. It had begun shortly after crossing the mountains. RX-138's left engine started throwing oil. Kosteff had no choice but land for repairs. Mindful of Auerbach's previous experience at this Treviso fighter base, and confident of an equally friendly reception, Kosteff had landed here.

Kosteff's assumption was not unreasonable. Normally, Danny Agronsky would have applied his wizardry, repairs made, and the airplane sent on its way. But Don Kosteff's luck ran doubly bad that day: a high-ranking civilian customs official happened to be visiting the base. He inspected the C-46's cargo. Before Colonel Bracci could intervene, Kosteff and his crew and passengers were hustled away.

To jail.

And I swear this is exactly how Colonel Bracci said it: " . . . ah, yes, your friends. Well, your friends are in ze–how do you say in Ingleesh?–ah, yes, zey are in ze hoosegow!"

Because the "case" now fell under Italian customs juris-diction–an entirely different bureaucracy–Colonel Bracci was unable to place the heretofore magic telephone call to Rome. So Kosteff and his crew remained in the hoosegow.

But the colonel certainly did not object to Auerbach phoning Rome, to Danny Agronsky who had already been advised of the incident but mistakenly believed that the air-plane and crew had been released. Danny promised to get right on it. In the meantime, he said, Auerbach was to get the hell out of Treviso the moment the weather cleared.

Clearance, at the earliest, was not expected until morning,

so we accepted Colonel Bracci's invitation to dinner. First, however, he arranged for us to see Don Kosteff.

Treviso, nestled in the Alpine foothills, is a lethargic city of some 30,000. The city center is quaint and charming, with a collonaded main street filled with shops and trattorias.

Not so charming was the jail.

A ramshackle building, two stories of cracked and dust-grimed windows, and a facade that was a collage of ragged splotches of peeling plaster and paint. It presaged what lay inside: the tile-floored, high-ceilinged rooms with barren white-washed walls and the wafting, constant stink of Lysol.

Accompanied by Colonel Bracci we were ushered into the Police Chief's office. Everything about the chief appeared heavy. Arms, hands, legs. He wore a wrinkled blue uniform, trouser cuffs caked with mud. He and Bracci engaged in a long animated conversation with continuous gesticulating and facial gyrations.

Finally, Bracci said to Auerbach, "If you wish to see Captain Kosteff, you must make a formal request."

"Didn't you just do that?" Auerbach asked.

"It must come from you," said Bracci.

So Auerbach addressed the Police Chief in English, which Bracci translated. More lively conversation between the two Italians, resulting at last in Bracci announcing that we would be allowed to see Kosteff.

Ten minutes later, escorted by two armed *carabinieris*, Don Kosteff entered the office. Unshaven, haggard, hair matted, his poplin flying jacket grease-stained, tan shirt and slacks dirty and rumpled. He certainly did not resemble the cool, confident thirty-five-year-old ex-airline pilot who only a month before had so eagerly volunteered his services. The same man who exclaimed good-naturedly, "This goddam war's put aviation progress back fifty years!"

He had apparently been told of our presence, so was not surprised. Neither did he seem pleased. "Thanks for stopping by," he said acidly.

"Don, how are you?" Auerbach asked, a question he immediately regretted.

"How am I?" Kosteff shouted. "How the hell do I look?"

Auerbach said, "How are the other boys doing?"

"Oh, they're fine," Kosteff said. "They're all just great. We're getting used to sleeping on a damp concrete floor. You'd be surprised how after two nights it grows on you! We have plenty of things to do. We look at each other, and when we're not doing that we play gin rummy for the one extra blanket! Now when do we get out of here?"

"Momentarily," said Auerbach, and told him of the phone call to Danny Agronsky.

"Yeah, well for your information, the minute we landed here, we telephoned Danny," Kosteff said. "The colonel here even dialed the number himself—"

"—that was before your airplane had been inspected," Colonel Bracci said, with an uneasy, almost embarrassed smile.

"—and Danny said he'd take care of it right away," Kosteff continued. "Yeah, he took care of it all right!"

"There was a little bit of a mix-up," Auerbach said, and again immediately regretted the words.

"Mix-up?" Kosteff shouted. "That's all it is to you: a fucking mix-up? A mix-up!"

The police chief said something. The two *carabinieris* seized Kosteff's arms and started herding him out. Kosteff pushed one of the soldiers aside and moved menacingly toward the Chief. The *carabinieris* blocked him. All this time he was shouting at the Chief.

" . . . can't hold us like this! We're American citizens! There's an international law that says an aircraft in distress can make a forced landing anywhere!"

The chief spoke. Bracci, with that same embarrassed smile, translated. "He says he knows of no international law protecting airplanes carrying one hundred and fifty machine guns and one hundred and twenty thousand rounds of ammunition. But he promises that the men will be released from jail tomorrow morning and taken to a hotel."

"Bullshit!" Kosteff shouted. "That's what they said when we landed." He looked at Auerbach, then me, then waved his fist at the chief. "This no good son of a bitch comes charging out to the airport and tells us he's taking us to a hotel. So like nice little boys we all pile into a truck and drive to town. The truck goes into a courtyard. The gate slams shut behind us, and there we were: in jail!"

Kosteff had more to say, but the Chief gestured the *carabinieri* to remove him. We could hear Kosteff yelling obscenities at his guards all the way down the corridor. Bracci and the Chief had another but briefer conversation.

Bracci said, "In the morning your friends will be sent to a hotel. Under guard, of course, but they will certainly be much more comfortable."

Short of storming the jailhouse and overpowering the guards, there was nothing further we could do. We had dinner with Bracci and then checked into a hotel ourselves. In the morning Auerbach went shopping. He purchased two hundred pounds of choice beef, fifty dozen eggs, and one hundred pounds of butter. We loaded the provisions onto the airplane. Our people at Zebra would eat well for a while.

Before leaving for the airport, Auerbach insisted on personally making certain that Kosteff and the others had in fact been transferred to a hotel. They had been, although their incarceration–albeit in a hotel–continued nearly four more weeks. When Danny Agronsky finally obtained their release, the Italians allowed Don and his crew to leave in RX-138, but without the cargo.

Scratch one hundred and fifty machine guns.

2.

In late July a second UN truce was imposed. It was briefer than the first, and broken by both sides almost from the start. In the five days following the end of this second truce, supported by their increasingly effective tactical air force—the three B-17s and dozen Messerschmitts—the Israeli Army scored an astounding series of victories. The Egyptians on the central front were routed. Lydda airdrome was captured. In the north Nazareth was taken, and the entire Galilee sector reduced to a small pocket. Jerusalem remained besieged, but supplies were getting through on the newly constructed "Burma Road."

The 101 Fighter Squadron—aptly named: the first and only IAF fighter squadron—achieved such tactical aerial superiority that sometimes, for days, their patrols flew unopposed. They took to routinely strafing enemy armored columns and troop concentrations. Egyptian ground forces grew so disorganized and demoralized the mere sound of distant aircraft engines drove them to cover. Cairo Radio claimed that to accomplish their Zionist dirty work the Jews sent teenage pilots on suicide missions.

Encouraging as all this was, it amounted only to pushing the invading Arab armies back toward the original partition lines. On all fronts, the Israeli Army was outnumbered and outgunned, especially in the Negev desert. There, a large Egyptian force had cut off an entire Palmach brigade. Not only were all attempts to relieve the Negev unsuccessful, but the Egyptians were tightening the ring. Israel lacked the manpower and resources to sustain a prolonged siege. If the Negev fell the war could be lost.

In the meantime, ATC flew. Our Zebra-Oklahoma airlift, the airplanes still operating as Panamanian flag carriers, delivered more tons of guns and ammunition, more Messerschmitts.

We obtained a C-54 which, like the Connie, flew non-stop from Zebra to Israel. And we were pushing the C-46s—and ourselves—to the limit. A blur of flying, eating, sleeping, flying. You lived in a waking nightmare of power failures on takeoff and wheels-up landings and feathered propellers and grossing fifty-five thousand pounds on flights over 16,000-foot mountains so that if you lost an engine you had no chance whatever.

We were isolated, cocooned in a world all our own, a vacuum that made the war almost a vague, distant incident. Yes, we brought weapons in and occasionally dropped bombs on the way out. We knew battles were being fought at places called Latrun, Faluja, El Arish, Gaza, Ishdud–and, of course, Jerusalem–but it was difficult to relate to them. To us, in truth, they were little more than names. We were too preoccupied with ourselves and our own survival.

We had little personal contact with the soldiers engaged in ground actions. We knew men were being killed and wounded. We suffered our own casualties after all, our own friends. But to us these others were really only numbers, statistics, associated with more of those biblical-sounding places. Later, when the airlift ended and Tel Aviv became our permanent station, some of those nameless, faceless people would assume dimension. They would become flesh and blood. We would know them, they would know us. But at that time, no. Then, that whole summer, our only close contact with Israelis came through either the Air Force staff officers, or the Aquir mechanics and ground personnel.

We got along well enough with the mechanics and ground personnel. We admired and respected them, mainly I am sure because they deferred to us. The staff officers did not; they expected us to behave as military subordinates, a category we refused to accept. We considered ourselves civilians, and autonomous. We were filled with our own importance.

But then, how could you not feel important, watching a flight of fighters overhead with Stars of David on their wings?

3.

In late August, in a single day, we lost two airplanes. The first, in Ajaccio, when someone drained the full fuel tanks of a Mosquito (a formidable combat airplane) being ferried to Israel. Since the pilot, an Englishman hired for this one flight, had personally supervised the aircraft's refueling the previous evening, he neglected to visually check his fuel prior to departure. The bomber crashed on takeoff.

The pilot walked away with a broken nose and fractured wrist. The airplane was demolished. I did not witness the accident but saw the wreckage just off the runway when we landed at Ajaccio. I was with Raab, en route to Zebra from Oklahoma. We recognized it immediately as a Mosquito, although not as ours. We had no idea it was bound for Israel until informed of this by Commandant Latour.

His gouty leg freshly bandaged, Commandant Latour hobbled out to greet us. He told us about the Mosquito, and that he suspected sabotage. Larry wryly agreed this was a distinct possibility, particularly since the tanks had been emptied.

"I intend to question the pilot," Commandant Latour said. "He might well have done it himself."

"Not unless he was suicidal," Larry said.

"It has happened. Believe me, my friend, it has happened before," said Commandant Latour. "Well, we shall investigate the matter thoroughly, I promise you."

I remember telling him in my mind, Sure, Major, sure you'll investigate the matter thoroughly. With the same thoroughness you investigated the meteorology reports a few weeks before. Erroneous weather advice had delayed three Zebra-bound C-46s for nearly two days in Ajaccio. Commandant Latour thus far had been unable to locate the person or persons responsible. His promise to investigate reminded me of Claude Rains's famous line in *Casablanca*: " . . . round up the usual suspects."

The usual landing and gasoline fees were paid, and we took off for Zebra. We arrived near dusk. As always, there were no control procedures; you came in from the south, over the town of Zatec, and let down straight-in to the runway. On the approach nothing seemed out of the ordinary.

Ahead and below, parked on the hardstand were the C-54, another C-46, and one of the two BT-13 trainers we had brought in from Millville and now used for instrument training. It all looked quite normal.

Until I heard Raab shout, "Jesus Christ, there's an airplane on its belly!"

I whirled and peered out Raab's window at the grain field left of the runway. I saw, first, four furrows of earth, long and straight, resembling four plowed trenches. The furrows ended abruptly and there, sure enough, was an airplane lying on its belly in the grass, four propeller blades bent into the ground.

RX-121, the Connie.

Except for Raab issuing crisp, curt landing instructions, the sight of the crippled Connie had silenced every-one in the C-46 cockpit. Closer, lower, we saw that the Connie's fuselage and wings appeared intact. Some dozen men, mechanics and pilots, moved in and around the airplane, talking, gesturing, inspecting the fuselage underside. Standing apart from the group, alone, was another man. As we roared past on our touchdown, I saw that he stood gazing mournfully at the Connie.

It was Sam Lewis.

Sam, whose "baby," whose pride and joy this Connie had been. Had been, past tense, for it was obvious this airplane would not fly for a long time to come. If ever. So, in effect, Sam was sitting *shiva*, the traditional Jewish ritual of respect for the dead.

Raab landed, wheeled the C-46 around, and raced to the hardstand. The instant the engines were shut down we scrambled out of the airplane and rushed over to Sam. He said nothing a moment, only stared vacantly at Raab and then at me. He was so disconsolate you almost wanted to put your arms around him and utter some "life goes on . . . " platitude.

He turned toward the hardstand in the near distance, the

C-54 parked there, and said, "Well, there's our new flagship!"

I learned later of Sam's valiant effort to save the Connie. The airplane had departed Tel Aviv with passengers, women and children, families of Israeli consular personnel residing in Prague. Marty Ribakoff was in the left seat. An uneventful flight but for a brief moment off the Yugoslavian Adriatic coast when a Yugoslav YAK fighter came up to look them over. The Connie's Panamanian markings apparently satisfied the Yugo pilot who waggled his wings and sped away.

Marty said he should have known they had pushed their luck. Not ten minutes after the YAK encounter, the Connie's main hydraulic line ruptured. Marty continued on to Zebra. He knew they were in trouble, but not how seriously until the landing gear was lowered. Only the left wheel came down. The right wheel and nose wheel remained retracted. Marty tried to raise the left wheel back into its well. Once retracted, he hoped all three might lower properly.

The left wheel would not budge; it remained locked in the down position. For two hours they circled the field while the Flight Engineer vainly struggled to manually crank either the left wheel up, or the right and nose wheels down.

Sam Lewis had a plan. He would fly a BT-13 alongside the Connie, slide the smaller airplane's right wing under the Connie's left wingtip, and then slam the wing up into the Connie's wing. Sam theorized that the impact could unfreeze the Connie's two jammed wheels. The collision was unlikely to harm the Connie but might severely damage the more fragile BT-13. In that event, Sam would bail out.

Sam waited until Marty had exhausted most of his fuel, then prepared to take off in the BT-13. Zebra maintenance chief Sam Pomerance thwarted the fanciful scheme, but only by physically restraining Sam Lewis.

A few minutes later Marty Ribakoff brought the Connie in. A belly landing is precarious enough but this belly landing, with one wheel down, required the delicacy of a brain surgeon.

And luck.

Marty came in, left wing down, so low it literally skimmed the grass. He cut the master switches and touched down on the left wheel, knowing that under the great weight it might instantly collapse. It held. Not for long, but long enough for Marty to keep the right wing up while he rolled along the grass and lost speed. It was, as he said later, a perfect "one-point" landing. It had to be perfect. At that rate of forward speed, if the right wing had fallen too soon the wingtip would have dug into the ground and careened the airplane around in a lethal cartwheel.

Skill and luck, the proportions unimportant, although in less competent hands it unquestioningly would have been a disaster. In all his years of flying Marty Ribakoff never made a better landing.

Sam Lewis was the first person to greet and congratulate Marty, whose immediate response was, "Sam, what the hell is the matter with you? You gone crazy, for Christ's sake? Trying to knock the wheels loose with that BT-13?"

"It might have worked," Sam said.

"Yeah, and might have killed you," Marty said. "How could you even consider such an idiotic idea?"

Sam shrugged. "We can't afford to lose airplanes," he said.

Marty's superb airmanship did not go unrewarded. He was ordered to Mexico City to take delivery of a brand new C-46, which he would then fly back to Zebra. The trip included a two-week delay en route in the United States, allowing him a long awaited reunion with his wife and young children. It was of course tantamount to a vacation.

No one begrudged him the good fortune, he unarguably had earned it. But then Marty Ribakoff was not the only man deserving a vacation, and he couldn't fly the C-46 alone. So who would crew it?

It turned out that only one additional crew member was assigned. Surprisingly, it was me.

I say surprisingly because others certainly were more entitled to the trip. Eddie Styrak, for one; not only had he been involved in the earlier crash with Moonitz, he was the radio operator on the ill-fated Connie. I later learned that Eddie had indeed been asked, but opted instead for a three-week furlough in Tel Aviv where he had fallen in love with a girl named Fanya. On her part, said Eddie, Fanya was probably not so much in love with him as intrigued with "old faithful," the celebrated gentile appendage that had won its owner his release from Acre Prison.

In any event, when Sam Lewis informed me I was to accompany Marty, you can be sure I did not question Sam's good judgment. Little did I dream that it would result in Marty and me being swept up in a wild and unpredictable adventure that matched any Alan Ladd–William Bendix film, and then some.

And it really happened.

The author at the former home of his uncle, Nuremberg, Germany, 1945.

The author at Payne Field officer's club, Cairo, 1946.

Norman Moonitz and the author,
Panama, April 1948.

At dinner, compliments of the casino, Panama City, April 1948. Left to
right: Sol Fingerman, Art Yadvin, the author, and Norman Moonitz.

"FLY LAPSA" postcard from Panama.

The author's LAPSA ID card, front and reverse.

Ray Kurtz, Panama, April 1948.

Sheldon Eichel and Norman Moonitz in the hospital after their crash, Tel Aviv, May 1948.

Ezer Weizman, Tel Aviv, June 1948.

Swifty Schindler (left, in leather jacket) tries to convince the RCMP that he had no intention of trying to take that B-17 to Israel. Halifax, Nova Scotia, July 1948.

The Altalena *beached in front of the Kaete Dan Hotel, Tel Aviv, June 1948.*

Al Raisin, Tel Aviv, July 1948.

Norman Moonitz (rear, third from left) with his B-17 crew.

Hal Auerbach in El Al uniform, Tel Aviv, December 1948.

Larry Raab.

Captain Sam Lewis.

Two C-46 crews. Left to right, Ed Styrak, the author, Harry Schwartz, Al Raisin, Cyril Steinberg, Eddie Chinsky, Gordon Levett, Sheldon Eichel (in shadow), Jack Goldstein, Len Dichek, Al Dobrowitz, and Eli Cohen. Ajaccio, Corsica, June 1948.

A gathering of Old Eagles at a fortieth anniversary reunion. Seated, fighter pilots Leo Nomis and Aaron Finkel. Standing, left to right, Sam Gal, Sam Lewis, Mike Flint, Lou Lenart, Sy Cohen, and the author. Santa Monica, California, 1988.

NINE

A TICKET TO CAIRO

One week after Marty Ribakoff left for the States and his East St. Louis, Illinois, home, I was supplied with expense money, an airline ticket to New York via Paris, and telephone numbers for the appropriate Israeli representatives–more Little Men. Marty was to meet me in New York, from where we would proceed to Mexico City.

I hitched a ride to Ajaccio with one of the Swedish crews, then caught the Air France Languedoc flight to Paris. The last time I saw Paris–from the song of the same name–had been shortly after VE Day, 1945. I loved the city, the broad boulevards, the sidewalk cafés, the parks, the museums, the food, the taxis, the weather, the women. I loved the fresh clean smell of the city after a rain. I loved the smell of the city, period, even the smell of the exhaust fumes of the automobiles and buses that somehow, magically–probably because they were so uniquely Parisian–seemed not at all unpleasant, indeed almost sensuous, even the cramped little cars of the Metro that always reeked of garlic.

Love at first sight, which was on the 31st of August, 1944, six days after the Liberation, and five days before my twentieth birthday. I had landed at Orly Field with seven other radio and control tower operators to open an AACS station. But Orly still lay in ruins from Allied bombings and was temporarily unusable.

The only U.S. Army personnel at Orly were some engineers, who told us to report back in a week after they had cleaned up the runways. Where were we supposed to go? Where to sleep, to eat? Since no one had an answer, let alone appeared to particularly give a damn, the city seemed the only logical place to go.

The Third Army had bypassed Paris. Not many Americans were in the city, only a few war correspondents, some deserters, and the eight of us. The streets were crowded, people cheered us and offered bottles of wine or champagne, and cried *"Vive Les Americains!"* A week after the Liberation they still celebrated.

We wandered aimlessly, stopping at a bar here, a bistro there, and in not a single place was money accepted. Not even in the Sphinx, a famed and fabled bordello where the madam insisted we spend the entire night. On the house. A small token of appreciation from those grateful ladies for our having liberated Paris from the despised Boche. I was by then so sodden with brandy and immersed in Chanel No. 5 that I not only accepted credit for liberating Paris, I think I nearly believed it myself.

So now, four years later almost to the week, I wanted to relive those times (unhappily not possible at the Sphinx, for in a series of inexplicable post-war paroxysms of morality the French government had closed all those convivial establishments). But this, too–a day or two stay in Paris–proved not possible: the Paris Little Men, my sole source of funds, insisted that I immediately board the first available New York flight.

I was given the Manhattan phone number of a man named Nat Cohn and instructed to report to him, and to also destroy my LAPSA identification papers. LAPSA was out of business: the Panamanian government had canceled all aircraft registrations. Upon arrival in the U.S., I should anticipate a thorough grilling. Any connection to LAPSA might prove troublesome.

To my relief–and, I must confess, chagrin–LaGuardia customs and immigration passed me through with hardly a second glance. Not being recognized as an international brigand was a little disappointing. I phoned Nat Cohn and was informed of a minor change of plan. I was to meet Marty Ribakoff, not in New York but in Miami, and from there continue on to Mexico City to pick up "the item." Detailed instructions would follow. However, because Marty was moving his wife and children to Israel, he planned to remain in Illinois another week helping them pack and prepare. Therefore, if I wished, I could briefly visit my family in Massachusetts. I had not seen my parents since March, nor spoken with them since a July telephone call from Prague.

Three days in Haverhill were more than enough. My father pleaded with me not to leave. My mother told me to do what I had to, although she had hoped I might stay the weekend to see my younger brother and sister. Both were away at college. Impossible under the circumstances: I was in the States on an "important mission," and unable to spare the time. The more I made this claim, the more convinced I was not only of the importance of the mission, but of my own importance.

I returned to New York and went straight from Grand Central Station to Nat Cohn's office in a dress manufacturing loft on Seventh Avenue. He was a middle-aged, brusque but friendly enough man who gave me a $100 dollar bill and told me to check into the Henry Hudson Hotel and await further orders.

The first person I saw in the Henry Hudson lobby was

179

Marvin Paris, one of our B-17 crewmen, an aerial photographer. With not even a How-are-you, he blurted, "They're looking for you!"

They?

They, he said, were the FBI.

The FBI? Looking for me. For *me*?

"Well, for any of us," Marvin said. "They're all over the place, coming out of the fucking woodwork! And all the hotel phones are tapped!" He went on to explain that he had come home on leave to visit his critically ill mother. He was returning to Zebra the following morning, but glad he could warn me because all hell had broken loose over a shipment of aircraft engines seized in Miami by U.S. Customs.

The shit, said Marvin, had hit the fan. Whereupon, immediately, he vanished. I hurried to an outside phone booth and called Nat Cohn's office. He had gone for the day; his switchboard operator refused to give me his home number. I stood in the phone booth a long moment, thinking, actually more exhilarated than concerned.

The challenge of pitting my wits against theirs.

"Theirs," of course, the FBI, MI5, the Deuxieme Bureau, Egyptian Intelligence, or whoever else might be watching my every move.

Ladd and Bendix.

But what was there to think about? I had to move from the Henry Hudson, and fast. I phoned a friend, Norman Seaman, a World War II buddy who knew of my Haganah association. I explained my predicament. Norman volunteered to go to the Henry Hudson, check out in my name, and collect my luggage (one B-4 bag) and bring it to another hotel.

It made sense. I took a taxi to the Belmont Plaza Hotel on Lexington Avenue. A half hour later Norman appeared with my B-4 bag.

"Were you followed?" I asked.

"I don't think so," he said.

"You don't *think* so?"

"I didn't see anybody."

"How could you 'see' them?" I said. "You don't even know what they look like! Neither do I."

"That's what I mean," he said. "Besides, they're not about to *let* me see them, are they?" His pleased grin and furtive over-the-shoulder glances annoyed me. He was enjoying the intrigue. But then, so was I.

Over a beer we reminisced. Norman reminded me this was not the first time he came to my "rescue." The other time was during the war, on a raucous weekend in Paris. I have less than a fragmentary memory of the episode, but he contended that I had refused to pay the extra charge demanded by the concierge of a Montparnasse hotel for a girl I brought to our room. According to Norman, after an altercation with this concierge, I raced around in my underwear collecting keys from the doors of vacant rooms and hurled the keys down the elevator shaft. Norman claimed that he got me into my uniform and shepherded me and our belongings out of the room and out of the hotel just seconds before the MPs arrived.

"And the girl?" I asked.

"She stayed," he said. "The room was paid for."

We shared a few more laughs and then he left. I checked into the Belmont Plaza as "Harold Ellis." I spent that evening locked in my room, listening to the radio, and gazing out at the rain-slicked street twelve stories below. In the morning I phoned Nat Cohn. He said he was unaware of any FBI surveillance and that Marvin Paris had an overactive imagination, but to be on the safe side I should stay put until time to leave for Miami. And not to contact anyone I knew.

More intrigue. I loved it.

That same afternoon, bored, restless, I went next door to the Shelton Hotel where I had lived for several months in 1947. I had a drink at the bar, then wandered into the lobby. To occupy myself, I picked up a house phone and asked the operator to ring Harold Livingston. Not surprisingly, she told me that no such person was registered. The switchboard operator's voice was warm, feminine, and encouraging. It made me feel less alone. I asked if Jerry Yulesman still resided in the hotel; he was a young man who had also lived at the Shelton.

"I'll ring the room," said the operator.

One ring, two. It was like an eternity. When he answered, what could I say? "Hey, kid, I'm on my back to Israel!" Jerry and I had become good friends. He was a photographer, a sometime stringer for *Look* magazine. He'd want my story. On the third ring I slammed down the phone and hurried away. And nearly collided with a bellhop, a leathery-faced man I did not recognize but who seemed to study me an observant extra moment before muttering, "Sorry," and continuing on his business.

I cursed myself for my foolishness, my self-indulgence, my loneliness. What a stupid way to pass time! But now I had to be sure about that bellhop. He might easily be an undercover agent. At that instant he reappeared. He walked past with not even a second glance. Which convinced me I had been "made."

I scurried out of the Shelton, back to the Belmont Plaza, and checked out. I moved to yet another hotel, and then another. Finally, three hotels later, and on my birthday, September 4–also the start of the Labor Day weekend–I decided to move into one last hotel. And stay.

Again with Norman Seaman's furtive assistance, I checked into the Barbizon Plaza on Sixth Avenue. Norman promptly went on his way and I was, again, alone.

And lonely. Saturday night is the loneliest night of the week. Particularly if it is your birthday.

But I had been exhorted not to contact anyone I knew. Security was of utmost importance. All right, I'd follow orders. For the first few hours of that evening I lay on the bed, trying to read, trying to pass the time. In a hotel room. I hate hotels. The sterility (no matter how sumptuous), the feeling of unbelonging, of impermanence.

Tolerable at least when you have company. Torture when you are alone.

I tried to sleep; impossible. I studied the pages of the Manhattan telephone directory for familiar names and thought about the next day when I would still be alone with nothing to do and no one to talk to. I stared out the window at lighted windows of other rooms on my floor. In the window of a room across the courtyard the figure of a woman was silhouetted against the drawn curtains. I tried to locate her room number on the hotel fire exit diagram. It looked like Room 907. I started to call 907 but hung up when the operator answered. My God, what could I say to the woman in 907? "Hi there, you look as though you might like to help me celebrate my birthday–." No, that would never work.

Some birthday.

To hell with it. I got dressed and went downstairs. Adjoining the hotel on 56th Street, directly accessible from the hotel side entrance, was a small bar. Gary's, a neighborhood tavern frequented by regulars or hotel guests discouraged by the Barbizon Plaza's exorbitant bar prices: Chivas and soda, for example, sixty-five cents.

Gary's was moderately busy, dimly lit, noisy with piped music, talk, laughter. I sat at the uncrowded bar and ordered a drink. No one paid me the slightest attention. I started feeling more relaxed and more confident. Here, in this typical Manhattan bar, I was safe. I might even pick up a girl. The place was loaded with women. I looked around, trying to be casual, trying to identify the unescorted ones, and began rehearsing my introductory speech: " . . . look, I realize we don't know each other, but I can see you're alone, and so am I, and tomorrow just happens to be my birthday . . . " It would work like a charm. No hurry, though, it was only 10:30. I had the whole night.

With my second drink I became aware of the man on my right, a middle-aged, graying man. He was discussing dinner plans with a younger man on his right. Both wore well-tailored suits and Windsor-knotted ties. In those days, in midtown bars or restaurants, you wore jackets and ties. The older man proposed a certain west-side restaurant he said served the best Shishkabob in town. Shishkabob, lamb grilled on a stick, classic Middle-Eastern food.

Shishkabob?

And he spoke English with that hard, harsh accent I immediately recognized as Arabic-based.

The younger man, clearly an American, said Shishkabob sounded fine to him, and he knew "Barbara" would agree. The least he could do was give her a decent meal, he said. He rose unsteadily and announced he was going over to get Barbara; he'd bring her back with him, whereupon all three would dine. He left.

After a moment, probably sensing my gaze, the older man turned to me. He shrugged and pointed at the stool just vacated by the younger man.

"Had too much to drink," he said.

"Looks like it," I said.

He was a heavy but compact man, with iron gray hair that was thick and curly, and a face pocked with acne scars, and teeth much too perfect for a man his age, which I judged between forty and fifty.

We exchanged a few more meaningless remarks and then he insisted on buying me a drink. We continued chatting, mostly I think about the relative sophistication of New York women. I was concentrating not on his words, but the accent, straining to hear every rolled "r," every inflection. It was then, certainly more for mischief than any conceivable precognizance, I asked him a question that had simply popped into my head:

" . . . haven't I seen you before? In Egypt?"

"'Egypt?'" He fairly snarled the word. "Listen, I'm a British subject!" He reached into his inside breast pocket and withdrew a British passport. He slapped the passport down on the bar. Unexpectedly, then, he smiled. "But I've been to Egypt."

"I'm sure I saw you there," I said; it sounded like the logical thing to say.

"Where?" he asked. "Cairo?"

"That's where it was," I said. "Cairo."

"When?"

"In '46," I said, which was when I had worked for TWA in Cairo. "August, or September."

Wordlessly, the man flipped the passport pages to an Egyptian visa. He propped the passport on the bar against my glass and tapped his finger on the visa's entry and exit dates. The date of entry was August, 1946. Date of exit September, 1946.

"So there you are," he said, pleased. "You did see me. Was I in uniform?"

In uniform? What was I getting into here? What had I gotten into? Whatever it was, it was fun, and infinitely preferable to a lonely hotel room.

I said, "I can't remember. What kind of uniform was it?"

"It doesn't matter," he said. "But what were you doing there?"

With no hesitation, as though I had carefully composed and rehearsed the words, I replied, "I was on a flying deal. It went sour, so I had to get away from the place fast."

"You don't say?" He extended a hand and introduced himself. "Bill Daire. What's your name?"

"Hal Ellis," I said, and we shook hands.

He told me he was the American representative for an English distillery. Fine whiskey, he said, but made by the cheapest bastards in the business. They allowed him "only" forty dollars a day for expenses, which he said might sound generous but was only half what he deserved for having tripled their business in his few short months in their employ.

We had another drink and then all at once he asked, "You said you had a 'flying deal.' You're a pilot?"

Again with no hesitation, I said, "Yes, I'm a pilot."

"Who do you fly for?"

Now, with the liquor and my imagination running wild, I really was Alan Ladd. In Singapore, at the Raffles Hotel bar, negotiating with Sidney Greenstreet for my not inexpensive soldier-of-fortune services.

"I fly for anybody for the right price," I said. "I just got back from South America. I'm looking for a job."

"What kind of planes do you fly?"

"C-46s, '54's, Connies," I said. "Any kind of transport. Hey, they have wings and a prop, I'll fly 'em."

"You and that fellow that just left should have a lot in common," he said. "He's a pilot, too. He'll be back anytime now." And with that, abruptly, he resumed the discussion of New York women.

A few minutes later the younger man returned, accompanied now by a fairly attractive young woman. Bill Daire ignored the woman and introduced me to the man, whose first name was also Bill. Bill Dunne.

" . . . Mr. Ellis is a pilot," Daire said, fixing his eyes on Dunne's as he uttered the word, 'pilot.' "He flies transport planes."

Dunne was impressed. "You were in the army?"

"ATC," I said. "Europe."

Dunne said, "I was in the Pacific. Fifth Air Force, B-24s. Where'd you go to school?"

Now, as fast as the smooth slick answers had formulated in my brain, they vanished. I could not recall the name of a single aviation cadet training field. I did not want to risk a questionable guess, so I said, "I had a commercial license before I got in the army."

The instant I heard my own voice I wanted the words back. To realize it was chronologically improbable for me to have had a prewar commercial license, Bill Dunne needed only to look at me closely. And I looked even younger than my twenty-four years.

But he was more interested in the woman, Barbara, and dinner. The older man, Daire, told Dunne and Barbara to go on ahead to the restaurant. He, Daire, wanted to talk more with me.

Daire and I had another drink. Daire said he was bored with Gary's, and suggested we go some other place. He was drunk, his speech slurred, his gait unsteady. We walked south down 56th Street to another neighborhood bar in the middle of the block, one of those saloons fronted by a wall of varicolored illuminated glass bricks.

It was in this bar, at two in the morning, that the man who called himself Bill Daire offered me a job.

Flying.

"Flying to where?" I asked.

He grinned, a narrow, smug, alcoholic grin. His too-perfect teeth gleamed white in the reflection of the roseate indirect bar lighting, and I recall with total clarity that I knew precisely what his reply would be. "To the place where you first saw me!" he said.

The place where I first saw him.

Cairo.

For an instant I was too astounded to speak, and I was unsure of what to say anyway. Daire read this as disinterest on my part. He said, "There's good money in it."

"How much?"

"Two thousand a trip."

Cairo! Two thousand a trip! Jesus to Jesus! Don't panic, I told myself, play it smart. Play the game. This is what I told myself, but my heart was pounding and my throat was suddenly sandpaper dry. I strained to keep my voice calm and steady.

"What kind of planes will I be flying?"

"C-54s," he said.

I wanted to laugh. This had to be some kind of practical joke. Yes, of course: my friend, Norman Seaman. It was just like him to pull such a stunt. But then how could Norman, or anyone else, have possibly anticipated my walking into that first bar, Gary's? Let alone knowing I would sit next to Bill Daire?

"Well?" he asked.

"Two thousand sounds okay," I said. I was completely sober now. He seemed more collected, too, but was starting on yet another, a martini no less. I had long since lost count of his drinks. I went on, "But first, I want to see the money."

"Don't worry about the money," he said.

"I always worry about money," I said, in my best Alan Ladd voice.

"Tomorrow, I'll introduce you to some people. If you pass muster, you'll have your money." He finished his drink in a single swallow and slammed the empty glass on the table. He rose. "It's late," he said. "Let's get the hell out of here!"

After agreeing to meet at five the following afternoon at Gary's, we walked back to Sixth Avenue. He asked where I was staying. "Downtown," I said. "At the New Yorker, on 34th Street."

"I'm at the Delmonico," he said. "Up on Park, Park and 82nd. Very nice digs." He flagged a cruising cab, shook hands with me, and got into the taxi. "Delmonico, please," he told the driver.

I watched the taxi drive off. I hailed another cab and asked the driver to make a U-turn and head downtown. My hotel, the Barbizon Plaza, was of course across the street, thirty yards away. But I wanted to take no chances. Somebody might just be watching. It turned out we both were taking no chances. Daire, I later learned, lived in the Great Western Hotel. On 56th Street, almost directly opposite the Barbizon Plaza.

2.

I slept little that night. I had obviously uncovered–blundered into, if you will–a major Egyptian aviation project. Although I had identified myself as "Hal Ellis," it seemed only logical that the Egyptians possessed dossiers on all

LAPSA personnel. I would have to be crazy, or suicidal–or both–to keep tomorrow's date with Bill Daire.

Since I had by now obtained Nat Cohn's home number, promptly at 7:00 that morning I phoned him. I explained the situation. He said he would contact the appropriate parties and get back to me. To this day I can hear the annoyance in his voice: I know he thought I was crazy, or drunk–or both–but he could not afford not to take me seriously.

In those pre-Mossad days, Israel's counterintelligence was a loose-knit free-wheeling organization composed mainly of volunteers taking time from their jobs with legitimate law enforcement agencies. The agent who contacted me was a NYPD detective on leave-of-absence. A fair haired, nervously energetic man of perhaps thirty, he introduced himself simply as Joe. Joe Shoo-shoo, he said, was what they called him.

Joe Shoo-shoo.

Shoo-shoo, he explained, is a Hebrew colloquialism implying secrecy. All Israeli counterintelligence agents referred to themselves in this manner. Bill Shoo-shoo, Fred Shoo-shoo, Irving Shoo-shoo.

Harold Shoo-shoo.

I told him the story. Unlike Nat Cohn, Joe was not at all skeptical. He said they had suspected such an Egyptian operation, but this was the first break. A hell of an opportunity. He urged me to keep my date with Bill Daire that afternoon at Gary's.

I mentioned my concern about the Egyptians having a line on LAPSA people. Not to worry, said Joe. Gyppo Intelligence could hardly tie their own shoes, let alone zero in on LAPSA. Joe's assessment may or not have been correct, but there was another, even more immediate problem: suppose Daire asked to see some valid aircraft operating licenses? All I had was a private single-engine permit.

"Yeah," said Joe Shoo-shoo. "That might be a problem."

"Yeah, *mine*," I said.

But then I realized how to overcome that: Marty Ribakoff.

I would tell the Egyptians that the CAA had revoked my papers, but I had a friend, a rated airline captain, who I was sure would be interested in the Cairo proposition. Marty held all the necessary licenses, including an Air Transport Rating ticket. He could vouch for me.

Joe agreed this was the perfect solution. He would summon Ribakoff to New York immediately. In the meantime, I was to meet with the Egyptians and learn all I could. Their faces, he said. Commit their faces to memory well enough to describe each wrinkle and wart. It was an old police method.

After he left it occurred to me that the method worked both ways. They might be committing *my* face to memory.

In New York, at 5:00 on a Sunday afternoon, neighborhood bar business should ordinarily be slow. Gary's, that Sunday afternoon, was jammed.

Men and women, all well-dressed, crowded the bar and the booths. Bill Daire sat at the bar with his young American associate, Bill Dunne. Daire acknowledged me with a casual salute. I slid into a stool beside Dunne, who offered me a cigarette and said, "You tying up with us?"

"Us?" I asked.

Before Dunne could reply, Daire leaned past him and said to me, "Bill works for me."

And then Dunne asked the question I had feared. "What kind of a license do you have?"

I said, "Multi-engine, land."

"Instrument-rated?"

"Of course, instrument-rated," I said, and waited to be asked to display the license. I had improved my tale of the "revoked" license: now I would spin a yarn about the CAA having pulled the papers after I had been caught smuggling dope from South America.

But Dunne seemed uninterested in pressing me further. He looked at Daire and nodded. Daire looked at me. "Good, very good," he said. "Let me buy you a drink." He signaled the bartender. "Scotch and soda, right? Chivas, or Pinch?"

"Chivas," I said.

"Only the best, eh?"

"That's why you're hiring me, isn't it, because I'm the best?" I said, and then told him of my friend, the ex-airline captain, my partner on "these deals." Daire said the more the merrier, and that he looked forward to meeting the new recruit.

I said, "Speaking of meeting people, last night you said you wanted me to meet somebody. When does that happen?"

"Tomorrow," said Daire. He waved his hand about the room; he seemed to only then have noticed the unusually large number of customers. "Kind of busy, isn't it?" he said to the bartender, who had just served my drink.

"Yeah," said the bartender, a short, powerfully built man whose name was Kelly, and looked it. "Must be a convention in town, or something."

It was "or something," all right, as I learned a few minutes later in the men's room. A man entered immediately after me and stood in the next urinal. A stout, balding man of middle years, he fixed his eyes straight ahead on the urinal's stainless steel trip handle and spoke blandly to the wall.

"Don't worry," he said. "We're here."

I looked at him. He faced me, smiled, and said he was a NYPD plainclothesman, "helping out." Wherever I went from now on, he said, someone would be with me.

"All these people in the bar?" I asked. "They're with you?"

"With *you*," he said, and smiled again. "You're okay, so don't worry."

Don't worry. The place was filled with strange faces. Faces now that I thought about it suddenly all looked Jewish. Faces that had already attracted the Egyptian's attention, and this guy was telling me not to worry!

I rejoined Daire and Dunne at the bar. The drink and the roomful of Israeli agents had emboldened me. "Now listen," I said, "I want to know who I'll be working for!"

Daire peered at me incredulously; it was almost as though

I had questioned the existence of God. He glanced around to make sure he was not overheard. His voice was low, but hard and condescending. "You will be working for the right side!"

"Which side is that?" I asked, again in the Alan Ladd voice.

"The only side which is doing the right thing. The side which has been persecuted!"

The side which has been persecuted. What side was that? The Israelis were the ones under siege. The Arabs, disdaining the UN partition, had invaded Israel's pitifully tiny allotment of territory and proclaimed a *jihad* to sweep all the Jews into the sea. And *they* were persecuted?

I said, "I don't want to get mixed up in any politics. All I know is I fly for money!"

"You'll get your goddamned money," Daire said. "Don't worry."

Don't worry. Everyone was telling me not to worry. But I still wanted to hear Daire admit he was an Arab. I said, "I have to tell you: I won't fly for the Jews."

"You will not be flying for the Jews!"

"Why didn't you say so in the first place?"

"I'm saying it now," he said, and told me to meet him the following day. Same time, same place, and to bring my "partner," for an interview with the man in charge of operations.

I had another drink and left, careful again not to go directly into the adjoining Barbizon Plaza, my hotel. I walked up 56th Street to Seventh Avenue, then to the Park, and then back down to Sixth Avenue. Finally, confident I had not been followed, I returned to the hotel.

Joe Shoo-shoo and the bald cop were in my room waiting for me. I told them of the conversation, and of tomorrow's appointment, and that I had no intention of keeping the date unless Ribakoff was with me. Joe assured me that Ribakoff would arrive momentarily.

Ribakoff did not arrive, not that evening nor the next

morning. He was delayed in St. Louis. This hardly deterred Joe. He urged me to attend the meeting, talk to the people, but imply mistrust. This tactic should successfully stall the proceedings until Ribakoff joined the party.

So once more I met the two men in Gary's. Their operations chief—and they identified him now by name, Art Chester, a well-known, world-class racing and stunt pilot—was unable to make the meeting. Tomorrow, they said, he would show up. But now Daire suggested we all have dinner.

We walked, stopping along the way at several bars, to a Lexington Avenue restaurant. Behind us, like a phalanx of Swiss Guards, trailed four Israeli intelligence agents. They waited patiently outside each place we visited. At the restaurant one went inside and sat at the bar.

It was a fairly uneventful dinner. By now Daire was drunk. While I certainly made no attempt to keep up with him, I did drink enough to make me slightly high. Enough to again convince me I was Alan Ladd. After dinner, when Dunne wandered over to the bar by himself, I asked Daire where the Cairo-bound C-54s were presently located.

"A country south of Florida," he said.

"What country?"

"You will know in good time."

"How do I get there?"

"By commercial airline."

"To where?"

"To Miami first," he said.

"And then fly to . . . to the destination?"

"Yes."

"Where's the money?"

Daire's face tightened with annoyance. He looked away. He tapped a spoon impatiently against a water glass and called, "Waiter, another round here, what do you say!" Without pausing for breath he turned to me. "As soon as you pass muster, you will have your damned money!"

The following morning Ribakoff finally arrived, and that

same afternoon at Gary's I introduced him to Daire and Dunne. Again, Art Chester, the celebrity pilot–operations chief, did not show up to "pass muster" on us. But Daire seemed impressed enough with Marty, so much so that he agreed to Marty's $2,500 per flight demand. A firm, conclusive meeting was set for the next day.

It was becoming routine now that immediately after each session with Bill Daire, I would report the results to Joe Shoo-shoo. But that evening, when Marty and I met him at an uptown dairy restaurant, it was Joe who did the reporting. He had learned that the man with the unlikely name of Bill Daire was indeed an Egyptian agent, and engaged in a very viable project to ferry airplanes to Cairo. Some half dozen American pilots had already been hired to fly the airplanes, which were B-24s, not C-54s.

This inept transposition of aircraft letter and number designators, said Joe, was only another example of Arab clumsiness. Marty disagreed. He believed it was deliberate, a recruiting ploy: a C-54, the military version of the Douglas DC-4, was a far easier airplane to fly than a B-24, the famous World War II Liberator bomber.

"A guy'd take on a job flying a C-54 a hell of a lot faster than he would a B-24," Marty said.

"Do you realize what this means to us?" Joe asked. "A B-24?"

It was the "to us" that tipped it off. Marty got it first. He looked at me and then at Joe. "You got to be kidding!" Marty said. He looked at me again. "They want us to really go down there and take the job! They want us to fly the fucking B-24 to Israel!"

"Oh, shit!" I said, and thought, Ladd and Bendix. Forget it.

"You guys bring over a B-24, it'd be the greatest *mitzvah* since the parting of the Red Sea," Joe said.

"Yeah," said Marty in his laconic fashion. "But they're sure to have a crew on the airplane. A navigator and a radio operator and probably an engineer. What the hell are we supposed to do with them?"

"Kill them," said Joe Shoo-shoo.

3.

When Joe Shoo-shoo said "kill them," it was at that instant I ceased being Alan Ladd. I told the Shoo-shoo boys—and Marty concurred—that this was as far as we went. We would attend tomorrow's meeting with the Egyptians, and we would attempt to learn specific locations of their aircraft. But it was to be our final performance. We were not tempted even by Joe Shoo-shoo's offer of a $25,000 cash bonus for bringing a B-24 into Israel. We were out, period, end.

Kill them. And Joe Shoo-shoo had meant every word.

That final meeting, despite the failure once again of the operations chief to appear, was eminently successful. It commenced with the usual pub crawling and ended hours later at the Russian Tea Room on West 57th Street. Somewhere along the drunken way we lost Dunne.

Marty matched Daire drink for drink. Now and then the two broke out into off-key duets, or exchanged bad, dirty jokes. I made no attempt to keep up with them, not from any particular sense of responsibility—under these circumstances, one of us, Marty or I, had to stay reasonably sober—but because I knew that any more liquor would make me deathly ill.

Daire was just drunk enough so that when I called him a liar and accused him of having no money and no airplanes, he pulled from his pocket a typewritten form. He waved it teasingly under our noses. Marty snatched the paper from him and flattened it on the table.

Marty tried to focus his eyes on the print. "What the fuck is this?" he asked. "A laundry list?"

"A schedule," said Daire. "A bloody goddam schedule! Nobody calls me a liar. I'm the bloody goddam governor!"

And with this, Daire snatched the paper away and crammed it back into his jacket pocket. But I had had time enough to read some of it. According to the schedule the airplanes would leave from Ciudad Trujillo in the Dominican Republic, proceed to Casablanca, then to Tripoli, and on to Cairo.

"Okay, so now we believe you," I said, all the while desperately straining to commit to memory that part of the schedule I had been able to read.

"Yeah, we believe you," Marty said.

"Good," said Daire. "Let's have another drink."

"No, let's go home, I think I'm about to be sick," I said, which was not entirely untrue and probably discouraged Marty from staying. He told Daire we'd meet him tomorrow, and I told Daire that he'd better have the money or forget the whole bloody goddam deal. We left him there, drinking.

In a taxi I jotted down the schedule as best I could recall it and presented it to Joe Shoo-shoo who awaited us at the hotel. In return, Joe gave Marty and me tickets for an Air France flight to Paris at 8:00 that same morning. It was too dangerous now for us to remain in New York.

As for the Mexico City C-46–the errand that brought us here to the States in the first place–someone else would do the job. We were now too "hot."

A few days later, in Paris awaiting transportation to Zebra, I sat in a barber's chair reading the *Paris Herald–Tribune*. On an inside page was this item:

> Tripoli, Libya, Sept 12 (AP)–
> A mysterious explosion at the airdrome here wrecked a large hangar last night. Two Argentinean Air Force B-24 Liberator bombers were completely destroyed. The possibility of sabotage is being investigated.

Ladd and Bendix.

What a way to fight a war.

I never saw Daire or Dunne again. Nor Joe Shoo-shoo, although some years later I was questioned about him by an Israeli military attaché. It seemed that Joe Shoo-shoo, along with $50,000 he promised to turn over to the Israeli government, had vanished. It also seemed that this $50,000 was the exact sum Joe Shoo-shoo had allegedly extorted from Egyptian agents whose activities he had been assigned to monitor.

4.

Marty continued immediately on to Israel to join his family, but I managed to cajole the Little Men into allowing me a few extra days in Paris. Larry Raab was in town; he had brought the C-54 into Orly for engine overhaul, a five- or six-day undertaking. So, accompanied by Larry, I finally did relive the old days in Paris. Nothing had changed. The food was marvelous, the early autumn weather perfect, the women beautiful.

A splendid week we would not soon forget, that ended too soon, and we returned to the war.

But not to Zebra.

Zebra no longer existed.

The Czechs, bowing to American pressure, had ordered us out. Another example of that befuddled U.S. foreign policy, influenced no doubt by the British and their U.S. State Department Arabist allies. In the space of twenty-four hours the entire installation was packed up, loaded into our airplanes, and transported to Israel.

The European airlift was over.

TEN

THE END OF THE BEGINNING

In wartime your entire existence is accelerated. From survival to food to camaraderie, your very senses are heightened. The pleasures of Paris notwithstanding, I was anxious to rejoin ATC. I wanted to get back in the air, and see my friends, and hear again the bitches and gripes, the wild stories—and to share with them my own wild stories. I wanted to see Moonitz, and Kurtz, Styrak, Eichel, Steve Schwartz, Sy Cohen, Phil Schild, Hal Auerbach. Chinsky, Raisin, Cubernik, Katz, Maseng. Sam Lewis, Al Schwimmer, Ray Foster, Ben Sklar, Willie Sosnow. All of them.

I wanted to feel again that warm flush of achievement and self-esteem, strolling along a Tel Aviv boulevard knowing I was recognized as an American volunteer. I wanted that exquisite sense of acceptance and belonging. As I told Raab when we flew back to Tel Aviv after our memorable week in Paris and had just sighted the Israeli coast, I felt as though I was coming home.

Home, in late September—with the Czech airlift over and the full ATC complement now stationed permanently in Tel Aviv—was the Bristol Hotel. If the Park Hotel was a three-star establishment, the Bristol was, generously, a half-star. It was no beachfront resort: a three-story, utilitarian building on a residential street surrounded by apartment buildings and small businesses that had been requisitioned for ATC's quarters. Our meals were prepared in the hotel's kitchen and eaten, family style, in the dining room. The Bristol Hotel resembled a barracks, which in truth it was, for in addition to ATC it also housed some dozen or so new pilots who had arrived during my four-week absence.

These were mainly fighter pilots, non-Jews, mercenaries rumored to be receiving handsome salaries. Additionally, however, the newcomers included a few American-Jewish volunteer multi-engine pilots who replaced ATC people sent to Italy to initiate a cadet training program for qualified young Israelis.

When I said "family style," I meant this literally. Women and children now lived with us. Families of married pilots and crewmen. Norman Moonitz's wife, Lillian, and their five-year-old son, Michael. Ruth Kurtz and her five-year-old, David. Marty Ribakoff's wife and three youngsters. Phil Schild's wife, Sylvia, and young daughter, Betty.

And others, even some girlfriends.

There were other changes. At Aquir, our once silvery C-46s were now a drab, camouflaged brown. Gone was the blue LAPSA logo, RX numbers, and Panamanian flag. Stenciled now on the airplanes' wings and rudder were Israeli Air Force numbers—and the Star of David.

A new airlift was in progress.

Operation Ten Plagues.

2.

From the air, during the day, it resembled a vast, undulating brown carpet. Waves of heat shimmered upward from it. At night, it was a cold and impenetrable blackness suggestive of some long dead alien planet.

It was the Negev. The arid, inhospitable desert in southern Israel encompassing nearly three fourths of the territory allocated to the new state. The very heart of the nation, defended valiantly from the start by a single, stubborn, Palmach brigade. But now, in September 1948, the Egyptian army pushing into the Negev threatened to overwhelm the besieged defenders and thereby split the country in two.

Relief overland was not possible. The only road into the Negev, one narrow artery—more literally a trail—came down from the north and wound uncertainly in and around the endless sand like a dotted pencil line on a map.

ATC was asked to prepare a plan to airlift supplies and soldiers. The fact that security mandated all operations to be conducted at night was almost academic: not a single airstrip existed in that desert, certainly none to accommodate our heavy transport aircraft. The runways would have to be built from scratch from sand.

Leo Gardner was sent into the Negev to survey the feasibility of establishing two airstrips. Leo, a thirty-year-old former USAAF transport pilot and one of the first Schwimmer volunteers, reported that building the strips was impossible, impractical, and unthinkable.

And therefore could be done.

And it was.

Engineers were sent in. Within days, two airstrips materialized, gouged out of the sand. The strips, called "Dustbowl One" and "Dustbowl Two," were constructed on a seven degree grade for our C-46s to land on the upslope and take off downslope. Tricky enough, and of course even more so for night landings and takeoffs, but workable. Workable, that is, when your visibility was not obscured by the constantly whirling sand.

Although the distance between Aquir and the Dustbowl strips was only thirty miles, flight time each way was thirty minutes. To avoid Egyptian ground fire we climbed to 5,000 feet southbound, 7,000 feet returning. We flew from dusk to dawn, slept through the day, then flew again all night.

The same night of the day I arrived from Paris I was flying to the Negev. Three flights that first night, four the following night. And, for the next two weeks, at least three nightly. The procedure never varied. You took off from Aquir loaded with ammunition or food or soldiers—or all three—climbed to altitude over Aquir, then turned south for the Dustbowl strips. Off to the left and right, east and west, in between the constant total darkness below, you saw the flashes of artillery from the guns of both sides. It provided a kind of corridor. You radioed the strip for runway lights—a single line of flare pots—and you landed. The flare pots were immediately extinguished. By the time you coasted to a stop on the upslope you had reached the unloading area. You turned the airplane around so you were headed downslope for takeoff and cut the engines. Before the propellers had stopped turning, a truck had backed to the airplane's door and soldiers were clambering aboard to unload the cargo.

I use "soldiers" generically, for not all served in the military. Some were old, men and women, many certainly grandparents. Others were very young, boys and girls, preteeners. They sweated as hard as the soldiers. These civilians, most of them sabras or long-tenured immigrants, came from nearby *kibbutzim*. All wore pistols or carried rifles, even the women.

I know it was here, in the Negev, that for the first time I saw another side of Israel. Not the well-dressed, caste-conscious, highly educated western European professionals or intelligentsia. Or the myopic religious zealots with visions of recreating a biblical kingdom. Or Zionists envisioning a socialist paradise. These were farmers and artisans, Jews with no religious or political pretensions, pioneers whom we likened to our own American pioneers. A conveniently romantic image, I suppose, but these were the people who had made a desert bloom.

This, in the vernacular of four-and-one-half decades later, was what it was all about, and was vividly demonstrated to me one night at Dustbowl Two.

We had delayed our takeoff to await the arrival of a squad of Palmach being rotated out. I went into the operations shack. Shack, literally, for it consisted of little more than a few wooden boards nailed haphazardly together. It functioned as a control tower, tool shed, and living quarters for the mechanics and other ground personnel stationed at the strip.

A youngster, a sabra, a girl no older than fifteen, was alone in the shack. She was eating stew from a can of U.S. Army rations heated on a Primus stove. She wore blue jeans, an army shirt, and a khaki forage cap under which she had neatly tucked her red hair. The building's only illumination was a kerosene lantern hung from a nail high on one wall. When the wind blew through the loose wall boards the lantern flickered brightly and highlighted her face, the delicate feminine contours of her mouth and chin. I never would have guessed her for a girl otherwise, for her voice sounded like that of any adolescent boy.

She spoke English quite well, offering me some stew in a mess-kit dish, which I refused. I said, importantly, "I had enough of that stew in the American army."

"I was right!" she said. She nodded, pleased. "I knew you were American!"

"Almost all of us here are American," I said. "In the air force, I mean. I thought everybody knew that?"

The admonition in my voice seemed to embarrass her and she apologetically explained that this was only her second day here at the strip. She was from a kibbutz ten miles to the south.

Now I felt foolish. As a kind of apology of my own I said, "You look American yourself."

She did not appear particularly flattered but was polite enough to pretend the remark a compliment. "Thank you," she said.

"It's true," I said, which it really was. In bobby socks, wool skirt, and cashmere sweater she might have been any American teenager. Except for the pistol butt protruding from her belt.

She said, "Is your home in New York?"

"Yes," I said, believing she could more easily relate to that than a small town outside Boston.

"I would like to go to New York some day," she said.

"To live?" I asked.

"Oh, no," she said. "Only to see it. The largest city in America, they say."

"In the world," I said. "It's a wonderful place. If you went there you could wear nice clothes and everybody would think you were American. You'd be just as pretty as any American girl. You could go to parties and dances. You'd love it."

"American girls?" she said. "Is that all they do? Go to parties and dances?"

"Girls your age," I said.

She shook her head solemnly. "I would not be very happy if all I did was wear nice clothes and go to parties. I am much happier here in my kibbutz, doing useful things."

Useful things, I thought, such as building a country. And I thought of the fifteen-year-old sisters of some of my Haverhill friends. They joined Junior Hadassah or Hadassah Buds or similar organizations, all designed to inculcate into those children a sense of their Jewishness. Which was almost pathetic, I thought. Almost laughable when you saw how Jewishness was manifested here: a fifteen-year-old in a desert shack, eating canned stew, a pistol tucked into her Levis.

It was also in the Negev that for the first time I directly

204

encountered Haganah combat soldiers. My only previous contact with Israeli Army ground troops had been those smartly uniformed, British-trained officers you ran into in Tel Aviv hotel bars. The ones we admired when they deferred to us, and resented when they did not.

It was at Dustbowl One this time. We had brought in barbed wire and artillery shells. We were to bring back some dozen wounded *Palmachnicks*, litter cases. They were already on board with an army nurse in attendance. Repair of a defective right engine propeller governor delayed our takeoff, which meant at least an hour's layover. I had intended to stay in the airplane and catch some sleep, but the whole cabin reeked with the astringent aroma of antiseptics and the foul odor of festering wounds and body gases. I not only felt guilty for feeling inconvenienced by this, I also felt inferior. I could hardly compare my contribution to the war with theirs.

I decided to go into the operations shack for coffee. In the cabin the litters were placed on the floor across the width of the airplane. It left a narrow aisle on one side. I hurried past the wounded men but near the door one man reached out to grasp my hand. He was a burn case, his face and body swathed in grimy, salve-stained bandages.

In English, he said, "Thank you."

"For what?" I asked.

He spoke little English, this soldier; the nurse, never taking her eyes from the IV bottle she was adjusting, translated. The soldier seemed to smile, although through the bandages you could not see this. It was the sudden brightness in his eyes. "For helping us," the soldier said in Hebrew, which the nurse translated.

"Tell him I'm Jewish," I said to the nurse.

She did, and the soldier grasped my hand again. He nodded. He knew.

3.

In mid-October, after ATC flew 5,000 tons of munitions and 10,000 troops into the besieged Negev, the Israelis broke out and routed the Egyptians. While not the beginning of the end it was, in Churchillian rhetoric, the end of the beginning.

The beginning of the end came shortly thereafter in the biggest tactical aerial operation of the war.

Mass bombing of Egyptian and Syrian positions.

Mass bombing? With three B-17s?

Three B-17s, plus seven *C-46s*.

For four days we flew round-the-clock. Our navigators, doubling as bombardiers, sighted on the B-17s leading the formation. When we reached the approximate position where the B-17s had dropped their bombs, the navigator signaled the bomb-chuckers.

Bombing from a C-46, of course, required the services of bomb-chuckers, all of whom by now were young Israeli soldiers remarkably proficient in that new "specialty." Indeed, bomb-chucking had been refined into a military science all unto itself. Now the bombs were one-hundred pounders (and larger), secured to the C-46 cabin floor in specially designed metal trays that released one bomb at a time along little tracks built into the floor. This task was performed by one bomb-chucker who rolled the bomb to the open cabin door where, on either side of the door, webbed belts tethering them to the fuselage, stood two other bomb-chuckers. One young man pulled the bomb's pin, the other kicked it out the door. It was state of the art bomb-chucking.

We hit Damascus, Gaza, Majdal, and Faluja. One morning we massed thirteen aircraft: the three B-17s, six C-46s, one C-54, and three C-47 Dakotas flown by South African volunteers. The "bomber stream" was escorted by five Messerschmitts. Our objective was the railway station at Gaza where the Egyptians were known to have stored huge stocks of gasoline and oil.

After rendezvousing at 4,000 feet with the B-17s, we proceeded toward the target in a loose V. I was flying with Moonitz. Approaching Gaza, greasy black puffs of smoke began dotting the sky in an uneven ring over a small section of the city.

Moonitz stared interestedly at the still distant antiaircraft fire. "Ex-Nazis are supposed to be on those guns," he said. "But if those are Nazis, now I know why the Krauts lost the war!"

What he meant was that the Egyptians had deployed their batteries in a perfect circle around the target, thereby obligingly providing us the target's location. At night, flying toward the searchlights, it was even easier. The target lay precisely within the ring of lights.

I remember Moonitz's expression of quiet pride as he glanced around left and right of us at the other airplanes. "This," he said, "is an impressive show in any army!"

More impressive were the results. With no losses from the Gaza guns and only a few near-misses, the rag-tag "bombers" plastered that railway station. For days afterward, thick black smoke billowed up from the rubble.

Now, truly, was the beginning of the end. By November, the ground forces, following up on all fronts, had driven the invading Arabs back to, and in some cases slightly beyond, the partition lines.

The Air Force, which had quadrupled in size since July, doubled yet again when the Czechs finally agreed to sell Israel those forty British-manufactured Spitfire fighter airplanes. Simultaneously, the Yugoslavian government approved Operation Velveeta: permission for the Spitfires, en route from Czechoslovakia to Israel, to land for refueling in Yugoslavia.

Velveeta would be implemented in two stages, the first stage to start in December when our C-46s ferried the fighter pilots to an airfield, code-named "Alabama," near Dubrovnik on the Adriatic coast. From there the C-46s, navigating for the smaller aircraft, would shepherd the Spitfires back across the Mediterranean to Israel.

Operation Velveeta.

The war, for all practical purposes, was over.

My war, however, was just about to begin.

My personal war.

4.

Israel's national airline, El Al–in Hebrew, "To The Skies"–is today composed of a fleet of Boeing jetliners, 767s, 747s, 737s. To a man, El Al's captains are all former Israeli Air Force pilots, graduates of the IDF academies, indigenous Israelis, second and third generation sabras.

It was not always so.

When El Al began flying, in the late autumn of 1948, its equipment consisted of a single C-54: ATC's C-54. When an El Al flight was scheduled, the C-54 was removed from active military status and tugged into a hangar. Shortly afterward, her desert camouflage removed, carpeting laid on the aluminum cabin floor, bucket seats replaced with plush recliners, that same C-54–transformed now into a DC-4– rolled out of the hangar. Freshly scrubbed and shiny, atop her now silvery fuselage was a decal, a distinctive Hebrew and English El Al logo, and on her wings and rudder was a blue-stenciled international aircraft registration designator, 4X-ACA.

And, flown by a smartly uniformed ATC crew, off she went. A flight to Paris to pick up former U.S. Treasury Secretary Henry Morgenthau and convey him back to Israel for a state visit. Or Geneva for Dr. Chaim Weizmann, bringing the new president of Israel to his homeland. On that Geneva flight–the very first El Al flight–Hal Auerbach (for Dr. Weizmann's benefit given the Israeli name of Hillel Bahir) was the captain. From ideal weather to superb cuisine, it was a letter-perfect flight. Dr. Weizmann, understandably impressed, complimented "Captain Bahir" on the excellent service and proficiency of the crew, especially the fluent English spoken by all these "Israeli boys."

"I'm happy you noticed that, Mr. President," Auerbach replied. "You see, sir, for this flight we chose all college graduates!"

Returning from an El Al flight, the airplane was towed into the hangar again, airline markings removed, repainted, and sent back into combat action.

Until her next "airline" mission.

This was how El Al started, as a division of Air Transport Command. ATC, which once had been LAPSA, which once had been Service Airways, and had all originated with Al Schwimmer's American volunteers. Many of those men–especially those with professional aviation backgrounds–had come to believe that the embryonic airline represented their future. A bona-fide commercial airline where qualified aircrewmen would not be victimized by the anti-Semitism of American companies.

But the position of ATC Director was held by an Israeli, Munya Mardor. All his administrative assistants were Israelis. The Americans functioned only in operational capacities. In other words the Americans ran ATC, but the Israelis controlled it.

Which, albeit with considerable bitching and resentment, the Americans accepted. They assumed that when the airline became a reality they–those interested in an airline career–would be the first hired. A not unreasonable assumption, which helped maintain a certain calm and spirit of cooperation.

Until a rumor spread that those infrequent El Al European flights were conducted on an actual commercial basis. With paying passengers, revenue freight, and an Air France mail sub-contract.

A commercial enterprise whose employees received no wages? Into whose pocket was this money going? Who were the entrepreneurs reaping profit at the expense of their workers? For this we had volunteered our services? For this we had risked our lives? This was our reward?

Aircrewmen of the world, unite.

The source of the rumor was unknown but it was reminiscent of Panama and Mexico City, those stories of similar commercial ventures using our aircraft and crews. Our toil and talent exploited for other's profit. Our sweat and blood. The Mexico City incident had nearly precipitated a minor insurrection.

This one would be worse.

To be sure, it was not the El Al story alone that started the trouble. Perhaps it was that the war was winding down. We had little to do other than sit around the Bristol playing gin or poker. Or indulge in petty rivalries and internecine bickering. Perhaps it was the weather: the winter rains had begun. Flying was minimal, even training missions.

Perhaps it was the growth of the tactical air force and the commensurate decline of ATC's importance. Or it might have been the influx of mercenaries. Whatever the reason, it was only another example of an accident—more accurately, an incident—waiting to happen, and it did.

The first meeting was held in the Bristol Hotel room of a pilot I shall call Harry Berger. I was there, along with Moonitz, Marty Ribakoff, Ray Kurtz, and Gordon Levett.

Harry Berger, a one-time Trans-Caribbean Airways pilot, had joined LAPSA in its waning days. One of the Constellations's captains before its crash, he now flew as a regular captain on the El Al flights. He had organized the meeting, as he said, "to protest the current bullshit situation."

" . . . if I'm going to fly for a commercial airline," he said, "I want commercial pay."

"Maybe you should go back to Trans-Carib, Harry," Gordon Levett said quietly. Gordon was English, one of ATC's two non-Jewish captains, but totally and selflessly dedicated to Israel.

"If this keeps up, maybe I will," Harry said. "Look, guys, we're being taken advantage of. It's one thing if we're fighting a war, but the war is over. Why should we fly a commercial airline on wartime pay?"

Ray Kurtz said, "Nobody told me the war's over." Ray's massive frame and muscular features belied his basic gentleness. But he disliked Harry Berger and never pretended otherwise. "You know something we don't, Harry?"

Harry's face tightened belligerently but before he could reply, Marty Ribakoff spoke up for him. "Come on, Ray," Marty said. "If it's not over, it might as well be." He continued to Harry, "What's exactly on your mind?"

"I say we should ask for a decent wage scale," Harry said. "A civilian scale—"

"—hold it a second," said Gordon Levett. "You don't know yet if this story about commercial flights is true. Wouldn't it be a good idea to check it out first?"

"Who do you check it out with?" I asked. "Ben-Gurion?" I recall this so well: I still hear my own voice and remember my excitement, my sense of importance. They had invited me into the meeting, the only non-captain. I had to say something to substantiate such recognition, didn't I? Besides, I had been consistently vocal regarding what I believed undue and unnecessary Israeli interference with ATC. ATC, our own exclusive little American club. Members only.

Harry laughed unhumorously. "Whoever we check it out with, you think they'd tell us the truth? Marty, did they tell you the truth when they brought your wife and three little kids over and promised decent living conditions? So where do you live? Right here, in the Bristol, with the rest of us. A whole family in two lousy hotel rooms!"

Marty seemed almost embarrassed. "My family's not the only one in this country with poor housing. Something'll open up, we can wait." He looked at Moonitz. "I don't hear you complaining."

Moonitz shrugged. "I only have one kid."

Ray Kurtz said, "I'm not complaining, either. Neither is my wife. So Harry, why don't you take your story over to the

Yarkon and ask Haman Shamir if it's true or not."

"You don't mean the Yarkon," Harry said sarcastically. "You mean that big building in Jaffa. The one they took over for ATC Headquarters, with Munya sitting in his office giving us all orders."

"I don't care who you ask, just find out if it's true," Marty said.

"And if it turns out true, if they really are making money off the flights, what will you do?" Harry asked.

"I won't be too goddam happy about it, I'll tell you that," Marty said.

Harry said, "That doesn't answer my question."

"I'll do something," Marty said. "I don't know what, but something."

Gordon Levett said, "I don't think you know what the hell you're talking about, any of you. I think you've all gone bonkers."

Ray Kurtz said, "Get the facts, Harry, and then come back to us. The facts."

"Hey, I'm only trying to help you people," Harry said.

"That's what Hitler used to tell the Jews," Ray said.

But even had Harry Berger obtained the facts it would have made no difference, for long before the rumor of revenue-producing El Al flights could be proven or disproven, it was given credence by the emergence of another rumor whose veracity was unquestioned.

This second rumor was confirmed in an Air Force Headquarters directive: ATC would no longer function as a quasi-autonomous, civilian organization. The unit was to be integrated—a clumsy euphemism for *inducted*—into the Army of Israel. As of January 1, 1949, ATC would become the 106th Air Transport Squadron of the Israeli Air Force. All flying personnel were to receive an officer's rank in the Israeli Air Force.

And so began my war.

ELEVEN

THE ULTIMATUM

. . . the following agreement shall be in effect for one year from the date of signature between the undersigned and the government of Israel:

The undersigned will be commissioned as an officer of the Israel Defense Forces, at a wage no less than he currently receives in his volunteer status.

The undersigned agrees to accept and obey rules as set forth by the Israel Defense Forces and the existing military laws of the State of Israel . . .

This was the text of the document to be presented us by the Air Force. No one had yet been offered an actual contract, and no official word had come down. Information concerning the document, and a true copy, was provided by sources close to Air Force HQ.

But no one denied its existence, even those in the know at

the Yarkon, although Air Force Chief of Staff Aharon Remez and his deputy, Haman Shamir, had thus far not been directly confronted. By now the story was widely circulated, the main topic of conversation, taking precedence even over the news that the first phase of Operation Velveeta would commence in three weeks, on December 18.

We talked about it, first in small groups gathered in the Bristol Hotel dining room or in someone's room. The meetings grew larger, and louder. "Showdown" and "acting like men" and "American pride" became battle cries. No meal or casual drink or card game was complete without a personal or hearsay anecdote of "Israeli ingratitude," "Israeli inefficiency," "Israeli selfishness." And all this heaped atop the El Al profit-making story, which by now not one pilot or his wife—or child—doubted. And all compounded by the very existence of the dozen-plus non-Jewish mercenaries whose presence under these circumstances could not have been more untimely.

For me, the issue was clearly defined. ATC was a civilian, all-foreign volunteer operation and therefore sacrosanct. In my view, ATC had brought in every gun, every bullet, every bomb, every airplane. Every screwdriver. As far as I was concerned, without ATC there might have been no State of Israel. As far as I was concerned, ATC was the new Messiah.

Messiahs are not drafted into the army.

Not even into a Jewish army.

It was like a divine vision. A heavenly message. I thought that all at once it answered the question that had plagued and confused me from the beginning: as a Jew, did I owe an especial allegiance to Israel?

The Air Force, by arbitrarily deciding I should become a member of the armed forces of Israel—simply, it seemed, because I happened to be a Jew—had provided me with the answer.

The answer was No.

An unequivocal No, resoundingly seconded by nearly all

my American and Canadian volunteer colleagues, for whom the same question had now been answered.

So now we knew where we stood. And we knew what to do about it.

In unity there is strength.

As in all such movements, if "movement" is a valid characterization—"lynch mob" might be more accurate—the loudest and most animated become, if not the leaders, at least the spokesmen. I was loud, one of the loudest, so I became a spokesman-leader. Or, perhaps even more accurately, one of the instigators. In point of fact, one of the chief instigators.

On a rainy Sunday evening, some forty ATC aircrewmen gathered in the Bristol Hotel dining room to state their case (or cause) to Al Schwimmer. Although he now held the title of Air Force Director of Engineering, he was the man who had brought most of us into ATC, the man for whom we worked. We merely tolerated the Israelis in titular capacities, the Munyas and the others. To us Al Schwimmer was and always would be The Boss.

His calm, quiet voice was the sound of reason, of logic, common sense. He said that yes, of course he had heard the rumors of ATC being inducted into the military. Yes, he believed them true (once and for all silencing any doubters), but . . .

But.

" . . . try to understand the Air Force's position," Al Schwimmer said. "They feel, rightly or wrongly, that ATC has become too big to continue as an independent outfit. It was different in the old days. In the old days the Air Force wanted ATC to operate independently. Now, in their judgment, it won't work."

He elaborated briefly on this—the legal, political, and military ramifications—and then someone asked the obvious question. "Where do you stand on this, Al?"

He had been packing tobacco into the battered Meerschaum pipe he always carried. He said nothing for a moment. He continued packing the pipe, very carefully, very deliberately. And then he replied.

"I happen to agree."

The whole room fell abruptly silent. You could hear cars sloshing along the wet street, and the steady beat of the rain on the pavement. You could hear people in the smoke-filled room breathing, lighting cigarettes, shifting nervously in their chairs.

You could hear the dismay.

They had not expected this of The Boss. Now, suddenly, everyone had to stop and think. Schwimmer wanted us to consider the Air Force's position. But we already knew their position: ATC was not to remain an independent entity. Yes, it had grown, but so what? Look what we had accomplished. Look at the record.

Someone called out, "What about El Al?"

Schwimmer impatiently waved the unlit Meerschaum pipe. "The stories about money being made? I'm trying to check it out, but personally I don't believe it."

Come on, Al, I told him in my mind, you can't get off that easy. I said, "Suppose it's true?"

A chorus of voices exhorted him to answer *that* one!

Al waved the pipe again, this time a signal for silence. "If it happens to be true, which I tell you I honestly doubt, then we'll deal with it."

"How?" I asked.

"I don't know," he said. "I don't want to even think about it until I have the facts, one way or the other. So let's put that aside and get back to the main issue." He paused to light the pipe now, drawing on it slowly and exhaling a slender flawless smoke ring. He seemed unhurried, and I remember resenting what I considered deliberate theatrics. Later, he confessed privately that yes, it was deliberate, but not for any effect. He needed the precious time to think.

"First of all, none of you can be forced into joining the army if you don't want to," Al Schwimmer said. "Believe me, nobody's holding a gun to anybody's head. Those who want to sign on, can. Those who don't . . . don't."

And that was his mistake.

For the obvious response to that was, "What happens to the people who choose not to join the Israeli army?"

An excellent question, none better, and one for which Al Schwimmer had no ready answer. But I did. I said, "I'll tell you what happens: we're all free to go back to where we came from! New York, Detroit, L.A., Miami, Montreal, Toronto, Wabash, Indiana, or Kalamazoo, Michigan!"

And Haverhill, Massachusetts.

"In other words," someone shouted from the rear of the room, "we're out!"

Out.

"Nobody said anybody'll be out of anything yet," Schwimmer said quietly, "But since you brought it up, what do you think you'll be out of? Out of what you came here for in the first place? What was that? A payoff? What payoff? I thought you all came here to help fight a war. To build a country. All right, you've done that. And now the country you came here to build has to think of the future. *Its* future, not yours."

We were in no mood for such overt flag-waving, not even from Al Schwimmer. The group reaction was immediate, and negative, and definitely surprised Schwimmer.

"Come on, Al, we tied our future in with theirs, didn't we, for Christ's sake!"

"My God, where did the bastards ever get the *chutzpah* to think they could pull such a sleazy stunt?"

"That's gratitude for you!"

"We risk our asses for them, and this is what we get to show for it!"

"We're *Americans*! We can't join a foreign army, goddamit!"

And more of the same, and more.

I was pleased no one mentioned what I believed the most

salient point of all, and the most apparent. I wanted the satisfaction of bringing it up myself: " . . . and by the way, guys, this little stunt of putting us in the army is supposed to happen two weeks after Velveeta! *After* Velveeta! Get it? *After* we've brought in the Spitfires! So we'll have done our jobs and they couldn't care less whether or not we sign into the army! They won't need us any more!"

I avoided facing Schwimmer directly. I could feel his displeasure. But to hell with him. The shouts and catcalls of agreement vindicated me. And I loved the feeling of power all this gave me.

Schwimmer raised his hands for silence. His voice hardened just slightly, but enough to carry that edge of authority and respect. When Al Schwimmer talked, you listened.

"I don't see anything so terrible about what the Israelis are asking," he said. "I happen not to believe they owe you— owe us," he added carefully. "They don't owe us a goddamned thing! If anything, we owe them!"

What, Al? What do we owe them?

"Our loyalty," he said.

But to preclude any debate on that delicate subject he hastened to say that this was his opinion, and that he felt he owed us some loyalty, too. He would therefore convey to the Air Force our vehement opposition to the induction plan. The Air Force, meaning Chief of Staff, Colonel Aharon Remez, and the Deputy Chief of Staff, Lieutenant Colonel Haman Shamir. It was evident that one or both of these gentlemen had miscalculated.

2.

The Air Force's response was two days in coming. Two days of more meetings and more rhetoric. More rumors: El Al was being financed privately by one Harold Rothenberg who owned the Palestine Electric Company. The mercenary wage, initially reported as $1,000 monthly, was really $1,500. The Air Force considered Schwimmer too powerful and was attempting to ease him out. Orders had been placed in the United States for four Douglas DC-4s. Once they got you in the army, they would demand you renounce your American citizenship. Once you were in the army, you *automatically* renounced it.

And on, and on.

It only fed our evangelistic fervor, for by now we were entirely convinced of the righteousness of our cause. By "we," I do not mean to suggest there were no dissenters: there were, several, but vastly outnumbered and their dissent was, at best, mild and measured. They were loath to offend good and trusted friends, men with whom they had fought side by side for a common goal. Men now in need of their support; a united front was essential.

In the two days, also, the main body elected a three-man committee to represent them. It was assumed Colonel Remez would desire a face-to-face explanation from his discontented ATC colleagues. The committee consisted of Norman Moonitz, Ray Kurtz—and me.

The deaf leading the blind.

So, again, we gathered after dinner in the Bristol dining room to receive Schwimmer's report. He wasted no words. "They refuse to discuss it."

It was like feeding raw meat to a school of hungry sharks. *They* refuse? Who the hell are *they* to refuse anything? Refuse? We weren't in their fucking army yet! Did they think we were a bunch of Boy Scouts?

Schwimmer raised his voice above the clamor. "Calm down, dammit! Let's figure out an intelligent way to handle this."

Harry Berger leaped to his feet, nearly upending the empty bridge chair in front of him. "Al, you know there's only one way to deal with these people! Give 'em a dose of their own medicine. I'm sick of all this! For my part, I'm willing to pack in right now and call it quits!"

"That's right, Harry!" someone else shouted. "Let's see them run their great air force with their high-priced mercenaries! If they don't want to talk to us, they sure don't need us anymore!"

And more of this, and more, all adding up to a consensus:

We had "asked," now we would demand.

Demand.

But, again—always—it was from Al Schwimmer we sought direction. "If you must 'demand,' don't antagonize," he said. "A tall order, I know, but it's the only way you'll accomplish anything."

Harry Berger said, "The first thing to 'accomplish' is either get rid of the mercenaries, or else put us on the same pay scale! I'm goddam sick and tired of doing the same work they're doing for a tenth of the money!"

"Harry, you *volunteered* your services," Al Schwimmer said.

"Not to fly commercially, I didn't!" Harry replied.

Schwimmer said, "I thought all this was about the army thing, not a wage scale?"

"It's all part of the same plot," Harry Berger said. "They get us in the army, they don't have to pay us. Come on, Al, it's plain as the nose on your face!"

The mob yelled their approval.

I said, "Let's write a letter to Remez, a group letter to put him on notice that none of us will ever go into the army! Signed by everybody. Everybody!" I waited for the cheers and shouts of encouragement to quiet. I said to Schwimmer, "What do you think of that, Al?"

"I think it stinks," he said.

But I suggested we put it to a vote. The vote was unanimous. The few dissenters were persuaded that the letter could be construed only as a not unreasonable request for the Air Force to reconsider the January 1 directive.

2 December, 1948

FROM: AIR TRANSPORT COMMAND
TO: CHIEF OF STAFF, ISRAELI AIR FORCE

SUBJECT: ARMY SERVICE

1. It has been brought to the attention of the persons named below that the Chief of Staff refuses to discuss with representatives of Air Transport Command an Israeli Air Force directive dated 1 January, 1949, said directive which concerns the contemplated induction of Air Transport Command into the Israel Defense Force.

2. The persons named below wish to go on record as stating their disapproval of such a directive.

3. The persons named below consider themselves civilians employed by a civilian contract carrier, and have no intention to change that status.

All forty-two men present signed the letter, a letter I had composed and typed. Schwimmer did not conceal his displeasure. We were playing with fire, he said, but agreed to take the letter to the Yarkon.

This time the response was instantaneous. Colonel Remez agreed to meet with the committee. He had finally seen the light. Seen the light? It was a thousand-watt Klieg light beamed straight into his face.

Schwimmer suggested we choose a different committee. One, in his words, that might be, " . . . well, let's say a little easier-going."

He was howled down. I can still see a pilot I'll call Sid Glickman, his face glistening with perspiration, screaming with clenched fist at Schwimmer. "No, Al, no changes! They'll know just what to say! They'll put those guys in their place! Sign into the army, bullshit!"

3.

Aharon Remez was a quiet, intense man of twenty-eight. Heavy-framed, leathery-faced, thick brown hair chronically rumpled, a classic sabra. He had served in the RAF in World War II and, long before we arrived with the Messerschmitts and the B-17s, he had flown the Taylor Cubs and Austers of Haganah's "Primus Air Force." He had paid his dues.

He was dedicated to the establishment of a true, indigenous, and independent Israeli Air Force. That the present composition of this air force was nearly one hundred percent foreign volunteers—most of them, fittingly, Jews—was an indignity he could temporarily endure.

It had never occurred to him that his Jewish volunteers might not desire Israeli citizenship, let alone object to induction into the army. The protests, therefore, came as a distinct surprise and shock.

We met one late afternoon in Colonel Remez's Yarkon Hotel office. Moonitz, Kurtz, and I sat in folding chairs placed in a semicircle before Remez's desk. A few feet away was Schwimmer and, facing him on Remez's side of the desk, the Deputy Chief of Staff, Haman Shamir.

Everyone was at first relaxed and amiable. Tea or soft drinks were offered, cigarettes lighted, a few bad jokes exchanged. Surprisingly good humor under the circumstances. It was a little disconcerting.

Haman Shamir said, "Well, I hear you fellows have a few gripes you want to get off your chests. So speak up and tell us about it. That's what we're here for, you know."

He appeared to have addressed me. Everyone looked at me. I stared at the large framed photograph on the wall behind Remez's head: the three B-17s flying in formation over the Tel Aviv skyline, their olive-drab fuselages emblazoned with white Star of David roundels. I had been rehearsing my presentation but now the words seemed trapped in my throat. Whenever I saw Haman Shamir I was always reminded of Panama, that eloquent plea for our understanding and cooperation, and his ready acknowledgement that our services were so essential to Israel's survival. But Schwimmer told me of Haman's outrage at our letter and I had promised myself not to let him intimidate me. Now, facing him, it was not so easy.

It was Moonitz who finally spoke, and to Remez. "We want to talk about this army story," he said. "About putting us in the army."

Remez glanced, perplexed, at Haman. Haman said, "What is it you want to know?"

I found my voice. "First, is it true?"

"Yes, it is true," said Remez. He had a deep, gravelly voice that intensified his heavy accent. This time he spoke slowly and distinctly. He wanted himself clearly understood. "Each man will be required to sign a contract that we call The Conditions of Service. It is for one year, at a minimum salary of $150 monthly for single men, up to $450 for married men. More than your present wage scale and much more, believe me, than Israeli officers are paid."

"Nearly twenty times more!" Haman said. "The average wage of an Israeli soldier is two pounds: eight dollars."

"Haman, we aren't Israeli soldiers," Ray Kurtz said. "And what makes you think we can sign into the Israeli army anyway?"

"That's right," I said. "We'll lose our citizenships." I pulled my passport from my shirt pocket and recited a paragraph on the last page: "' . . . American nationality may be lost through taking an oath or making a declaration of allegiance to, or serving in the military forces of a foreign state.'"

Remez gestured impatiently at the passport as I slipped it back into my pocket. "We can see to it that you have no trouble with your government," he said.

"How?" Moonitz asked.

"Norman, for God's sake, after all you've been through here, can't you take our word for it?" Haman said.

"Frankly, Haman, when it comes to this—" Moonitz leaned over and tapped the top of the passport protruding from my shirt pocket. "Frankly, I don't take anybody's word."

"Is that your main objection, Norman?" Remez asked. "Problems with the American government?"

"No, Aharon, that's only part of it," Moonitz said. "I didn't come here to join the army. I don't think any of us did. I just got out of one army, I'm not about to go into another."

I glanced at Schwimmer. His eyes were calm, almost contemplative, but his mouth and jaw were set rigidly. I felt bad for him. We had put him in an awkward position. Now he looked at me and shrugged. I could read his mind: okay, you asked me to arrange this meeting, I did, so now put your money where your mouth is.

I said to Remez, "Aharon, why are you so determined to have us sign into the army? Why is it necessary?"

It was a foolish question, although I did not think so then. Only much later did I realize—more accurately, did I allow myself to realize—why it was inevitable that ATC could not retain its autonomy. It had grown too large, too unwieldy. The Air Force could no longer tolerate this group of free-wheeling Americans, these self-proclaimed soldiers-of-fortune, these would-be adventurers, gamblers, lovers, gourmets.

These Bagel Lancers.

Aharon Remez was not so unkind as to put it in those terms, but that is certainly what he meant when he said, "We have reached a point in our growth where without military discipline, we will have chaos. Anarchy. Can't you see this?"

"I can only see that we've done pretty well not being in the army," I said. "I don't think it's fair to ask us to change now."

Ray Kurtz was growing impatient. "Look, Aharon, we made our feelings plain in the letter–"

"–what letter?" Remez asked.

I glanced at Schwimmer again. He shrugged; he shared our surprise at Remez's apparent unawareness of the letter. He said, "I gave it to Haman."

Remez whirled to Haman. "What letter?"

"Oh, just something they sent up," Haman said.

"What kind of letter?" Remez asked.

I said to Remez, "Do you mean to say Haman didn't show you the letter? Isn't that why you agreed to meet with us? Because of the letter?"

"I know of no letter," Remez said. "I agreed to the meeting because Haman asked me to." He turned to Haman. "Now I want to see this letter."

Without a word, Haman rose and left the office. He returned almost immediately, letter in hand, accompanied now by Dov Kinardy. Kinardy, which was his Hebraic name, was a slender, bespectacled, pleasant-looking man of medium height. An American-born Israeli citizen, a graduate aeronautical engineer, he was Haman's deputy.

Remez read the letter. His face reddened. He read it once again. Then, holding it antiseptically between thumb and forefinger, he elevated it to eye level and let it drop. The single sheet of white paper fluttered down toward the desktop.

"This is disgraceful!" Remez cried. He smashed his fist down onto the paper, pinning it to the desktop. "You should be ashamed of yourselves! How dare you!"

"You can't send a letter like that," Kinardy said. He pulled the paper out from under Remez's fist and waved it in the air. "Where the hell are your brains? This is a military organization!"

"Maybe you're in a military organization, but we're sure as

hell not," Ray Kurtz said, as Kinardy put the letter back on the desk. He leaned forward and flicked his fingers against the piece of paper. "Now let's cut the double-talk and decide what to do about this!"

"I want to tell you something, all of you," Remez said. He was straining for control. He peered a long moment at each of us. "As far as I am concerned, you are no better than mercenaries. Worse: you are traitors! Jewish traitors! Betrayers of the Jews!"

Ray Kurtz stood. He gripped the edge of Remez's desk. "'Jewish traitors?' That's what you call us? Jewish traitors! We risk our necks every day for this country, we sweat our buns off, our men are killed! And you call us Jewish traitors?"

Remez was unimpressed. "Your 'sacrifices' are no greater than those of any other Jew in this country!" He rose. He stood facing Ray an instant, then pushed back his chair and strode across the room to the door. He opened the door, turned, and called to Haman. "I'm through with them! You do anything you like!"

Slamming the door behind him, Remez left the office. For a moment the room was deathly silent. Then Haman rose and moved over to Remez's chair. He sank wearily down, at the same time gesturing Ray to resume his seat. "Listen, hear me out," Haman said. "These Conditions of Service aren't as bad as you think. In fact, they give you quite a break." He nodded at Kinardy. "Dov has a copy. Read it to them, Dov."

Moonitz said, "We already know what's in it, Haman. What we can't do is sign our names to a paper that says we agree to take an oath of allegiance to Israel."

"An oath of *obedience*," Haman said.

"The same difference," Ray Kurtz said.

Looking at Ray then–his eyes hard and angry, that square jaw menacingly jutted; and at Moonitz, lighting a cigarette and tossing the match disgustedly into an ashtray–not in my wildest imagination could I guess that three short years later I would be summoned out of a Brandeis University classroom for an urgent long-distance telephone call. From Moonitz, then an El Al Captain, who had just landed in New York from London with tragic news: Ray Kurtz, ferrying a Mosquito bomber to Israel, had gone down in a Greenland fjord. Neither he nor the wreckage was ever found.

Requiem for a Jewish traitor.

That afternoon in Aharon Remez's office, Ray faced Haman Shamir and said, " . . . Aharon said it was up to you. What's it to be?"

Haman flattened the letter on the desktop with the palm of his hand, placed a fingertip against the side of the paper, and slid it across the desk to the edge. The paper fell to the floor.

"That's your answer?" I asked Haman.

"That's my answer," he said.

Late that same evening after hours of debate, argument, name-calling and browbeating, another letter was drafted. Thirty-six signatures were affixed to this second document.

It was an ultimatum.

4.

4 December, 1948

FROM: AIR TRANSPORT COMMAND
TO: CHIEF OF STAFF, ISRAELI AIR FORCE

1. The following named ATC personnel hereby notify the above that, as of 0500 GMT, 9 Dec., 1948, all ATC operations will cease.

2. The following named ATC personnel hereby notify the above that the IAF Directive known as "Conditions of Service" is refused and rejected unconditionally.

3. The following named ATC personnel hereby notify the above that unless said directive is withdrawn on or before 9 Dec., 1948, the persons named below unconditionally resign from ATC and request immediate repatriation to their respective homes.

Al Schwimmer, called away to the B-17 base at Ramat David, was unable to be present when we reported the Yarkon meeting results to the assembled ATC group, and did not know of the ultimatum until after it was delivered. He had urged us to cool down and not do anything foolish. He felt sure Aharon Remez and Haman Shamir might also cool down and then he, Schwimmer, believed he could negotiate some compromise acceptable to all parties.

But "compromise" to me meant turning the other cheek, so I took it upon myself to deliberately not inform Schwimmer of our ultimatum plans. I knew he would be unalterably opposed and might express that opposition by delaying his Ramat David business to attend our meeting. As I said, when Al Schwimmer talked, you listened.

But then again, his presence might not have made the slightest difference. It was too late. We were storming the Bastille. No one could stop us, not even Schwimmer. Although this time six men refused to sign the letter, no one really cared or even condemned the dissenters. We were all too swept up in the frenzy.

Schwimmer, however, upon his return from Ramat David the following day, did relay to us the Yarkon's reaction to the ultimatum. Outwardly at least, Schwimmer did not appear offended or perturbed that the ultimatum was issued without his consent. If anything, he seemed frustrated. He asked everyone to gather shortly before lunch in the Bristol dining room. We were all there, all except Auerbach and his crew who had gone off on a flight to Paris, and some half-dozen others on various operational or training missions.

Schwimmer waited until the civilian kitchen crew finished setting the tables. Then, when the last worker disappeared through the swinging door into the kitchen, Schwimmer said, "I just came from the Yarkon." He paused to step into the center of the room; he wanted to be heard and seen by everyone. "There's an awful lot of activity going on down there, and it's all got to do with you. With your ultimatum."

He paused again to remove the Meerschaum from his pocket and I thought he was looking directly at me. I remember adjusting my chair just slightly so that someone's head obscured Schwimmer's view of me, and I remember saying to myself, Here it comes. Here's where he laces into you for not letting him know about it in advance.

But he cradled the pipe in the palm of his hand and said, "I'm going to ask you to retract your letter, your ultimatum. I think it was a rash, ill-considered act. A goddam silly one. But you did it, and there's no point kicking around the 'whys' and 'wherefores.' And there's also no point in reminding you this is as close to an act of mutiny as you'll ever see. That word, by the way–'mutiny'–hasn't been used yet. But it will."

He paused again, now to slip the pipe back into his jacket pocket. I glanced at Moonitz; he looked away, down at his hands, carefully examining his fingernails. Ray Kurtz was slouched in his chair, legs stretched far out before him, staring stonily at the wall behind Schwimmer. Someone in the back of the room changed chairs. The chair legs scraped abrasively along the hardwood floor.

"Oh, I'm as much to blame as anybody," Schwimmer continued. "Maybe even more: I should have been more forceful about it the first time. I should have known Aharon would resent it, and I should have seen where it would lead. So now I'm asking you to retract. I'm not doing this on behalf of the Air Force or anybody else. Only myself–and you. Because what you're doing–" he paused once again, now for breath, and I remembered that at the first meeting he had pointedly used the word "we," thereby in effect including himself in with us. Now he was distancing himself from us. I didn't blame him.

But he surprised me. "What we're doing is wrong," he said, not emphasizing the "we," but nevertheless making it implicit. "If ATC ceases operations, it jeopardizes the Velveeta project. And Velveeta's already balanced on the head of a pin. The Yugos are under tremendous pressure not to go through with it. Any delay, they're liable to use that as an excuse to pull out. Israel needs those Spitfires, I don't have to tell you how much.

"All right, sure, with or without the Spits we'll probably win the war now. And, sure, maybe the Air Force is inefficient and nepotistic, and maybe they do take advantage of us. But, believe me, this is not the way to cure any of that. All this can do is make it worse."

With this, he fell abruptly silent. For a few moments no one spoke; no one was certain he had finished. But then he returned to his table and sat down. Immediately, the room was loud with the buzz of private conversations. Moonitz's booming voice drowned out the others.

"Al, don't you think if we back down now they'll take it as a sign of weakness and really shove it into us?"

"No, Norm," said Schwimmer. "In fact, just the opposite. I think they realize we mean business and they'll be a lot more careful of what they say and what they do. I guarantee you they'll rethink the army affair."

Someone suggested the "rethinking" be done first, as a condition to withdrawing the ultimatum, instead of the other way around. Schwimmer said he thought that would be too humiliating for the Air Force; it would be an admission of their inability to control the men under their command.

" . . . but more important," Schwimmer continued. "If the ultimatum isn't withdrawn, it negates everything we came here to do. Everything we've done. Please, think about that."

Ray Kurtz said, "Al, you may be right, but I can see now that all this is more than just a protest about signing into the army. That part of it is just what's on the—" he groped for the proper word. "What's on top, on the surface. Sure, we bitch and gripe, and we piss and moan. We bitch about Israelis that don't know an airplane from a tractor but try to tell us how to do our job. We bitch about not getting enough money to feed our families. We bitch about flying in airplanes that we're afraid will fall apart if we breathe on them too hard!

"Listen, we take our lives in our hands every time we get off the ground, whether it's a check ride or a bombing run. We fly missions that even with the best equipment in the world nobody in their right minds would dream of doing. But we do it, and nobody asks for medals. Hey, I don't think anybody *wants* a medal! But it seems to me that it's going just a little too far, when either because you're a Jew or because you volunteered to come here, the State of Israel thinks they own you body and soul! No, fellas—for me at least—that's pushing it too far!"

The spontaneity of the applause and shouts of encouragement seemed to embarrass Ray. He seemed almost surprised at his own eloquence. He grinned self-consciously and switched into a kind of parody of his Brooklyn accent. "Youse hear me good, youse guys?" Immediately, he was serious again. "But now that I said all that, I have to also say it's got nothing to do with the fact that I love this country and I'm proud of what I did here!"

More shouts and applause. Ray looked at Schwimmer and nodded grimly. And then he turned and strode to the door. At the door he turned again. "You people do what you want. I'll go along with the majority, but I just want you to know how I feel!"

I had listened to Ray with half my mind still focused on Al Schwimmer's words: by sending the ultimatum we were negating everything we came here to do. The more I turned all this over in my head the more I wondered what I, personally, expected from it all. I loved and was proud of Israel as much as Ray Kurtz or anyone else, but hadn't I already decided that America, not Israel, was my country?

Then what did I want from Israel?

Fair treatment, I told myself, but I think I knew even then that fair treatment, as I defined it, was Aharon Remez or Haman Shamir personally apologizing, on behalf of the Air Force and the entire country, for their temerity in ever even considering ATC as a less than hallowed institution. And the apology should be followed by an Israeli demonstration of profuse gratitude for my heroic contribution to the nation's survival.

The meeting went on. More points and counterpoints. Someone proposed that we withdraw part of the ultimatum and, until our case was decided one way or the other, continue to fly operational missions. Velveeta, or any combat mission, but no more commercial transport flights.

Moonitz vetoed that. "Yeah, but they'll say it's not for us to determine what trips are commercial. And they'll be right!"

At this point we took a break. While most of the men barraged Schwimmer with questions, Moonitz and I went out onto the dining room terrace. It was a warm, sunny day, the first decent weather in nearly a week. We leaned our elbows on the stuccoed balcony rail and gazed out at the street. Directly adjacent to the hotel was the *Tenouva* dairy restaurant, a favorite ATC hangout. In good weather you could sit at the sidewalk tables and enjoy a breakfast of eggs and fried potatoes with onions, which we all preferred to the Bristol Hotel's typical Israeli breakfast of cheese, yogurt, and raw garden vegetables. Even more preferable, of course, were good old-fashioned bagels and lox, but the *Tenouva* manager claimed there was not a bagel to be had in all Israel. Unlikely as it sounds, it was true.

Bagels brought Ray Kurtz to mind. His wife's family owned a chain of small bakeries in New York. Ray once said if he settled here he would open a bagel factory.

232

I said, "That was quite a speech Kurtz made."

"Schwimmer's wasn't bad, either," Moonitz said. He turned, his back against the terrace rail now, and faced the dining room. He stared unseeingly through the open French doors into the room. The men milled about in groups of twos and threes but a number remained bunched around Schwimmer. There seemed to be more conviviality now, too.

"All the guys that signed," Moonitz said. "You think they'd like to change their minds? You think they'd like to retract?"

"I think they'd like nothing better," I said.

Moonitz said, "Schwimmer was right, you know."

"So was Kurtz," I said. I could still hear Ray's voice: " . . . *I love this country and I'm proud of what I did here!*" I wondered if Kurtz's pride about what we'd done here included being proud of the past few days. No, I thought, for sure not of the past few days, although at the same time I knew we were right. We were right, but we were wrong.

I fixed my eyes on the people at the *Tenouva* tables. Two young soldiers appeared to be enjoying their food while they flirted with a graying, motherly waitress. She seemed to be enjoying it, too.

I said to Moonitz, "I think we made a mistake."

I wish now I could say this came to me through some sudden insight, or a dramatic mind-opening revelation. For example, if I had happened to see at that moment an old man from my grandfather's *shtetl* in Russia, who knew my grandfather, and was the sole survivor of an entire family that had perished under the Nazis. And this old man embraced me and spread his arms in a broad circle to take in the tree-lined streets of Tel Aviv and the high-rise buildings and lush green parks, and thanked me for helping make it possible for him and others like him to continue to live as free human beings, and Jews.

If that had happened, then my decision to retract the ultimatum would have been admirably motivated. Instead of what really happened which was, simply, that I had recognized the whole business as nothing more than a childish tantrum.

Not to mention being just plain dumb.

So in reply to my suggestion that we had made a mistake, Moonitz said, "Yeah, I think maybe we did."

"What do you want to do?" I asked.

Moonitz said, "Schwimmer was right: this really does blow everything we came here for." He looked at me a moment, his forehead creased in a series of three almost geometrically perfect lines. "How did Al say it?"

"Negates it," I said.

"Yeah, negates it," Moonitz said.

The vote to withdraw the ultimatum was unanimous. Schwimmer scanned the upraised hands and raised his own hands in a victory gesture. "If it's okay with everybody, I'll get right down to the Yarkon and tell them!" He sprinted through the crowd to the door. At the door he stopped. "And guys . . . thanks!"

So the war was over and I had lost it. But I was glad it was over, for it had not been a dishonorable defeat. This is what I thought. I was wrong. It was far from over. It had hardly begun.

And there would be little honor.

TWELVE

DESTINATION ISRAEL

It rained for three straight days. Cold, unrelenting December rain that on the fourth day, all at once, stopped. The sky was blue and clear, the sun bright and warm. We considered it an omen, for we had heard that in return for our retracting the ultimatum the Yarkon would forego the Conditions of Service. We also heard that ATC was to remain an autonomous, civilian volunteer unit–at least until the war was officially over.

An omen, all right, the wrong kind. A day later, with the fine weather continuing, word came down of an impending Air Force action to once and for all "smash the mutineers." I remember telling someone it sounded like Haman Shamir's rhetoric. It was bullshit, I said.

It was no bullshit.

Five days after the withdrawal of the ultimatum, an Air Force sergeant, a young woman, smuggled a copy of a Yarkon document to her then boyfriend, an ATC captain. He showed it to Ray Kurtz and me.

It was simple and succinct. Each man who signed the ultimatum was required to retract his signature, in writing. Refusal to sign became an automatic request for repatriation.

(Name of individual)

I AGREE TO RETRACT MY SIGNATURE ON THE LETTER DATED 4 DECEMBER, 1948, ADDRESSED TO CHIEF OF STAFF, ISRAELI AIR FORCE

Signature . . . .

THE ABOVE NAMED REQUESTS IMMEDIATE REPATRIATION IF HIS SIGNATURE DOES NOT APPEAR AS INDICATED

You signed, or you were out.

Ray said, "Moon really called it, didn't he?" He was referring to Moonitz's prediction that the Air Force would interpret our withdrawal of the ultimatum as a sign of weakness and, as Moonitz had said, "really shove it into us."

Yes, I thought glumly, Moonitz called it. They were shoving it into us. But Moonitz wouldn't know about it for days, perhaps longer. He and Gordon Levett had gone off that morning as co-captains on an El Al Paris flight.

"Okay, so we stick together and refuse to sign their paper," I said. "What can they do? Repatriate all of us? It's a bluff. So we call it."

My flippancy angered Kurtz. He was like that; if you failed to see what he considered obvious, he immediately lost patience. "'Bluff?' What the hell's the matter with you? They may be dumb, them *mavins* in the Yarkon, but they're not crazy! They're not worried one fucking bit about us sticking together! 'Sticking together,' for Christ's sake! You just offer any one of our heroes a sure El Al captaincy and you'll see how fast he signs up. You think somebody like Harry Berger wouldn't sell you out in a second? Hey, smarten up!"

I said nothing. I was thinking of Moonitz's explosive temper, and of Gordon Levett who had been away on another El Al trip at the time of the first meeting and therefore had not signed that first letter, and would not have in any case. From the beginning Gordon was coldly disdainful of what he termed our "juvenile plotting." He had categorically refused to sign the second letter, the ultimatum. The whole bloody foolish affair disgusted him, he said. *We* disgusted him.

Although official word did not come down for another day, the rumor of the retraction-in-writing demand spread fast. There were howls of anguish and cries of outrage. To a man, all vowed not to place their names on this disgraceful document. We had retracted the ultimatum. We had admitted our error. Why rub our noses in it?

So we would stand fast, united.

Late the following morning I was summoned to Haman Shamir's office. I did not hurry; it was another lovely day, clear and sunny, warm for December. I stopped at the *Tenouva* for coffee. I was preparing to leave when Al Schwimmer and Ray Kurtz appeared. They joined me at the sidewalk table.

"You're on your way to the Yarkon?" Schwimmer said. It was a statement, not a question. "We were just there."

"Al resigned," said Ray. "So did I."

The words did not immediately register. "Resigned from what?" I asked Al.

"My lofty position," said Schwimmer. "I told Remez that if they insisted on going ahead with this retraction, I was through." He gestured the waiter for coffee for himself and Ray. "So I'm through."

"You *resigned*?" I said to Schwimmer, as though the word held some new, unfamiliar meaning. "Why the hell did you do that?"

237

Schwimmer laughed dryly. "Let's say it was 'irreconcilable differences.'"

I looked at Ray. "And you resigned, too?"

"At precisely 8:20 this morning, twenty minutes after I walked into Haman Shamir's office," Ray said. "Hey, he even sent a car over to the Bristol for me. He couldn't wait to tell me Harry Berger and two others already signed the retraction."

"The other two were captains?" I asked.

"Yeah, captains," said Ray. "Haman's no dummy. I'll lay a thousand to a penny he got to Berger last night and made a deal. Guaranteed the bastard an El Al captaincy. But that's how they'll break this thing wide open, you know. Get the captains to sign–especially the senior pilots–the other crewmen follow like blind mice."

"They don't have any choice, Ray," Schwimmer said.

Ray acknowledged this with a grim nod, then said to me, "Before you ask, I'll tell you: I signed."

At that instant the waiter brought their coffee; it was served in glasses that were inserted into small metal containers with handles, like the ice cream sodas in the States. The waiter fussed with napkins and sugar but Ray ignored him and continued speaking.

"Shamir showed me Berger's retraction, and the other two. So I signed . . . under protest," Ray said. "Whatever the hell that means," he added. "And then I resigned."

Schwimmer said to me, "Hesh, are you going to sign?"

"Do you want me to?" I was hoping he would say yes, relieving me of any decision. Make it easy for me. I, like Ray, would sign and then resign. Sign and Resign. A nice slogan.

But Schwimmer said, "I can't tell you what to do."

I looked at Ray. He shrugged.

"I don't know if I'll sign or not," I said, but I did know. I had known from the very first moment. In my mind, you see, it had all become confused with "Honor," and "Pride," and what I believed perhaps most important of all, "Principle."

Jewish honor, American pride, Personal Principle.

American honor, Jewish pride.

Honor, Pride & Principle, Inc.

A wholly owned corporation of which I was CEO and sole stockholder. It was not listed on the NYSE, or AMEX, or on the Bourse. Not even on the Tel Aviv Stock Exchange.

"I don't know," I said again.

"Do what you have to do," Ray said.

I remember almost laughing; those were my mother's exact words the day I informed her and my father I had joined the Haganah. I said to Ray now, "Yes, I will. I'll do what I have to."

2.

At the Yarkon, on the third floor outside Haman Shamir's office, six or seven ATC pilots and crewmen milled about, conversing in quiet, determined voices. I heard one pilot say, "I'll never sign! Never!"

Just then a navigator, a close friend, emerged from Haman's office. Eyes averted, he walked sullenly past us. Someone gripped his arm and asked, "What did you do?"

"I signed!" said the navigator, and pulled free and rushed down the stairs.

The next man interviewed was a pilot I shall call Jack Goldbaum, another close friend, one of the original LAPSA group, a seasoned captain. Jack grinned confidently at me and winked when he entered the office. Fifteen minutes later, leaving, he strode past, head down. No one asked him if he signed. We all knew.

Two radio operators were next. Each remained inside only a few minutes. The first one came out glowering defiantly. "Nobody's goddam business what I did!" he said.

The second radio operator was inside an equally brief time. Where the first one had been defiant, this one was remorseful. "I couldn't help it, could I?" he said.

239

Now it was my turn. Shamir's secretary, a smartly uniformed young woman corporal, called my name and ushered me into the office. Haman sat comfortably at his desk, flanked on either side by Dov Kinardy and the secretary. A spiral-bound stenographic pad lay open on the secretary's lap, her fountain pen poised above the blank page like a runner awaiting the starter's gun.

Haman smiled pleasantly and gestured me into an armless, straight-backed wood chair. The chair was positioned directly in front of the desk, in the exact center, the way police interrogate suspects.

"Thanks for coming, Harold," he said. "Can I get you something? Coffee? Cigarette?" He extended a cardboard packet of Israeli cigarettes, Green Death, we called them; they were stronger than Gaulois.

I cursed myself for leaving my own cigarettes at the hotel. I wanted desperately to smoke, but I said, "No thank you." Accepting a cigarette from him would have been a sign of submission. Honor, Pride & Principle, Inc.

Immediately, Kinardy handed me a sheet of paper. The retraction. On the top, typed in bold black capital letters, was my name.

"Please read this," he said.

I did.

"Do you understand it?"

A dozen wisecracks rose to my lips: *Hey, this is a literary masterpiece! Listen, whoever wrote this deserves the Nobel Prize!* Or, *Sure, I understand; anytime you get something shoved up your ass, you understand it, believe me!*

I said, "Yes, I understand it."

Haman said, "By not signing this retraction you automatically request repatriation."

"Haman, we retracted the ultimatum," I said. "So why this?"

"It was a verbal retraction," he said. "We need the written statement of each person."

Of each mutineer, I thought, but did not say it. I glanced

240

at the secretary-corporal effortlessly taking down the conversation, writing right to left, in Hebrew. I watched her a moment, envying the ability to so adroitly translate one language to the other.

"Why?" I asked Haman. "Why do you need it in writing?"

Dov Kinardy said, "You retracted as a group, not individually. The Air Force cannot give recognition to a group."

Ah, now I have you! I told him in my mind. You walked right into my trap! I said, "If the Air Force doesn't recognize a group, how could it recognize a group letter? That's what the ultimatum was, wasn't it? A group letter?"

"Please, Harold," Haman said, almost amused. "No semantics, huh? Let's get on with this. A dozen other people are waiting outside. Either sign it, or don't."

You son of a bitch, I told him in my mind. I make a perfectly sound point, the logic of which is irrefutable, and you call it semantics. But he had swept my "logic" aside with such deft finality I knew that pressing the point could only make me look a fool.

More of a fool.

I wanted time to think. I wanted to ask them for some time, but that too would show weakness. I glanced at the corporal again, idly wondering why the procedure required a Hebrew transcription. Dov Kinardy and Haman Shamir were American-born; their first tongue was English. Oh, yes, Hebrew for the records, the archives.

Very nice, I thought, the archives. Which would contain the ultimatum, and now the confessions of the plotters' guilt. Forever, for all to see. The disgraceful behavior of the Jews from America. And who could deny it? The proof was right here in writing. Signed by their own hand.

"I made a mistake," I said. "I apologized. I will not put it in writing."

"Everyone else has," Haman said.

Everyone except Moonitz, I thought, but did not say it. I saw no purpose in making him an issue. By the time he

returned from Paris the entire incident would be long finished, history, blown over. The signature of one man more
or less would by then hold little importance; it could be conveniently and expediently overlooked.

Even more to the point, Moonitz was a senior captain, a
pilot whose services ATC could ill afford to lose. I, on the
other hand, was hardly indispensable. A radio operator with
fantasies of one day sitting in the left seat. Left seat? I hadn't
even reached the right seat yet, not even unofficially.

No, they were going to make an example of me.

But not if I signed. Then, if I signed, it meant I was back
in good graces, no longer a Jewish Traitor. On the contrary, I
might even be considered a Good Jew.

"Everyone's signed," Dov Kinardy said. "They have no
reason not to."

"I can't sign," I said, thinking *I* have a reason not to, but
not saying it, not wanting to be asked the reason. I felt foolish and childish even turning the words over in my mind.

Honor, Pride, and Principle.

But, foolish and childish it might have been–indeed, looking back on it, as it most assuredly was–I was now determined to play it out to the end.

I'd be damned if I'd let them beat me.

That day, back at the hotel, to all questions of whether I
had signed the retraction my reply was a curt "No!" Which, as
I quickly saw, instead of earning me my friends' admiration,
only embarrassed them. I was living proof of their own stu-
pidity. But they had atoned for their sins, and been forgiven.

I had not atoned, and would not, nor would I be forgiven.

Not until and unless I signed.

3.

For two days nothing happened, except that the Yarkon
persuaded Kurtz and Schwimmer to withdraw their resigna-

tions. In view of the mass signing of the retraction, for them to resign was pointless now. In truth, the whole damn affair was pointless now.

In truth, it was all only a matter of pride now. Pride that unfortunately—and foolishly—impugned the very reasons for which I had initially come here. Reasons now totally obscured in my own rage and frustration.

I was determined to win. Or, if defeated, to go down with honor, all flags flying.

But win what? It reminds me today of a dream that occasionally recurs. In this dream I am playing 21 at a Las Vegas casino. I am dealt blackjack. But the dealer never pays off, only deals again. Another blackjack. Again, no payoff. And he deals again, yet another blackjack. No payoff. And again, and again. An eternity of no payoffs.

And as for the flags, they apparently were all that would fly. I found my name excluded from the crew lists for the forthcoming Operation Velveeta. I did not bother to ask why. The reason was obvious: I was grounded. Ray Kurtz made a special trip to ATC HQ in Jaffa hoping to convince Munya Mardor to rescind the grounding order. Munya said the order came straight from the Yarkon. My grounding was indefinite.

On the third day they summoned me back to the Yarkon. This time Dov Kinardy alone interviewed me. It began pleasantly again, coffee and cigarettes. Kinardy was actually quite civil, almost friendly.

He informed me that the Air Force would defer to those men objecting to The Conditions of Service. On January 1, when ATC was integrated into the military, an oath of obedience would not be required of anyone unwilling to give it. And that, as Dov Kinardy said, was what all the fuss was about. So we got what we wanted. We had won after all.

But he wanted that signature.

We rehashed it all, over and over. Their positions, and mine. I said I regretted ever having initiated the letters. He said my apology was acceptable only in writing. I said this amounted to a signed confession, which I considered totally unnecessary—not to mention vindictive—a humiliation to which I refused to subject myself.

The Air Force, said Kinardy, similarly refused to subject itself to the humiliation of subordinates issuing ultimatums. So for God's sake, sign. Sign, so the whole incident can be forgotten.

And forgiven.

No, I will not sign.

Kinardy, still not unfriendly, dismissed me. "I want you to think about it," he said. "Think about it very carefully."

"There's nothing to think about," I said.

"Think about it, anyway. We'll talk more tomorrow."

And the next day we did talk. And the day after that, and for two more days. Each morning, promptly at 11:30, a staff car arrived at the Bristol to drive me to the Yarkon for my interview with Kinardy. I began to feel quite important, like a Koestler character. No more Ladd and Bendix now. Now I was the hard, cynical revolutionary the state resolutely intended to break. My wits, my guts, pitted against theirs. I enjoyed the role.

On the fourth day Haman Shamir joined us. He entered the office, waved cheerily, and drew up a chair beside me. He wore a fresh uniform, crisp and knife-creased with embroidered IAF wings over the left breast pocket. The wings were gold with a silver Star of David in the center. They were very handsome.

Haman listened interestedly to the discussion, which was brief and covered the now tired old ground: their reasons for wanting me to sign, mine for refusing. Haman remained silent until we were almost finished. Then he sighed, a sigh of sadness, resignation.

I smiled to myself. I had outlasted the bastards. I could almost hear Haman's voice telling Kinardy to forget it, drop the whole damn thing, let it go. I looked at Haman and waited, preparing my reply, something clever and witty. On the other hand, I might just tell him to go and fuck himself.

Haman said, "Look, Harold, we're trying to build something here. Namely, an air force. The Israeli Air Force. And we *will* build it. We *are* building it. Maybe not the way you approve, but frankly I don't give a damn whether you or anybody else approves. We're doing it *our* way! Right or wrong, it's our way. Our way, friend, because it's our country. You came over here to help us, and we're grateful. But you have no right to question any decision–" he paused and swept a document from Kinardy's desk, the ultimatum–"and certainly no right to do this!"

I started to speak but he raised his hand to silence me. He slammed the ultimatum back down on the desk and continued, "Now it's a policy decision that every one of you–" his lips curled downward as he hesitated to use the word but then decided to say it anyway–"cry babies. Every one of you cry babies–because that's all you are, goddammit! Every one of you has to sign that retraction! Sign it, or get out!"

He fell abruptly silent, his eyes leveled on mine. I wanted to rebut the "cry baby" accusation. I wanted to say, Why are we cry babies? Because we refused to surrender our American citizenships to join your army? Because we came over here and fought a war for you and objected to your acting as though you're doing us a favor? Because we resented your charade that the pilots and crewmen of your marvelous Israeli Air Force are all sabras fresh off some kibbutz, when in fact there are exactly three–count them, three–Israeli line combat pilots in the whole Israeli Air Force? The Israeli Air Force, friend, whether or not you like it, is ninety-nine and ninety-nine one hundredths percent *American!*

Well, maybe ninety percent, but the other nine percent are Canadian, so it's practically the same country. All right, so maybe another five percent are South Africans. So it's eighty-five percent American, which sure ain't chopped liver, and still leaves only those three lone Israelis.

245

I wanted to say all this, but did not. It had all been said already, a dozen times over. Besides, I was too preoccupied trying to stare him down. Another point of honor. Which I lost; he really did intimidate me. I looked away and concentrated on the IAF wings on his chest. I coveted those wings. I envisioned them on my own uniform. I knew they were not standard issue, there was no standard issue. I wondered where he had them made. I knew that if I signed the paper I could wear those same wings.

"I can't sign it," I heard myself saying.

"You won't sign, you mean," said Kinardy.

I looked at him, relieved at finally being able to look away from Haman. "Whatever," I said.

Haman said, "Have your bags packed and be prepared to leave for Haifa in two hours."

I said nothing, but I thought, My God, they're really going to do it! They are really going to repatriate me! My heart beat faster. My hands trembled. I lit a cigarette and inhaled. The smoke knifed deep down into my throat and seemed to expand like a metallic balloon inside my lungs. I got up and mashed the cigarette into the hexagonal yellow and black ceramic ashtray on Kinardy's desk.

I faced Haman. I strained to keep my voice steady; at that moment nothing seemed more important than keeping my voice steady. "Anything else?" I asked.

"Get out," he said.

I rushed downstairs to Al Schwimmer's office. He had gone for lunch to his hotel, the Yarden. I found him in the dining room, alone. I blurted out the story. He listened patiently. He seemed quite unperturbed, which annoyed me.

"You had lunch?" he asked when I finished.

I had left the Bristol with no breakfast and was famished when I first sat down with Kinardy. But now my throat felt constricted, my stomach knotted.

"Want some lunch?" Schwimmer asked again.

I shook my head, no, intending to say I lost my appetite. I

swallowed the words. I suddenly felt completely foolish running like this to Schwimmer. What the hell was wrong with me? Couldn't I fight my own battles? I took out a cigarette and started to light it. My lighter was out of fluid. Schwimmer tossed a matchbook across the table. I lit the cigarette. Schwimmer was saying, " . . . so you tell them that I hired you, and that I'll fire you."

"That won't do me much good if they bring along a couple of MPs to make sure I go," I said.

"They wouldn't dare," said Schwimmer. He resumed eating. "You just sit tight. I'll take care of everything."

Al would take care of everything. It was like a pardon at the door of the death chamber. The Shamirs and Kinardys would not prevail after all. I had been thinking more and more that perhaps it was time for me to leave Israel, anyway. But if and when I made that decision, I intended to leave at my own pleasure, and with honor, not hustled off in the dead of night.

That evening, Avram, the young sabra who was too young for military service but old enough to work at the Yarkon as an office boy, rode over on his motor scooter to the Bristol Hotel.

"In one hour," he said to me. "In one hour, your transportation for Haifa will be ready."

Schwimmer was standing with me in the hotel lobby. "Tell them he's not going," he said.

"The order came from Colonel Remez," said Avram.

Schwimmer said, "Well, tell Colonel Remez he's not going, and that I said so!"

Avram left. He did not return. I slept fitfully that night, and with my little Skoda pistol, loaded, under my pillow. I had this picture in my mind, you see, of several MPs coming to fetch me. Even now, remembering, I cringe at my own silliness. What the hell could I have done with that gun?

No one came for me. Not that night or the next day, or that whole week. Schwimmer said he had talked with "some people" who promised to look into the matter. He never once suggested that I sign the retraction, or continue resisting. To him, that was no longer an issue. To him, I think the issue had become almost personal: I was one of "his boys," and he therefore considered the Air Force's handling of the affair entirely inappropriate.

Other than my grounding order remaining in effect, it was as though nothing had happened. I hung around the hotel during the day, playing gin or poker with the people not on duty, going to movies at night, or to the Park Hotel bar. I even went out to the fighter base at Herzlia to watch the arrival of the first five Spitfires from Yugoslavia, the initial phase of Operation Velveeta, in which I had not been allowed to participate. The very sight of those airplanes thrilled me but at the same time left me feeling empty and left out.

The Spitfires' arrival was not the triumphant event it should have been. Sam Pomerance–the crack pilot and mechanical wizard, he who had devised the ingenious fuel supply system that made it possible for the Spitfires to fly nonstop from Yugoslavia to Israel–Sam Pomerance was dead. Ferrying one of those same Spitfires, he had smashed into a Montenegrin mountain.

At Herzlia, I ran into Dov Kinardy. He asked if I had changed my mind about signing the retraction. No, absolutely not. He said I was behaving like a child. Sign, he said. Get it over with! Do yourself a favor. Do us all a favor. He was as obsessed with obtaining my signature as I was not to give it.

The only other holdout was Moonitz, whose name was never mentioned in that regard. As though he did not exist. He was due back any day. I knew that if I asked him to, he would refuse to sign; and I knew, too, no action against him would be taken. No action against him meant none against me. So I would end up winning.

Honor, Pride, Principle.

By default.

But winning–or losing–all at once was academic, for now I also knew I had to leave this place. I had begun considering this seriously only after that day at Herzlia. Watching the Spitfires land, the Spitfires that had been acquired without my help. Whatever the symbolism, if any, I think it was then that I realized it was time for me to go. I had, if you will, outlived my usefulness to Israel.

Needless to say, Haman Shamir and Dov Kinardy shared this opinion. I had not signed the retraction, nor would I, so my departure would set the example they sought. The irony, now, was that I wanted to leave. But on my terms, not theirs. If I left of my own volition, it was not dishonorable.

I spent two whole days mulling this over in my mind. The more I thought about it, about leaving, the more I knew it was the answer. The morning of the third day I woke early, consumed a huge breakfast at the *Tenouva*, and fairly ran to Schwimmer's office at the Yarkon. I intended to ask him to arrange my repatriation. I gave my name at the gate but before the sentry had even picked up the phone to call upstairs for clearance, Schwimmer strode from the building.

By nature a taciturn man, that morning Al Schwimmer's whole face fairly glowed. "I was on my way to see you," he said. "I just got word from Ben-Gurion's office. The old boy said he'd struggled forty years to bring Jews into this country, and he sure as hell wasn't about to throw one out! He said he wanted all this–and this is a direct quote: 'I want Shamir to stop all this nonsense and I don't want to hear another word about it!' And," Schwimmer added, smiling, "you're back on flying status."

For one split-instant, when he said that, I actually saw myself wearing those IAF wings. But in the same instant I realized that to wear the wings I had to join the army, which I could not and would not do. Gold and silver IAF wings or not, however, I had won. I had proved my point. But it was all anti-climactic because I did not want to stay on in Israel, nor did I want an El Al job. It was time to go home.

4.

At Lydda—now of course in Israeli hands, and now the civil airport of entry and departure—I awaited the arrival of a Trans-Caribbean Airlines DC-4 that would take me to Rome. This was my first glimpse of Lydda since it had been refurbished and transformed into Israel's main airport. There was little traffic: Israel was theoretically still at war. A KLM DC-4 landed, and a TWA Connie took off. From the KLM airplane, a handful of passengers disembarked, businessmen or diplomats from their dress. The Connie, with less than a dozen passengers, was en route to Athens.

The Trans-Carib DC-4 arrived. She was a special passenger charter, fully loaded, so it was not an auspiciously smooth landing. She taxied to a hangar near the terminal. Atop the hangar roof a blue and white Israeli flag fluttered in the brisk December breeze. Above the building's entrance was a large neatly painted sign in Hebrew and in English.

IMMIGRATION SERVICE—GOVT. OF ISRAEL

A ramp was wheeled up to the DC-4 door, which had just been opened by a young, blue-uniformed stewardess. She stepped out onto the platform and beckoned to someone inside the cabin. A moment later an old woman appeared. A kerchief was tied *babushka*-like over her head and chin. She wore a shabby overcoat and, incongruously, shiny new high-topped men's work shoes. The stewardess guided the old woman across the platform to the ramp's first stair. The old woman gripped the handrail and started to descend. Then she stopped. Shielding her eyes against the noon sun, she gazed out at the airdrome, and at the flat brown land on all sides. She shook her head slowly, wonderingly, and with not a little uncertainty. After a moment she continued down the stairs.

Behind her came others. Single file, men and women and

250

children, all dressed similarly, all carrying on their backs or clutching in their hands their sole and total possessions. I am sure I only imagined it–or wanted to see it that way–but it seemed that each refugee, upon viewing the flag atop the hangar, and the sign, entered the building with head held slightly higher.

It took an hour for the DC-4 to unload and refuel. It gave me more time to think, and remember. And wonder. Wonder what might have happened had I not become so deeply involved in the foolish events of the past month and, indeed, why I became so involved. There were a thousand answers, and there were none. It was the same as wondering what might have happened had I turned left one day instead of right, or not answered a certain telephone call, or smiled at a certain woman.

If Bill Gerson had waited an hour before taking off from Mexico City that day, or Moe Rosenbaum had come into the cockpit and not remained in the cabin. If I had reenlisted in the U.S. Army and not taken the TWA job, and therefore never met Milton Russell who introduced me to Swifty Schindler.

If my aunt was my uncle.

For that matter, under different circumstances, I might well have stayed in Israel, probably married an Israeli girl, and almost certainly joined El Al. Many of us did stay (and marry Israeli girls). Schwimmer, for one. He founded and for many years managed IAI, Israel Aviation Industries, and saw it grow into a huge conglomerate, the nation's largest employer and one of the world's most prestigious aviation enterprises. Tryg Maseng and Bill Katz settled in Israel, and Julie Cubernik, Steve Schwartz, Coleman Goldstein, and Ben Sklar.

And many others, including two South African friends, Lou Mazerow and Mendy Vons, both of whom coincidentally traveled with me to Rome on that same Trans-Caribbean Airlines flight. Both were ATC radio operators who, like me, aspired to one day occupy the left seat. As it turned out both succeeded: both eventually became El Al pilots, 747 captains, when they recently retired, the last of the non-Israeli pilots.

But that 1948 day at Lydda, as the Trans-Carib DC-4 rolled down the runway and flew into the air, an airline career was the farthest thing from my mind. I knew only that I felt better than in weeks, months. I felt healthy. I felt free.

I glanced out the window, down at the flat scrubland receding behind us and, directly below, the highway littered with the burnt-out wrecks of trucks and armored vehicles. Climbing, heading west toward the water, off to the right were the brown hills of Jerusalem; to the left, the Tel Aviv skyline. I thought whimsically that if this DC-4 could somehow climb to an extremely high altitude, say 50,000 feet, you might see the whole country. It would be laid out before your eyes, end to end, side to side. North to Haifa, east to the Sea of Galilee, south to the Negev.

It was, after all, a very small country.

We had just reached cruising altitude when, out my window, I caught a flash of sunlight. Off to the left, probably a thousand feet below headed in the opposite direction, was another DC-4. In an instant, its silver wings and fuselage outlined against the blue of the ocean, the airplane was abeam our DC-4, and then gone. It was another refugee charter.

Its destination was Israel.

THIRTEEN

RETURN

One by one, they seem to go. An engine fire over the Arctic Sea, not enough power at Mexico City, an incorrect altimeter setting near Zurich, a bad guess at Aquir. You remember them, the names recalling faces and voices and things they did. You try to be tough and cynical about it, and concentrate on remembering the good and crazy way they were, and you count on your fingers the ones still left. You seldom talk about them—except in a professional sense: "He should have feathered number three." "I told him a hundred times that was a dangerous approach." "I always said that fucking airport was an accident waiting to happen." You let the shock wear off inside. You get drunk, refuse to think about it, laugh. And maybe, because you are getting used to it now, just a long sad sigh.

I wrote that paragraph as an epilog to my novel, *The Coasts of the Earth*. Now, all these years later—albeit perhaps youthfully maudlin—it seems more appropriate than ever. Except now of course it is through age or illness that they "go one by one." Sam Lewis is gone, and Tryg Maseng, Eli Cohen, Willie Sosnow, Haman Shamir, Paul Dunsky, Len Dichek, Danny Agronsky, Charlie Winters, Wayne Peake. And others, too many others.

To all of them, however, to a man, that year in Israel was the penultimate experience. Nothing before or since can equal it. A truly life-changing experience. Nothing, afterward, was ever the same.

Through the years, understandably, most of us have maintained close, almost intimate contact. A band of brothers, tied inexorably by that one singular bond. To be sure, some have simply vanished: Milton Russell, Marty Bellefond, Jim Wilson, Sol Fingerman, Ted Applebaum, Don Kosteff, Buddy Rosensen, Sam Klausner, Elliot Polansky, and the others, so many others. Whether still alive, or dead, they represent a time never to be forgotten.

Al Schwimmer, as noted, remained in Israel and went on not only to head a giant industry, Israel's largest, but to become a formidable figure in the nation's affairs, a participant on the highest level of the government. He is currently engaged in the struggle to push through the Knesset a plan for reform of the Israeli electoral system, of which he is one of the main architects. In absolute seriousness, a prominent Israeli—the former press secretary to Menachem Begin—once told me that had he so desired, Schwimmer could have been Prime Minister of Israel. I believe it.

My good and close friend, Norm Moonitz (who claims to still possess his white Panama suit!), continued flying until the mandatory sixty-year-old retirement age, as an El Al captain and, later, for Lufthansa and then Trans-America Airways. Another close friend, Gordon Levett, the World War II RAF Wing Commander, our "good goy," turned down an offer to command ATC but stayed on for a time in Israel where he flew what is disingenuously referred to as "government special missions." Substitute "secret" for "special," and you understand the true nature of those missions. Gordon, himself a writer of no small distinction, now lives in the south of England.

For Hal Auerbach, even at a healthy and affluent age seventy-six, "things have never looked brighter," as he continues to pursue his post-aviation career of business consulting. Auerbach's cousin, Bob Luery, after a long, distinguished career, which included several years as president of Manhattan's famous Empire State Building, now lives in comfortable retirement in Laguna Beach, California. Larry Raab flew as a captain with El Al and then Lufthansa, and capped that with an adventuresome tour of flying munitions to Biafran rebels. He is now a successful aviation broker.

Swifty Schindler left aviation to build a thriving Florida realty business. "The Polack," Ed Styrak, still sails as a Merchant Marine radio officer. Eddie Chinsky, after settling in Detroit, only recently retired from his own accounting firm. Sy Cohen owns and operates a Los Angeles travel agency. Julie Swing, just now retired from his fashionable retail dress store, also lives in Los Angeles.

Al Raisin, my dear friend (despite our never-ending feuds and arguments, which even to this day have hardly diminished) remains busily occupied putting together various industrial complexes. Arnie Ilowite, whom Sam Lewis labeled a "pilot's pilot," not long ago disposed of his chain of New York dry cleaning establishments to move to Florida where he can play golf year round. Another Florida resident is Leo Gardner, who concluded his aviation career as an El Al executive both here and in Europe. Lou Lenart, the flight leader of that very first Messerschmitt fighter sortie, is a major Hollywood film producer. Ezer Weizman, who also participated in that first sortie, went on to command the modern IAF, and then became Defense Minister, and today is President of Israel.

Phil Schild, the pilot on my first memorable flight into

Israel, finally realized his medical aspirations: he went on to become one of America's foremost gastroenterologists. Julie Cubernik never did return to his Chicago pharmacy, opting instead to marry an Israeli girl, settle there, and teach high school. Sheldon Eichel, he who pulled Styrak from the flaming wreckage of their C-46, now runs, of all things, an antique shop in Miami. Marty Ribakoff, my "espionage" partner, also finished out his flying days as an airline captain and now lives in retirement in Florida.

Another retired airline captain is Ray Foster, who in 1948, along with former USAAF fighter pilot George Lichter, established the flying school for young Israelis that was the direct forerunner of today's superlative Israeli Air Force cadet program. Their cadets trained the cadets who in time trained those who wrought the miracle of the Six Day War and Entebbe, and they in turn trained the ones who in 1981 flew all the way to Baghdad to destroy the Iraqi nuclear reactor.

Sam Lewis, who died in 1992 at the age of eighty, devoted his entire life to aviation; for years, El Al's chief pilot and, until the day of his death, actively engaged as a flight instructor. And there was the aforementioned Charlie Winters, the righteous gentile who served a prison term in our cause, who was granted his final wish to be buried in Israel. Another righteous gentile, fighter pilot Wayne Peake, also lies in the Haifa military cemetery.

Gone, too, is Hank Greenspun. Hank, the decorated World War II hero, whom Schwimmer literally kidnaped from his Las Vegas PR agency to take on the task of procuring munitions for us. In 1950, the U.S. government indicted Hank—and some eight other "conspirators," including Schwimmer and Sam Lewis—for violations of the Neutrality Act. After a sensational trial, all were found guilty, and like Charlie Winters the previous year, faced a prison sentence. But Charlie had been sentenced by a Miami court, not an empathetic New York judge (a man named Pierson Hall, a sixth-generation Yankee whose great-great-grandfather fought at the Battle of Bunker Hill) who deemed a fine of $10,000 adequate punishment for the crime. Hank returned to Las Vegas where he built a small newspaper into a Nevada power, and himself into a Nevada legend. And, I should add, a champion of mine: whenever the *Las Vegas Sun* received a review copy of one of my novels, although I am reasonably certain Hank never read a single one–he never had time–the reporter he assigned to review the book invariably received a stern memo that in effect read, "I find this to be an excellent book, repeat: *excellent*! I am confident that you will share my opinion."

2.

Not so strangely, on a sunny winter morning in 1979, gazing out the window of a Sabena 707, I was thinking of that epilog from *The Coasts of the Earth*. I had flown in from Brussels, and the airplane was just touching down at the airport I had known as Lydda, the same airport I had taken off from when I left Israel, in 1948. It was my first time back in Israel in those thirty-one years.

Steve Schwartz was right: I hardly recognized the airport. The one-story, flat-roofed, prefabricated wood structure that once served as the airport terminal was gone, replaced by a multi-storied gleaming glass and metal building with separate gates for a dozen different international airlines. The rickety shed with the sign IMMIGRATION SERVICE–GOVT. OF ISRAEL, had long since been replaced by a cavernous, modernistic facility capable of serving hundreds of simultaneously arriving and departing passengers. Huge steel hangars lined the tarmac now, and the runways were nearly two miles in length, and endlessly busy with airplanes landing and taking off. Jet airliners–747s, 767s, 737s, Airbuses, DC-10s, L1011s– no more battered old war-surplus C-46s, DC-4s, or Connies.

And, of course, no longer was it known as Lydda Airport. Now it was Ben-Gurion International.

Steve's first words to me when I entered the terminal were, " . . . don't worry, all is forgiven." This said with a kind of smug, winking grin. What he meant was that my role as a "mutineer" had long been forgotten. In retrospect, as I quickly discovered, a trivial incident, remembered only by a few, and then as no more than a grimly amusing footnote. I, obviously, was the only one who attached any importance to it now.

And I must have indeed been forgiven: Steve had presented a note to the customs official that immediately resulted in my being waved through the double line of passengers, my passport stamped, and a cheery "Enjoy your stay in Israel." Within five minutes we were outside the terminal, in Steve's classic 1967 Mustang, driving out of the tastefully landscaped airport entrance to the new four-lane highway.

"What was in the note?" I asked.

"A request from the Foreign Ministry for VIP treatment," he said.

"All of a sudden I'm a VIP?"

"Al insisted on it."

Al insisted on it. Al, of course, Schwimmer.

Some weeks before, I had phoned Schwimmer, asking if he thought I'd have any trouble entering the country.

"Don't be silly," he had said. "I'll take care of everything."

He'll take of everything.

That much, at least, had not changed.

I had come to Israel to research a film I was to write for an American production company, an assignment I knew would provide me the opportunity of seeing old places and faces, renewing old friendships. From the airport, Steve had driven me into Tel Aviv, to my hotel, the Tel Aviv Hilton. And that same evening he took me to dinner at the Rishon Cellar, which was where he made the wisecrack about the Schnitzel probably being the same piece of meat I had left on my plate that night we were ordered out of the restaurant because of a threatened Irgun attack.

I spent some three weeks in Israel, doing my research, talking to people, formulating the story for the film. But what I really did was relive the past. I rented a car one afternoon and drove out to Aquir, now called Tel Nof. I suppose I expected it to remind me of the movie, *Twelve O'Clock High*, the old USAAF base abandoned, runways cracked and weed-clogged, control tower a rotting wood hulk. Instead I found a modern airbase, crammed with jet fighters, helicopter gunships, and transports. I was disappointed, and at the same time, pleased.

During my three-week stay I was busy working much of the day, but during the late afternoons and sometimes after dinner at night, I walked the streets. The once posh Park Hotel was now a run-down second-rate establishment, the Bristol an empty, boarded-up relic, the Yarkon Hotel a vacant lot. But the city itself had grown into a dynamic metropolis with high-rise office buildings and imposing apartment buildings, and broad tree-lined boulevards and fine residential areas not unlike Bel Air or Grosse Pointe.

Yes, and Jewish police and Jewish jails and Jewish criminals. Israeli millionaires and Israeli indigents. Israeli Nobel laureates and Israeli schlock motion picture producers. Israeli doves, Israeli hawks, Israeli supermarkets, Israeli automobile dealerships, Israeli stock exchanges. Lawyers, butchers, candlestick makers.

And an air force, unarguably the finest in the world.

Each evening I visited with someone from the old days. Ben Sklar, now a prosperous aircraft parts dealer. Julie Cubernik, the high school teacher. Bill Katz and Tryg Maseng and Coleman Goldstein, flying for El Al. Steve Schwartz, commuting between his Tel Aviv and Toronto commodities company offices.

I was feted and greeted, wined and dined, and urged to for Christ's sake come back here and live. You helped make this place, so finish it out here. This is where you belong.

Where I belong.

It reminded me of the red-headed nurse, Zippy. I wondered what had become of her. I remembered thinking that she would have been close to my age, fifty-five at that time. I remembered thinking that had I stayed in Israel, I damn well might have married her. I also remembered fantasizing: I am sitting at the Hilton bar, and she walks in. I recognize her instantly. Even in her mid-fifties, she is still one hell of a good-looking woman.

"Hello," I say to her in the fantasy. "Do you remember me?"

She peers at me. "No, I don't believe–" And then her face brightens. "Why, yes, of course. The American flyer!"

"That's right," I reply. "The American."

"And you're here on a visit?"

"How do you know it's a visit?" I ask.

She nods gently, knowingly. "Someone like you would not come here to live. I knew it then, I know it now."

"'Someone like me?'" I ask.

"A person who turns away from his heritage."

"Because I won't come here to live, to you that means I'm turning away from my heritage? I explained all that to you that last time we met. I said I couldn't live here because I was an American, which is what I want to be."

In the fantasy, for a long quiet moment, she studies me. Then she shakes her head. She seems almost sad. She says, "And I said, you are also a Jew. This is where you belong."

"Where I belong is America," I say. "And I can still be a Jew. I can be both."

Once again, she studies me. She seems even sadder, and I am annoyed because it is as if she feels almost sorry for me. "I was wrong," she says. "You are not a Jew. You've chosen not to be one."

"I've chosen not to be an *Israeli*," I say. "There's a difference."

Then, again, that sad shake of her head. "You happen to

be quite mistaken," she says. "There is no difference, none."

The fantasy lingered in my mind, accompanied of course by that same resentful ambivalence, that same unsettling search for identity.

But then it vanished.

It happened almost magically, without warning, on the morning I left Israel. At Ben-Gurion International, just before I boarded the TWA 727 for the first leg of my flight back to America.

The flight was briefly delayed, allowing me nearly an hour to browse around the terminal. Three weeks before, when I arrived, I had been whisked through customs and immigration. I had had no time to really stop and look around.

Now, for the first time, I took careful note of the terminal interior, the vastness of it, the modernity, the activity. The scores of fashionably dressed people serenely hurrying about, the smartly uniformed El Al flight crew members and ground personnel, the well-stocked gift shops and surprisingly good restaurants. I was enveloped by a feeling I had not known—not with such intensity—since my very first flight into Israel thirty-one years before, a sudden and unexpected sense of pride and achievement. I suddenly realized that I had helped make all this happen. I had helped build this place.

And then, in my mind, the handsome new terminal was superimposed with a panoramic view of the city itself, Tel Aviv, the skyline and the hotel-lined Esplanade, the beaches, the parks, those expensive residential neighborhoods. The bustling airfields I had visited with the sleek fighters, the F-4s, the F-15s and F-16s and the superb Israeli-manufactured Kfirs, all bearing the Star of David on their wings and fuselage. The high-tech control centers at the airfields—not the primitive airstrips we knew with the asphalt runways and creaky old RAF wooden control towers—modern airbases with two-mile-long concrete runways and underground bunkers brimming with state-of-the-art radar and television screens and electronically projected sectional maps, and manned by crisply uniformed young men and women (any one of whom you wouldn't at all mind having for a son- or daughter-in-law).

The image stayed with me when I was in the TWA airplane, taxiing out, and then in the air and, much like that time thirty-one years earlier when I had left Israel in an ancient DC-4, I gazed off to the left, at Tel Aviv. Sparkling in the sun, so much bigger now, so much more permanent, so much more real.

And I knew now where I belonged, which was in America and not here, for the deceptively simple but very sound reason that I was an American and chose to remain one, and because Zippy in the fantasy was wrong: I could indeed be both an American and a Jew, and I had not turned away from my heritage, not at all. I knew all this because I knew that thirty-one years ago I had done what I came to do in Israel.

I had helped make it a reality.

43694 KB6